REDEEMING MULATTO

REDEEMING MULATTO
A Theology of Race and Christian Hybridity

Brian Bantum

BAYLOR UNIVERSITY PRESS

© 2010 by Baylor University Press
Waco, Texas 76798-7363

Scripture quotations, where not the author's own, are from the New Revised Standard Version Bible, ©1989, Division of Christian Education of the National Council of the Churches of Christ in the United States of America. Used by permission. All rights reserved.

Cover Design by Cynthia Dunne, Blue Farm Graphics
Cover Art based on *Childhood Is Without Prejudice* by William Walker, © 1993. Photograph by the Chicago Public Art Group. Used by permission.

Chicago Public Art Group's mission is to establish creative partnerships between local artists and communities in an effort to transform and enhance the lives of residents in urban Chicago neighborhoods. CPAG projects combine legibility, accessibility, craftsmanship, and artistry to create monuments to local history, identity, values, and concerns. For more information, visit www.cpag.net.

"Christ in Alabama" and "Mulatto" from *The Collected Poems of Langston Hughes* by Langston Hughes, edited by Arnold Rampersad with David Roessel, associate editor, ©1994 by the Estate of Langston Hughes. Used by permission of Alfred A. Knopf, a division of Random House, Inc. Reprinted by permission of Harold Ober Associates Incorporated.

The Library of Congress has catalogued the hardcover edition as follows:

Library of Congress Cataloging-in-Publication Data

Bantum, Brian, 1975–
  Redeeming mulatto : a theology of race and Christian hybridity / Brian Bantum.
  243p. cm.
  Includes bibliographical references (p.   ) and index.
  ISBN 978-1-60258-293-4 (hardback : alk. paper)
  1. Jesus Christ—Person and offices. 2. Race—Religious aspects—Christianity. 3. Racially mixed people—Religious aspects—Christianity. I. Title.
  BT205.B165 2010
  270.089—dc22
                                2010000803

The paperback ISBN for this title is 978-1-60258-349-8.
© 2016 paperback edition.

Printed in the United States of America on acid-free paper.

In loving memory of my mother and father,
Wendy and Joseph Bantum

CONTENTS

PART III
IMMERSION
Christian Discipleship *or* the New Discipline of the Body

ACKNOWLEDGMENTS

As with any endeavor, this project is the sum of many people's encouragement, support, and guidance. This manuscript began as an inkling of a question that has prodded me since my entrance into the Master of Theological Studies program at Duke University Divinity School and that matured into larger questions that I pursued while earning my Ph.D. in the graduate program in religion at Duke. Throughout my coursework, exam preparation, and dissertation writing I received funding from the Fund for Theological Education, first as a doctoral fellow and then as a dissertation fellow. The Fund not only allowed me the financial freedom to pursue this work and still eat more than macaroni and cheese, but through conferences and mentoring the FTE guided me through the often-perilous world of academia. Additional funding from the Ford Foundation as a Predoctoral Fellow allowed me more time to develop the project as well as actually participate in life with my wife and three children.

Duke University has been my intellectual home for nine years. During that time I benefited from the guidance and wisdom of many faculty and staff members. I cannot name them all, but to all who supported, encouraged, and prayed for me I am deeply thankful. Stanley Hauerwas, with an encouraging and subtle hand, has allowed me the freedom to pursue this research. I have appreciated his pushing reminders to be as clear as possible, and was encouraged by the fact that these rejoinders were always grounded in his belief in my work. In Jay Kameron Carter I have been blessed by a seemingly endless reservoir of ideas and enthusiasm. In the moments when I thought this project insignificant or at a dead end, it was his enthusiasm or a timely book suggestion that helped me to regain my own excitement and momentum for writing. To Amy Laura Hall I must extend my deep thanks for the courage of her teaching and life. In the first class I took at the Duke University Divinity School my eyes were opened to a way of doing and inhabiting theology that set me upon this wonderful path. It was due to her example and encouragement that I imagined that I could and should do this work. In Willie James Jennings I have been blessed with a mentor and a friend who welcomed me into a new theological world. While in this world, I found no distinction between questions of family, world, theology, church, intellect, feeling, art, music, and so on. Instead, all of these questions and realities of life seemed to swim together in his own life, his own questions, and his own teaching. Willie has taught me to be a theologian. His most profound lesson has been in teaching me ideas, lessons, and a way of being in the world that I did not understand but could only grow into over time. There are too many others to mention here, but in many ways this book represents the collective encouragement of many who thought I had something to say before I knew I had something to say.

I am especially thankful to those who took time to read drafts and chapters as I finalized the manuscript, particularly Amey Victoria Adkins. Carey Newman and the staff of Baylor University Press have been incredible in their enthusiasm for this project and their guidance in the process of editing and refining the book's focus. But most importantly I must thank my family. My beautiful wife Gail and my three wonderful children Caleb, Ezra, and Joseph have been sources of constant joy and wonder. My boys have loved me not as one with good ideas or well-turned phrases, but simply as their daddy. The simplicity of this fact returns me again and again to the nature of this theological task, that we are loved and this God who loves us is present for us. I have my children to thank for that reminder every day. Of course my deepest and most profound thanks must go to my wife. Before any crazy ideas of graduate school entered our lives, Gail loved me, comforted me, pushed me, and most importantly laughed at my jokes. If there is anything good in these pages, it more often than not began in her beauty, grace, determination, and sacrifice. Her faith and her faithfulness, her receptivity to the Spirit's promptings, her joy and love have taught me more than my many years at Duke ever could have. Thank you, Gail, for loving me and for teaching me.

INTRODUCTION

In the modern world the realities of the slave ship and the encyclopedia converge within the life of the church. As Christians have reflected and lived in the world, theology has been both complicit and confined in the collection of knowledge and peoples. Theological claims have accompanied and impelled missions of conquest. But theological claims have also been catalogued and classified as part of a prior "universal" religious phenomenon. In modernity the church became both a servant of conquest and became itself contained within the "limits of reason" alone.[1] The peculiar confluence of power, enforced submission, and resistance forms the subtle framework of contemporary theological imagination, of the problems set before the church, and the possible range of answers to these problems. And yet, in these responses to the crisis facing Christian existence in the modern world, what actually constitutes the challenge to identity has been conceived in different ways. Black Theology, Feminist Theology, Radical Orthodoxy, Liberation Theology, and various appeals to "tradition" are just a handful of examples that are responding to the legacies of domination. In responding, these theologies have also conceived the problem in different ways and thus also begin to outline a possible answer. The questions that are asked are bound to the answers that are found.

Contemporary theological projects have either sought to reassert the value of the dark body, the native or ethnic body, the female body, *or* reclaim the intellectual proclamations of a "tradition" that had been seemingly abandoned.[2] Consequently theology (and the church) exhibits two related and perhaps necessary, but distinctly problematic, tendencies to the modern condition: disembodiment of ideas or an idealization of a body. In both of these moments the body becomes once again an object to be read apart from other bodies, a tool of classification to be escaped or utilized, to be freed or to be thought beyond.

In the fifteenth and sixteenth centuries the ships that disembarked from the ports of Europe left with Bibles and guns. Moving throughout the world these ships disseminated both knowledge of God and the imprint of European culture (while also accumulating a tremendous amount of knowledge and material and cultural wealth.) The children of this encounter can be seen in the faith and faces of cultures throughout the world. But what made these encounters possible was the idealization of a certain body that dehumanized all others, making them the "object" of both conquest and conversion, and thus instantiating an economy of white over dark. In the years to follow colonization dark Christians would not capitulate to these claims but would begin to imagine themselves anew, within the very same claims that God had entered into the human condition.[3]

Despite efforts to expand the light of the gospel, the church found itself confined within the limitations of the encyclopedia.[4] The encyclopedia grew out of the Enlightenment and its greater and greater dependence upon scientific inquiry and the classification of knowledge (and the ordering of modern lives that inevitably grew out of these observations). The pages of knowledge began to enclose God within a body of knowledge, as a god among many gods, the Bible as a book among many books, and its doctrine as set alongside the stories of Zeus or Medusa. Christianity did not crumble beneath the weight of knowledge but adapted to flourish within it, mastering the art of knowledge and wielding it in defense of itself against the onslaught of secularization.

The church today, as well as theological reflection, exists between these two tectonic shifts, living in the aftershocks and wreckage of the claims made about the human body and the contorted claims made about our claims. As such, theology finds itself situated between the legacy of these claims as well as their definitive rebuttals. Responding to the dehumanization of certain bodies some seek to narrate the centrality of dark and female bodies within Christ's own life. Resisting the secularization of Christian ideas, others seek to reclaim the ancient doctrines, the ideas of Christian faith considered as "tradition." These two projects of reclamation seek to not only thwart the effects of the problem conceived so long ago (colonization, the Enlightenment), but can also be seen as the centers of two distinct paradigms of theological formation that participate in the development of Christian intellectual and pastoral leadership.

Two examples of responses to the echoes of the slave ship and the encyclopedia can be seen in theologians James Cone and John Milbank. Cone and Milbank, each in their own way, have worked to define the problems confronting theology and the church, but in doing so also display themselves as modernity's progeny and thus envisage the difficulty for all Christians in imagining a new way forward. These two theological giants have effectively marked *the* theological trajectories before the contemporary church. While it is difficult to capture the nuance of each theologian's significant contribution, the theological programs of Cone and Milbank are inclined in one of two directions. Cone emphasizes justice and the particularity of racial identity while Milbank emphasizes orthodoxy as a practice; orthodoxy is a mode of identity. Both of these theological postures, despite their best efforts, have either slowly abandoned the particularity of Christian confession and reception of God's presence in the world (read: decolonial) or hardened a particular reading of tradition into weapons to further concretize a particular way of being in the world (read: colonial).

We begin to see this impasse most clearly when we look at how Cone sought to theologically describe the reclamation (or redemption) of black bodies in the United States and throughout the world. In order to do this he saw the necessity of a movement away from the ideas of Western theology. Reflecting on his slow movement away from his reliance upon Western theological categories in *Black Theology and Black Power*, Cone asserts that "as in 1969, I still regard Jesus Christ today as the chief focus of my perspective on God but not to the exclusion of other religious perspectives. God's reality is not bound by one main manifestation of the divine in Jesus but can be found wherever people are being empowered to fight for freedom."[5] The possibility of freedom and redemption did not lay in the doctrinal pronouncements of a white, colonial Christianity, but in the historical moment of Jesus as a child of oppression. Cones' movement away from what he viewed as Western theology was an attempt to rearticulate the presence of God among peoples whom so many Western theologians not only seemed to have overlooked, but participated in subjugating. However, Cone's theological vision has also served to enclose the image of God within the lives of the oppressed, and it rendered primary a different particularity in reflecting upon who God is in the world and for us. While Cone rightly points to the contextual reality from which all theology is done, the question remains whether God is also bound by those contexts and if the church might imagine not only the transformation of the oppressed into those who are free, but what that transformation might mean for all people.

In John Milbank's work we see a different reclamation project whose aim is not bodies in particular, but rather a set of ideas. In Milbank's widely acclaimed *Theology and Social Theory*, Milbank sought to retrieve meta discourse theology as an organizing set of ideas above all ideas. This position is again seen perhaps more clearly in *The Word Made Strange*, in which Milbank outlines his primary concern, "philosophy as autonomous, as 'about' anything independently of its creaturely status *is* metaphysics or ontology in the most precisely technical sense. Philosophy in fact *began* as a secularizing immanentism, an attempt to regard a *cosmos* independently of a performed reception of the poetic word."[6] Theology has been subjugated to an assertion of knowledge that claims to be without a context and thus threatens theology as a body of knowledge that is radically received.

Cone's attempt at reclamation renders Jesus discernible primarily within black experience, as a black body. Why he needs to do this is obvious; but in order to do so he must also distill the totality of Jesus' person and ministry into the negotiation of a politically oppressive reality. Cone seeks to disentangle theology from the chains of the slave ship by rendering Christ's divinity as located within a particular political (and racial) moment, the black and oppressed Jesus. Jesus is not the captain on the ship, but he is the chattel. Theologically, Cone wants to suggest it is Christ's divinity that enters into this mode of existence and thus redeems it.[7] But while the departing flight is clear the return leg seems absent. I think this is because for Cone, Jesus as the Word becomes overtaken within Cone's experiential (black bodily) framework. For Cone, Jesus' particularity effectively becomes inverted from Jesus, Jew/oppressed to oppressed/Jew. Ultimately this leaves not only Jesus as fundamentally a body, but also redemption as primarily bodily.

Most notably this circumscribing of Christ within a dark body is seen in Cone's conflation of Jesus' particularity as a Jew completely within his sociopolitical position as an oppressed Jew.[8] Cone sought to describe this transformation of possibilities through God's taking up of this particular position. Yet, the reconciliation imagined through this moment takes place primarily within black, dispossessed life as an assertion of black identity and community.[9] This enclosure of Christ's redemptive moment into not Jesus' body but black bodies, positions Black Theology as a perpetual space of self-preservation that maintains black reflection within the ever-threatening onslaught of white colonial theo-imagination.

In this respect, the cries of justice and equality serve to unchain the oppressed from the desperation of poverty or exclusion. And yet there grows a chasm between the activity of empowerment and the life of discipleship. Is the church more than political advocacy? Is salvation our participation within the political, economic system, or does Jesus call our bodies and lives into something that encompasses this and more? While confirming and exclaiming the beauty of the black body, the Latina body, can these exclamations also enclose dark bodies? Does the "contextual" imagination allow African Americans, Latino/a, Asian/Asian Americans to theologically imagine beyond ourselves? The reflex of a practical embodied self-preservation is a crucial one given the dearth of Christian intellectuals of color within the academy and their struggle for reception within their respective fields. But do not the claims Jesus made about himself seem to suggest a transformation that complicates identities rather than confirms them? Does Jesus' presence among us as God, as a Jew, as oppressed, but also divine and human, born of Spirit *and* flesh, make possible not only a wider set of allegiances, but require it of our lives as disciples? Can we speak to the church without these claims about who God is among us and for us?

Against the trend to diminish Christian doctrine, Milbank shows us how the reclamation of the *idea* of Jesus renders us not bodily, but reduces our bodies to our ideas. In this way the attempt to reclaim orthodoxy and redeploy it against the intellectual degradations of the late twentieth century have had little to do with our bodies and our lives together. Radical Orthodoxy and its various permutations have not accounted for the complicity of theology in the formation of the modern world, in the fathering of the strange-looking child that is the New World's theology. Instead, practices and the bodies that perform them have become occasions to display a system of thought. Milbank's attempt to reassert a meta-discourse that organizes all knowledge recapitulates the work of the encyclopedia with a particular reading of tradition as its organizing and disciplining principle. And through this mechanism bodies become little more than indicative of ideas that animate them, and practices little more than icons of an ideal that become transformative through the perfection of their liturgical performance. In Milbank the words are indicative of Jesus, not the bodies that utter them.

The clarity Milbank's Jesus offers us is another means of organizing knowledge, "a Christological poetics."[10] For Radical Orthodoxy, clarity concerning Jesus' identity is joined to an intellectually gauged set of practices that become demonstrative of an inward mental operation. Theology is a grammar, a discursive practice that is bodily because words are bound to language and language is an outworking of human interaction, but does the primacy of the Word suggest humanity can be understood primarily through a hermeneutic of grammar and discourse?[11]

While those within Radical Orthodoxy may want to suggest that they too are for the embodiment of theology, that they are fighting against the separation of thought and practice, the question here is not the *intent* of Radical Orthodoxy, but rather whether Radical Orthodoxy has actually done what it set out to do. To this I ask, if they have so effectively reconceived the fissures of body and mind, an inheritance of the Western colonial project, why do these expressions of orthodoxy seem to reproduce the exclusion of peoples of color within academic theology? Why do these accounts of the body seem unaware of the atrocities engendered in the name of right belief? Why can (or will) orthodoxy not theologically account for the rape of the New World and its mixed-race children? Is it possible that this theological trajectory guides our thought *about* God, but does little to open our lives to a substantial transformation of desire, of the economy of our everyday lives? We cultivate an understanding of a tradition, and with it train disciples to speak the creed properly and delineate between a bad performance of the Eucharist and an appropriate performance. Perhaps the most astute of these students will drive the connection between how Eucharist is performed and whether or not we are giving to the poor or the needy, but it will seldom drive them to question the faithfulness of not worshiping with the Spanish-speaking congregation that rents their sanctuary at seven o'clock every Sunday evening. This proper thought about Eucharist concretizes the positions of those who seemingly confess properly within their pews. Confession thus fences imagination of what constitutes salvation around thoughts *about* worship, rather than rendering their very bodies as worship.

These two attempts to address the reality of our bodies and the "rightness" of our theology ultimately delimit the language about Jesus' life and our possibilities. The fruit of these theological trees leave us to fight for justice without a theological language for the faithful in our pews, or binds us within the walls of intellectual circumspection. The church is left only with the options of becoming embodied without hope or with no body of hope. We are bodies or minds. We are thought or justice.

To remake the practices or life *of* Jesus into thoughts about the practices and thoughts *about* Jesus is to reiterate a form of human life that makes our bodies subsidiary to our minds. This process of abstraction deifies the intellect (and certain bodies) and dehumanizes those bodies that cannot enter into the salvific dialogue of the transcendent. Or, the church is left with the perpetual critique of these ideas in favor of the lived experience of particular peoples that idealizes their own image within the life of the one who was, in fact and ironically, a stranger to them. The uplift of *our* people becomes the mantra of the church, a gospel of preservation its aim. But to reject the traditional claims about Christ is also to reject the substance of who he was. Jesus was not just a body without an idea, nor is he an idea without a body. His salvation was not the reclamation of our thoughts about him, nor was it solely the redemption of our bodies from systems of oppression.

Misunderstanding Jesus, we misunderstand our own bodies and we must account for them differently, but we must also account for the Word more deeply. To struggle forward we must begin to reimagine the body, our bodies, as a problem. This notion of the body as a problem echoes the reflections of W. E. B. Du Bois as he answered the implicit question posed to him, "How does it feel to be a problem?" The question, asked in a hotel lobby over one hundred years ago, obscured the fundamental assumption of the European colonial project, "How does it feel to be the answer?" As Du Bois noted with the question never put to him, the question of whiteness as the answer is seldom raised in the new world of the twenty-first century and yet remains the legacy of the slave ship and the encyclopedia.[12] The reality of the slave ships and the encyclopedia were not only men and women packed in chains and the collection of scientific data. The slave ship was bound to the classification of peoples. The encyclopedia was not merely about the collection of knowledge, but those who could know. As dark peoples seek to escape the grip of oppression and tyranny they have not only struggled against brute force, but dark peoples have sought to resist the power of classification, of the disciplining whip of "knowledge."

But while bound together these two phenomenon are more than poles vying for power. The encyclopedia and the slave ship are parents of bastard children whose lives bare the mark of each. The shadow of

the slave ship became embodied in the modes of racial classification. But
more than this, those who were classified were born of both the African
slave and the white masters. In the birth of these strange children we see
the confluence of knowledge and bodies, the ordering of desire and intellect and its lustful transgression. These children are at once classified and
defy classification. The encounter between the Old and New Worlds has
produced and is producing children (theological, biological, and cultural)
who exist across the boundaries modern theology has struggled against
and exists within. As such, these theologies have become mechanisms of
resistance or sustenance that seek to maintain or protect a particular vision
of humanity within an already changed world.

In theologically accounting for our bodies we must account for race
in the modern world. Sitting on the precipice of a "post-racial" world, we
have yet to account for how all of our bodies are questions *and* answers,
seldom stated, but perpetually asked. Cultures throughout the world are
marked by a hybridity, and yet there remain patterns of differentiation
and violence that persist as nations and peoples vehemently declare their
purity and their traditions. Notions of purity and destiny and law became
intertwined in the upholding of an illusory race. While Cone and Milbank respectively postulate about their own bodies as answers, we have yet
to account for *the possibility that our bodies ought to be problems but that we
are not the answer.* We must look to another.

Christ was an emblem of a way out of the slave ships and the encyclopedia, but this way out became a new form of misperception. At the center
of modernity's birth was Christ, or more properly a messianic emblem that
served to establish purity within a people. The pattern of establishment
was not merely a process of doctrinal obfuscation, but a constellation of
practices that served to delineate who was inside and who was outside.
In the midst of demarcation was a profound misconception concerning
the answers and the problems that bodies posed. Even more central was a
misperception regarding the problem and the answer Jesus' body offered
to humanity. But in this use of bodies or systems of thought to delineate
a position within modernity, Cone and Milbank could not account for
the children of the modern encounter. They accounted for themselves, for
their ancestors bound upon ships crossing the Atlantic or as heirs of an
intellectual tradition. In either case their theologies could not apprehend a
central aspect of Christ's life among us. Christ came to us so that we might
become something different. For Cone and Milbank, modernity's theological mode of differentiation, of theological refusal, became redeployed

as the reclamation of bodies or minds. Their theologies resist the birth of children who do not look like them, who do not recite their words. Contextual Theology and Radical Orthodoxy are theologies of reproduction that ultimately foreclose the mulatto, the child among them born from the transgressions of modernity and the presence of God upon Mary.

Cone and Milbank are not alone. That we have all imagined Christ's body as ours allowed us to mistake our own bodies for salvific bodies; failing to see our bodies as problems, we could not see the answer Christ's body offered us. This book will begin with the description of a particularly problematic body, the mulatto body. The mulatto is one that confounds classification, and as quickly as it was identified, it slipped into light or dark to raise havoc within the walls of purity erected for self-preservation.

In the American colonies the mulatto, a Spanish-derived term to classify a child of African and European parentage, was present early on. As early as the mid-seventeenth century, colonies in the Americas began to distinguish between Africans and mixed-race children. The process of classification was not straightforward. Mulatto children were more commonly described as Negro, thus clouding the actual population of mixed-race children, and these children existed.[13] As the American slave system became more entrenched the process of classification also hardened, as fears of miscegenation and the diminution of white purity became more explicit.[14] The presence of mulattos was a constant conundrum in the New World that indicated the presence of white desire for dark bodies. But at the same time legal codification that resisted either sexual intercourse between races or the continual distinction between mulatto and white bodies served as means of identification through differentiation. That is, by denying mulatto bodies as a fruit of white desire and maintaining that the mulatto was essentially a black body, white identity would be created and maintained in the New World.

The church exists in the wake of this racial world, and for this reason mixed bodies still trouble the waters. Mulattos were bodies that troubled the waters for all of us because they existed on both sides in a space that could not sustain such a possibility. That we no longer characterize mixed-race children as mulatto does not mitigate the growing fact of these interracial children. But perhaps even more important, these children continue to pose a problem because the patterns of faith, education, and marriage still flow along the trenches of a world forged by race. The ambivalence of our racial condition is no clearer than in both the

election of a mixed-race president, Barack Obama, as well as in the vehe-
ment questioning of his faith, birth, and citizenship. Just as darker and
lighter Americans alike are reimagining the possibility of political life in
the United States, so too are the numbers of militias swelling, and chants
of "we want our country back" growing. The possibility of post-racial is
only an illusory bridge. To enter into such divisions we must recognize
interracial children and their perpetuation in our own lives in the subtle
and glaring ways we seek to reinforce our difference and refuse the possibility of becoming something different.

The reality is that the church cannot resist these patterns; but while
not the answer itself, the church worships a God whose body is both the
problem and the answer. In order to understand how this is so, we must
first begin to discern the shape of our condition more carefully and in
doing so we will begin to see not only the shape of our unfaithfulness
but also the outlines of our salvation anew. It is not solely a matter of our
proper confession or the righteousness of our acts, but the reality that our
confession of Christ is bound to the particularity of Jesus' body as born of
flesh and Spirit. In this confession we not only speak of him, but we enter
into his body and become something new. The church, its theological language, and its people must be reborn. It must enter into the baptismal
economy of renunciation, confession, and incorporation to see the contours of its refusals and thus the outlines of its possibilities, of a new hope
for ourselves and one another. In this process we will come to find that
accounting for Jesus cannot be articulated within the reductions of his life
to ideas about him or to his body, but must be confronted by the problem
of Jesus' body, the intermixture his life promises us, and the intermixture
our lives must become with him and each other.

PART I

RENUNCIATION
Racial Discipleship and the Religiosity of Race

Chapter 1

I AM YOUR SON, WHITE MAN!
The Mulatto/a and the Tragic

Mulatto

I am your son, white man!

Georgia dusk
And the turpentine woods.
One of the pillars of the temple fell.

> You are my son!
> Like Hell!

The moon over the turpentine woods.
The Southern night
Full of stars,
Great big yellow stars.
> What's a body but a toy?
> Juicy bodies
> Of nigger wenches
> Blue black
> Against black fences.
> O, you little bastard boy,
> What's a body but a toy?
The scent of pine wood stings the soft night air.
> *What's the body of your mother?*
Silver moonlight everywhere.
> *What's the body of your mother?*
Sharp pine scent in the evening air.
> A nigger night,

A nigger joy,
>A little yellow
>Bastard boy.

>>*Naw, you ain't my brother.*
>>*Niggers ain't my brother.*
>>*Not ever.*
>>*Niggers ain't my brother.*

The Southern night is full of stars,
Great big yellow stars.
>O, sweet as earth,
>Dusk dark bodies
>Give sweet birth
To little yellow bastard boys.

>Git on back there in the night
>You ain't white

The bright stars scatter everywhere.
Pine wood scent in the evening air.
>A nigger night,
>A nigger joy.

I am your son, white man!

>A little yellow
>Bastard boy.

—Langston Hughes[1]

INTRODUCTION

"I am your son, white man!" In the New World the children of slave ships and the children of the encyclopedia produced unexpected and problematic children. The refrain of Langston Hughes' 1927 poem represents the fruit of this encounter and the difficulties the interracial, the mulatto/a body presented to theology and the economy of white and black. The ensuing dialogue between a mixed slave and his master/father is a contestation of kinship and classification. The dialogue is a demand and a refusal to account for the black blood in white faces and for the white desire of dark bodies (for work and for pleasure). More profoundly this altercation of master and slave is the reverberation of the desire that built the slave ship and the hubris of classification that imagined all knowledge within the pages of the encyclopedia.

The confrontation of kinship and classification in the New World is not only about bodies but illicit desire and contested recognition, the

struggle to account for difference and to control that difference. This dia-
logic moment is iconic of a deeper incongruity, a deeper misconception
among those who imagined themselves disciples of Christ and Christian
theologians. While intermixture quickly became a fact of New World
existence, it was also vigorously resisted and disciplined. The refusal and
disciplining of intermixture, and the bodies that represented it, is bound
not only to relations of power, but to theological misperceptions regarding the shape and possibility of Christian life. Consequently, the church
and theology in the Americas (and the West more broadly) would be
built upon altars of their own self-creation. These altars would envelop
the whole of society within a religiosity of race whose practices served to
further classify its citizens and enclose all people. Within the dichotomy
of the slave ship and the encyclopedia all the citizens of the Old and New
Worlds would enter into an economy of racial subjugation or interpretation. The New World became marked by a violent severance between
bodies that were enslaved and demarcated "colored," while "white" bodies
possessed the power to discern the meaning of all bodies.

It is within the lasting and violent effects of classification and slavery that the modern world now contends with the question of race, but
also with the question of Christian identity. In modernity the possibility
of Christian personhood has unfolded within the riddle and tragedy of
domination, power, and enslavement. Europe's colonial project inserted
itself throughout the world into the various peoples of the world in such a
way as to assert European particularity above all other particularities. We
exist in the wake of this modern moment not only as children of particular
racial, cultural, or national realities, but as those for whom such identities
signify possibility or impossibility, blessing or curse.

The presence of Europe (its people, its culture, its colonial legacy)
among the various peoples of the world was not mere political or economic expediency; it served to recreate the world. The particularities of
any vision of life—those things that bound peoples together or the hopes
that compelled them forward—were circumscribed within a European
vision of possibility and fulfillment.

Ironically, we come to see that the reality of identity within the modern world is imaged through the bodies of those who are born out of this
encounter between the Old and New worlds. Children of rape, illicit desire,
and even possibly love were born in this colonial encounter. Mixed-race
children were in between the categories of colonizer and colonized, human
and nonhuman, slave and free. That these children were even categorized

as something in-between indicates the power such distinctions held within these societies. Mixed-race bodies display and make visible a drama of identity that every body, every life engaged in then, during its time, and now, during our time. Race is the drama of our present condition.

As such the color line outlines the contours of everyday life in the modern world.[2] While claims to racial purity are, on one level, less explicit in contemporary discourse, they continue to be persistently conveyed through the daily exigencies of political and social life in the United States. Although the United States is no longer explicit in its "calculus of color,"[3] the nation (and the Western world in general) nonetheless maintains a certain myth of purity. Our collective and individual desires (marriages, homes, churches) persistently display such myths of purity as matters of tragic inevitability. In the midst of such articulations of race (either its absence or its nature, the colonial deployment or the nationalistic response) what is often unarticulated are the ways these racialized lives are deeply bound to each other in such a way that renders their various claims to purity illusory and tragic.

The interracial or mulatto/a body is the site that unveils race as a tragic illusion.[4] The tragic, so often accounted to mulatto/a peoples as a bodily inferiority or a profound loneliness, is instead seen as the necessity of negotiation within multiple worlds that refuse them or which they themselves refuse. That this negotiation of different worlds is required is bound to a necessary cleavage of self, brought on by the discursive power of purity that renders the interracial body in-between. Tragic lives, in this regard, are lives that are fashioned in-between, lives that exist perpetually on the precipice of death or in cycles of perpetual performance. Yet this notion of tragic must be understood as not only bound to these particular bodies, but to all bodies in the modern world.

Theological investigation of these encounters and the mixed bodies they produce has been notably absent, but is crucial to begin to reflect on the patterns and substance of Christian existence in the wake of the colonial encounter.[5] The mulatto/a body points us back to our "birth" in the modern world. To imagine a life in Christ we must begin to reimagine the shape of our unfaithfulness, our complicity in the economy of race, in order to faithfully imagine what it might mean to participate in the renunciation of an old life marked by the tragedy and violence of race. This act of renunciation must begin with that peculiar and troubling child of the modern world, the mulatto/a and his tragic refrain, "I am your son, white man!"

I AM YOUR SON, WHITE MAN! THE TRAGIC AND TRANSGRESSION

Discourse regarding intermixture became crucial as the "encounters" of Europeans and native or "imported" peoples became a topic of serious scrutiny. Lawmakers, writers, and others sought to account for these encounters, but more importantly, the children of these encounters. Such accounts gave rise to a complicated system of classification: mulatto/a, mestizo, mestizo/a, mestizaje, quadroon, octoroon.[6] These classifications policed the racial lines that had been erected and transgressed. Racial classification served to demarcate a standard of whiteness, thereby displaying an important reality of racial life in the West—purity was something that was not inherent, but was something to be articulated, maintained, and upheld.[7] The precariousness of white claims concerning race is revealed in the various attempts at racial classification. More importantly, what these interracial bodies display is first, the fundamental denial of racial purity, and second, the ways all bodies have become tragically entangled in the racialization of the world.

The process of forming racial fidelity and the notions of personhood that operate out of these formations can be understood more clearly if race is interpreted as a religious modality. Racial identity constitutes a form of discipleship that must be theologically accounted for and resisted. That racial performance exists as a social phenomenon is certainly a challenge to Christian discipleship. But to suggest it is a religiously grounded form of being in the world is to infer a theological response that must be more precise in its description of the problem and the way forward. Racial performance is not simply a sinful behavior that must be avoided, but a way of being in the world that is more than difficult to resist, for it is the air we breathe. In a way, theology must begin to suggest how we become "new creatures," those who breathe differently. The contention that race is a mode of discipleship will be discussed as the chapter unfolds, but it is important to highlight here why this distinction is important.

Recent scholarship has suggested that race is a social construction. It is a discursive category rooted not in true biological differences, but in meanings attributed to perceived differences coupled with power that can enact economies and social structures that reinforce and reproduce these categories as "true." This theory of social construction has been widely accepted, but has struggled to work against the very real perceptions of "natural" or essential differences. Racial essentialism is the view that there are, in fact, biologically distinct people groups, each with gifts or skills that are particular to them. These gifts or particularities are to be preserved and protected in order to maintain a distinct peoplehood.

Race as a social construction and race as essential: each approach offers some important insights and neither can be easily dismissed in the acuity of its approach or the reality of the condition. The notion of discipleship mitigates these two approaches by suggesting that race and ethnicity is a way of being in the world that seeks to live into something beyond itself. In doing so, it enacts, adopts, and implicitly absorbs certain practices, habits, and desires that allow the person to enter into this aim. The life of discipleship is one that is cognizant of its personhood, but also bound to a certain community. This life of following and being formed is the negotiation of what it means to be a part of a people and how their individual desires, gifts, and sucn are to participate within the wider aims, hopes, and desires of their community, nation, and race. Discipleship is the deliberate conforming to certain aims, but it is also a more subtle process of being formed to become a citizen or a participant. It is the process wherein citizens may or may not discern themselves as citizens of a nation, but nonetheless their pattern of life is pointed toward and determined by being "a good American."[8]

Revelatory of racial fidelity and its transgressions as well as raising the assertions of moral or biological purity, mulatto/a existence signifies an inevitability of encounters among peoples. Claims of purity, citizenship, being and nonbeing are present as interracial people negotiate their everyday existence. The literary trope of the tragic mulatto/a has often pointed to the perpetual homelessness of the mixed body (better than black, not quite white).[9] However, these bodies also indicate the ways all lives are marked by the encounter, the union of "different" bodies, as well as how such realities are resisted in modernity's assertion of purity, rendering all lives tragic.

Hughes' "Mulatto" highlights the way racial lives were not only predicated upon difference, but also how such descriptions of difference were deployed in order to articulate the inner life of those responsible for the naming. This articulation of identity through differentiation was expressed through the language of purity. Here purity serves to establish the lines of identity and consequently power, which allowed for full participation in Western life. Within the West these intonations of purity were not only signified through political programs (laws, statutes, etc.), but instantiated through the mundane aspects of daily lives as those who participated or desired to participate were slowly immersed in the waters of racial existence.[10]

It is through these mundane moments of assertion and denial that racial existence becomes more than a claim of an essential identity or a construction placed upon a people in order to maintain their inferiority. Rather, racial existence becomes a performance that is lived into, inhabited, and rearticulated (or given back) to the world. This economy of performance becomes clearer through the language of discipleship in that racial identity takes place within an interplay of formation and agency. In this interplay individuals are formed through what Pierre Bourdieu would call a *habitus* that "enables the institution to attain full realization . . . Property appropriates its owner, embodying itself in the forms of structure generating practices perfectly conforming with its logic."[11] Identities were not fixed or natural, but represented various attempts to live into these norms that had become so hidden they appeared natural. Racial fidelity requires the invisibility of race as a system of beliefs and yet forms the scaffolding of modern self-understanding.

Identity in the modern world thus displays a dynamism of formation and reception. Personhood is a process of call and response that is mediated through mundane, day-to-day realities as well as through institutions.[12] It is this interplay of formation and agency that I want to describe as performance or the discipling operation of race that requires a religious lens to perceive its end as well as its structures. The process of racial performance or discipleship begins to outline the ways that identity is received, but then participates in the widening of the structure that forms its inhabitants. In this way those who perform race become its unwitting evangelists, further creating a world grounded in a racial economy of identity and identification.

Race is a phenomenon of racial performance that forms disciples. Race is not merely a form of social organization, but more significantly a form of religious expression and identity that shape who a person is. But race as a system of belief also indicates more than who a person is. Structures of racial formation articulate the telos of the inhabitant's life, what she will live in to, and what she will not. In this regard race becomes a category that organizes and guides the very presumptions people make about themselves and their world. However, this performance of race remains, the ways it is lived into and acted out of, hidden even in the midst of competing visions of racial life.

Through the violation of these boundaries—the contamination of purity—such a performance of race becomes manifest or unveiled. In the sexual encounter between races (violent or tender) the myths of these performances become apparent and resisted. These claims of personhood,

bound to these racial lives, are articulated and lived into via the renegotia-
tion of boundaries and resistance to their transgression. Ultimately, the
religiosity of such performances as racial discipleship pose a deep challenge to the sojourn of Christian life and must be resisted not merely as sin,
but as deeply idolatrous notions of human striving. They are not merely
practices that can be given up, but these lives of racial discipleship can be
seen as an idolatry that must be confessed and resisted in the lives of those
who confess the name of Christ. In this regard, interracial existence is seen
not as a hope or mediating reality. Rather, interracial bodies constitute an
interruption of racial "faith" and unveil the illusory notions of racial purity
that serve to shape and form our social imaginations.

Hughes' haunting assertion, "I am your son, white man!" frames
the power of this social imagination. In the midst of the claim to sonship
Hughes displays the tragic reality of mulatto existence as frustrated self-
assertion, as well as the inevitable reality of sonship that marks American
(and Western) society. Mulatto/a existence is portrayed not only as a bitter
product of the white torment of black women (or the fruit of forbidden
love in other cases) but mulatto/a existence is also shown to be the very
fabric that constitutes southern (and greater Western) society. Such conceptions of race and purity are themselves tragic moments of self-assertion
and denial built upon a distorted, but constant relationship between light
and dark serving to maintain the certainty of the racial imagination. To
begin to see the shape of mulattic interruption and revelation of racial
fidelity, Hughes' poem must be examined more closely.

Hughes' articulation of the tragic mulatto/a points us to a broader
understanding of the tragic within the modern world that can be described
through three important tropes: transgression, hybridity, and contestation.
These interrelated themes serve to outline how interracial or mulatto/a
existence marks the modern world. In attending to the display of these
realities we begin to uncover the various ways racial lives are asserted or
denied in contemporary societies. The tragedy of mulatto/a existence is
the instantiation of a wider problematic of modern racialized society.

Through the poetic imagination of Hughes we see "the tragic"
mulatto/a first narrated through the complex and violent transgression
of the slave owner upon the slave woman. The nature of the relationship is unstated in the poem, but within slaveholding society such sexual
encounters were common as an assertion of power, as well as a means of
increasing one's slave population. The presence of the mulatto/a child on
the plantation signified a deeper transgression not only of one person upon

another, but of one people upon another.[13] Here the mulatto/a's existence, their very body, is witness to the violence of the slave owner's objectification of the slave woman. Such terror is captured in the haunting account of Harriet Jacobs. Writing about her time as the slave of Dr. Flint in North Carolina she recalls the beginning of her "trials of girlhood."

> Soon she will learn to tremble when she hears her master's footfall. She will be compelled to realize that she is no longer a child. If God has bestowed beauty upon her, it will prove her greatest curse. That which commands admiration in the white woman only hastens the degradation of the female slave. . . . My master met me at every turn, reminding me that I belonged to him, and swearing by heaven and earth that he would compel me to submit to him. If I went out for a breath of fresh air, after a day of unwearied toil his footsteps dogged me. If I knelt by my mother's grave, his dark shadow fell on me even there. The light heart that nature had given me became heavy with sad forebodings.[14]

The stark and brutal reality of these encounters is the dust from which so many mulatto/as rose in American "civilization." But in Jacob's aversion to Dr. Flint not all white bodies represented death. In another "white unmarried gentleman," who seemed to exhibit a kind of care foreign to her, she found the possibility of relative safety. Here she found "something akin to freedom in having a lover who has no control over you, except that which he gains by kindness and attachment."[15] The child she bore out of this encounter remained bound within a distortion of affection and power, a tragedy deeply layered with hate and longing that makes visible the interconnections between white and dark bodies in the West.

Jacobs' account points to a deep tension also found in Hughes' poem. Where the vast majority of these encounters in the South were tragically violent, complicated feelings of loathing and desire were also present: Dr. Flint's desire for Harriet, Harriet's desire for the unmarried gentleman, and the mulatto son's desire for recognition from his father. These brief instances suggest that the violence of these encounters lie not only in the horrific transgression of white masters upon black slave women, but in the ambivalent tensions that preceded and resulted from these encounters. Such complications are seen most vividly in the literature that takes place after slavery and the Civil War, when such relations are less often forced; instead, the parties enter into a tenuous relationship of desire and fear. Here the violence is no less present, but it has now shifted as each encounter becomes pregnant with the possibility of death.

Jacobs repeatedly notes the pains with which Dr. Flint, with such haunting and all but limitless power, will take to hide his desire and pursuit of his young slave because his transgression is not only one against her black, enslaved body, but one against a wider Western myth of purity.[16] Here Jacobs' narrative also points to the myth of purity that pervades the social moment: appearances are still important because there are boundaries that must be maintained. In such a mythic world the mulatto/a child's existence becomes a witness to the violent transgression of the white (male) body against the dark black (female) body. The child's very face points back to the violence of white objectification which has rendered the black female body a dark abyss of pleasure to be hovered over. The products of these transgressions are the "yellow stars that fill the southern sky." The yellow stars witness to the very violence that begot them, while their faces point to a distorted joining of man and woman.

Hughes' descriptions of the moon and stars that hover over the darkness allude to a virtual creation of the modern world. The light of the moon hovers upon the dark night and the dark trees receiving its light, for they are nothing but receptacles. The darkness is that which receives the light and exists to be hovered upon. Yet Hughes' "creation" narrative exhibits a deeper significance in the transgression of a white man upon a dark woman. For Hughes, the tragic is not only bound within the interpersonal contestation of the relationship or the violent transgression of one with another. Rather, the tragedy for Hughes lies in the very fabric of southern (and Western) society, grounded upon the creation of these children and the transgressions and denials that constitute their existence. The night is full of stars. Mulatto/a bodies are not only individuals who desperately seek recognition, or pitifully fail to embrace their lives as black men or women. Mulatto/a bodies, as such, are iconic bodies witnessing to the transgressions of bodies, myths, and the possibility of any claim to purity.

Thus "mulatto/a" refers to an individual or a particular location, as well as to the multiplicity and hybridity of relations that constitute identity. These "yellow stars" point to a violent admixture: their father's nose and grey eyes, their mother's high cheeks and full mouth. Mulatto/a bodies make their father's face, the image of the master, visible among the slaves in the night. Their bodies represent the complicated intersection of race and gender that cannot be neatly theorized apart from one another, but are constantly interpenetrating the other. Their presence reveals the possibility that what was thought "to possess beauty and virtue which have never been black and which is the color of daylight"[17] is now present among the lowly. The purity of the owner can, in fact, inhabit the "least" in the world.

The faces of mulatto/a children are tragic, for their admixture is suffocated in the claim of purity and denials of paternity and kinship. The father shouts "Like Hell!" while the brothers reply "Niggers ain't my brother/Not ever." White lives exist in a delusion of their own independence, purity, and identity as light in the midst of darkness. The refusal of the mulatto/a is turned upon the claims of the father and brothers who remain blind to who they are and who their sons, brothers, and sisters are. The father, son and mulatto/a are all bound up in a tragic chimera.[18] The very social fabric of the South (and West) is one of hybridity, born of this drama of encounters, claims, and refusals. Cultural theorist Stuart Hall highlights this complicated interrelation in this way, "The play of identity and difference which constructs racism is powered not only by the positioning of blacks as the inferior species but also, and at the same time, by an inexpressible envy and desire."[19] Here Hall points to the way identity in the West has been constituted by a rhythm of assertion and resistance, when in fact identity is composed by these poles present within all lives in the Western world, "and this is something the recognition of which displaces many of our hitherto stable political categories, since it implies a process of identification and otherness which is more complex than hitherto imagined."[20]

In the midst of these assertions and refusals of hybridty we are left in the tragedy of contestation where the previous two moments of transgression and hybridity become the underlying discourse of southern society. Modernity is this moment of contestation, of assertion and denial concerning who is who and what are the relations of those in and out of power. Here the mulatto/a is constituted by contestation and self-assertion, seeking recognition yet meeting only denial. But in this refusal what cannot be silenced is the very existence of the one who speaks and bears the image of the father and mother in one face and consequently speaks by the virtue of their being. The mulatto/a's presence contests the father's denial and reminds him of his transgression, of his desire for dark flesh despite his own claims to moral and bodily purity, simultaneously attesting to the complicated love of a mother who sought to protect her children from the violence that begot them. We are reminded here again of the contestation present in Harriet Jacobs' account where Dr. Flint's desire for the appearance of propriety is disrupted by his desire for Harriet. There was an understanding that any verbalization of Dr. Flint's pursuit of Jacobs (or any other slave) was to be met with dire consequences. The severity of the punishment belies the seriousness of Dr. Flint's understanding of his own transgression, yet is complicated by his persistent pursuit of that which he ought not want to possess.

While the tragic in mulatto/a existence becomes visible in the refusal of white recognition, we must also attend to the difficulty of how such bodies become haunting reminders of these transgressions among their own kin. Historians have pointed to the deep racial hierarchy that has penetrated slave plantations as well as black life throughout America's history.[21] Here tragic claims of whiteness serve not only to exclude, but also mark black cultural life. Delineations between high yellow and brown skin, house slaves and field slaves, all mark the internal distinctions such transgressions manifested among slaves in the South and free blacks throughout the United States. Such mulatto/a bodies formed "in-between" societies among themselves, or had to navigate often-tenuous relationships among their black brethren.

This reality is also evidenced in the literary "tragic mulatto/a" throughout nineteenth and early twentieth century literature.[22] Most often set after the Civil War, these texts explore the world "freedom" created and the negotiation of this freedom by white and black folk alike. In these works the tragic mulatto/a is one who has been rejected by a white father but who also senses a certain distinction between him or her self and the "negro" race, while yet remaining politically dark and enslaved.

We see a marked developmental shift in the way the tragedy of mulatto/a existence is envisioned in the early eighteenth and nineteenth centuries, as compared to Harlem Renaissance depictions in the early twentieth century. In these later accounts the tragedy is construed in terms of the mulatto/a's weakness (or refusal) to recognize the beauty of their "dark" bodies, thus pitifully mimicking white life and living in perpetual self-deception.[23] In each of these moments we see the deep effect of racialized existence penetrating the mulatto/a body. Ties (both tragically violent and desirous) to white and black bodies are continually present, contested, asserted, and displayed. These interconnections require a cultural negotiation that is not foreign to other bodies of the West, but in the mixed-race body becomes explicit.

DISCIPLESHIP: RACE AS A MODALITY OF FAITH

In the midst of these three moments, transgression, hybridity, and contestation, within Hughes' "Mulatto" we are confronted by the deep paradox mulatto/a existence makes visible. The transgression of purity must be continually refused, avoided, and legislated against. Society moves forward upon a belief in white bodies and their antitheses. But this was more than a belief; it was knowledge related to certain facts about the world. The racial economy of the West was a veritable faith in the possibility and telos of white flesh upon which a great temple had been erected. But in the mulatto/a body, Hughes tells us "a pillar of the temple falls," revealing that in each verbal refusal there is a secret lust, for every law there is a dark violation, for every obstacle the slave raises there is a persistent aversion. The mulatto/a body of the South is the paradox of white loathing and "loving," the desire for that which one is not.

This mulatto/a body is the "great yellow star" under which we sleep. The tragedy of the mulatto/a body is the tragedy of the claims to racial purity rendering *all* bodies ultimately as lies and false performances. Within modernity all bodies and lives seek to live into something beyond them. This transcendental hope is a religious yearning that is bound to faith in God, made incarnate in the racialized societies of the Western world. This yearning that marked the West's turn to modernity would ultimately have the most immediate and deadly consequences for darker peoples, but would inevitably kill all in the inevitably illusory salvation of whiteness. But lest we mistake this particular historical peculiarity as localized and isolated we must be reminded that the southern moment is merely an intensification of a wider Western transgression. Its mulatto/a children are not only constituted through political enslavement or cultural power, but through a profound embodiment of a religious ideal and hope regarding white bodies.

This illusion of purity that the mulatto/a body renders visible belies a religiosity concerning the telos of white flesh that begins to characterize the movement of all racial lives in the West. Here I am not seeking to make a phenomenological claim concerning the nature of religious yearning. Rather, what I hope to highlight here is the way the claim to racial purity can be seen as a "quasi-religious" performance, where the ideal of whiteness served as a telos toward which the Western world sought to incorporate its adherents through a particular architecture of legal codes, social mores, and cultural matrices. That is, while the Western world would articulate its mission through the language of Christendom, what we see in actuality is a certain religious performance of race with whiteness serving as its axis. In this world, the actual modes of existence were arbitrated through the language of race. In this way it is not merely a sociological or anthropological phenomenon, but more profoundly a religious moment into which peoples became incorporated and transformed by its claims and its implicit (or explicit) hopes.

As early as the eighteenth century, Africans in America began to sense the deep disparity between the Christianity of their white nation and the "true" God and Creator. In his *Appeal to the Coloured Citizens of the World*, David Walker draws a parallel between the treatment of heathen nations and Christian nations regarding slavery. In doing so, Walker points to the deep unfaithfulness of American Christianity, painting in clear terms an idolatrous nation grasping for a glory that was not theirs to claim.

> While they [Europeans] were heathens they were too ignorant for such barbarity. But being Christians, enlightened and sensible, they are completely prepared for such hellish cruelties. Now suppose God were to give them more sense, what would they do? If it were possible, would they not *dethrone* Jehovah and seat themselves upon his throne?[24]

This assertion does not seek to deride Christianity, but makes apparent the idolatry American Christianity fell into. For Walker, white Christianity is no more than a heathen religion that fails to worship the God of Israel who brought Israel out of Egypt. It is no better (in fact, it is worse) than the Egyptians who were crushed beneath the waves of the Red Sea.

Walker's analysis frames the savagery of American (and Western) slavery in terms of a violation of God's justice and a deep perversion of the Christian faith. Frederick Douglass highlights this disjunction similarly as the incoherence between slaveholding religion and the Christianity of Christ, writing, "For between the Christianity of this land, and the Christianity of Christ, I recognize the widest possible difference—so wide, that to receive the one as good, pure, and holy is of necessity to reject the other as bad, corrupt, and wicked . . . Indeed, I can see no reason, but the one most deceitful one, for calling the religion of this land Christianity."[25]

The conclusions of Douglass, Walker, and others uncover the deeply religious character of Western racial society. Their jeremiads utter harsh judgments against a nation's claims, rendering these claims meaningless in light of the extortion of African bodies. The subtext of idolatry makes such prophetic utterances intelligible and renders visible the way white images, grafted upon the flesh of so many Europeans, have usurped God's primacy in the lives of its bearers. What these writers so keenly understood was the way white Christians were so thoroughly bound to a god other than Jesus. Their political and social realities did not participate in or point to the kingdom of heaven, but were a tragic and deadly rejection of God that bore more resemblance to the "heathens" of the world than to Jesus, the Son of God.

Such an indictment against heathen religion is indicative of the problematic shape of racialized thinking in the West. While racism and colonialism ravaged populations and did much to malign the darker inhabitants of the world, these accounts cannot be understood only in terms of power or social injustice. A theological account of such injustice, suggesting it is "simply" humanity's sinfulness (race and idolatry), is to diminish the challenge Walker and Douglass present to Western Christianity. In their characterizations of Christian "heathen" religion we see what Karl Barth would later characterize as "the sin of unbelief" where "there is no such thing as an undisputed heathendom . . . heathen religion is shown to be the very opposite of revelation: a false religion of unbelief."[26] Like Walker and Douglass, Barth understood the world theologically, as that which either conforms to or resists God's presence and judgment.

Walker's indictment of Western Christianity is intensified in Barth's claim of religion as "unbelief," not only as a rejection of revelation, but a rejection through the formation or participation in something outside of Christ (even if it confesses it is within Christ.)[27] The seemingly rigid formulation of reception and rejection highlights the religious nature of every aspect of human life and striving. Even in our most trivial moments we are either refusing or seeking God's revelation. Such a conception does not require our intelligible attestation of our own greatness or desire "to be like God." Rather, everyday existence displays particular forms of life that make visible this rejection of God's revelatory work and our self-understanding as creatures made to "live and move and have our being in Him." (Acts 17:28) For Barth, this structure of unbelief is grounded upon a form of life where "in this loving and choosing and willing, and in the activity determined by it, one becomes something which is human but supremely non-human." Barth's conception of unbelief has less to do with a set of intellectual denials and more to do with the way people's lives are bound together and to what end. In this way unbelief has a deeply material character that can even pervade "its purest and noblest and perhaps its most pious and philanthropic forms."[28]

While Barth has been received in the late twentieth century as a defender of orthodoxy we must also be reminded of how the cultural and political realities were bound, in Barth's view, to the theological claims the church refused to make. The failure of the church in the face of Germany's assertion of dominance was bound to the perversion not only of dogmatic claims, but how dogmatic claims became embedded within nationalistic hopes.[29] Barth understood the connection between religion and unbelief was connected not only to the explicitly religious movements away from "orthodox" Christologies as exemplified by Friedrich Schleiermacher, Friedrich Strauss and later Adolf von Harnack and Adolf Schlatter, but Barth understood the lives of German Christians especially to be performing into something very different than the life of Christ.[30] What Barth points to in the religion of unbelief is the reflex of the encyclopedia that inhabits modern theological inquiry and consequently the church. Theological reflection for Barth, Douglass, and Walker had become subsumed within the economy of the encyclopedia. The power to classify and to order lives within those classifications became the fundamental practice of theological reflection and Christian belief.

The performance of unbelief or heathen religion demarcates a certain form of humanity at its center so that "all that he does when he arrogantly assaults the limits marked out for him is to attain pseudo divinity. He does do that. And as a pseudo divinity he secretly worships himself, appearing as such and even outside and deceiving others as he has first deceived himself. Even if man is quite powerless to become anything more than himself, his attempt to do so is real."[31]

The divinity such lives point to is real, though one may or may not consider themselves "religious." But as with both Walker and Barth, we here begin to see all lives are caught up in such a rejection or reception of one's life. That said, Barth points to the ways such lives must continually circumscribe the lives of others in order to make them intelligible. Thus unbelief is hardly an individual act, but a deep distortion of the communion of saints.

The communion of saints, a congregation of God's people, could be said to be marked by their mutual creation, by a mark of being marked, of being gathered together by one who was not them, but became them. In a heathen mimicry the communion of whiteness forced the communion of "others" who were corralled neither for adoration nor out of their own recognition. Dark bodies were instead gathered to form the margin and the limit. Their bodies become the demarcation of the center's glory.[32] In his connection between an internal belief and an external "evangelism" Barth points to the way unbelief as a religious performance demarcates or asserts itself. This assertion of pride at the center of unbelief involves both an individual and communal reality seeking to enfold others into its lie and concealment. Such a performance is significant for conceptions of race (and what I am seeking to describe as racial performance) as a religious performance, in that race similarly seeks to compel one into a life of worship where the outline of dark bodies make possible the inner "light." This relationship is one of pure self-centeredness, where dark bodies revolve around and constitute white self-assertion. Here the heathendom of unbelief is made possible only by the distinction of light and dark.

This relationship between unbelief and material life is a crucial one. Here again Barth exposes unbelief as an intellectual rejection of presumption, pointing to the complex interrelationship between desire and assertion that is required of adherents or believers. This racial-religious performance is certainly an instantiation of pride that seeks to resist God's revelation, but Barth points to its performative nature. He suggests that "religion is the action of sinful man which will inevitably involve flagrant continuations and confirmations and repetitions of his unfaithfulness and therefore sheer self-contradictions, with the continual rise and influence of the alternatives of doubt and skepticism and atheism."[33] Thus religious performance is not only one among many, but the central act of self-assertion with, in this instance, whiteness as its operative mechanism. These acts of discipleship serve to shape and inhabit virtually every aspect of society's daily life. In this regard religious performance inhabits racial idolatry serving to not only frame the assertion of one group over another, but to organize society within its outlines.

THE CULT OF WHITENESS: RACIAL RELIGIOUS STRUCTURE

Racialized life in America and the West, then, is not a statement of biology, but an assertion of belief. The claim of whiteness becomes comprehensible less as provable fact and more as a creed. "I believe" is materialized in the daily refusals and assertions that would mark daily life in America. The denial of the white father in Hughes' poem can now be read more powerfully as an attempt on his part to live into this creed regarding himself, his family, and the slave. It is the attempt to affirm and assert his belief and thus his own identity. What his denial reveals is the power of the claim the son is making upon him. The father must assert himself and his purity to remain faithful to his race. Some may argue that the father's denial is a question of power. I do not disagree. But what is crucial to note is the question of adherence and fidelity.

Whiteness serves as an invisible deity imaged through the father and thus rendering who can be called blessed.

The religious structure of race can be further delineated through an examination of religious practices and the ways these practices are bound up with ideas concerning religion in general. Drawing on the work of Paul Tillich, I would like to highlight theologian Kelton Cobb's discussion of ultimate meaning, religious symbol, and myth to outline the religious character of Western racial imagination that served as the structure that would give birth to the tragedy of mulatto/a and all racialized bodies.[34]

The quest for ultimate concern is characterized by Cobb as the reality that "out of the multitude of things we value in life . . . something makes an unconditional claim upon us, and we organize our lives and all of our other values in accordance with it."[35] Ultimate concern has a triadic character comprised of demand, threat, and promise. In this triad the object of ultimate concern demands the adherent's surrender and utter loyalty, threatens exclusion from fellowship when disloyalty is discovered, and promises fulfillment to those who are faithful.[36] The reality of demand, threat, and promise, which mark the religious expression of an ultimate concern, can be seen as unfolding racially in American (and Western) political and cultural life. Seen through such a matrix, demand, threat, and promise are racially infused within American legal codes, sacrificial lynching, and baptismal practices. In each of these moments racial logic serves not only as a means of control and power, but also as an overarching or transcendent reality which enlivens daily existence in the United States (and the West), creating adherents and displaying a sacral reality into which all people must live.

The triad of legal structuring, sacrificial punishment, and practices of initiation demonstrate particular bodies that become grafted into the hope of citizenship and display whiteness as a racial religious moment in the West. Whiteness as an ultimate concern is clearly an integral moment of America's self-identity. Racial logic demanded surrender and loyalty, marking the tragic life of the mulatto/a that Hughes pointed us to earlier. The refusal of the father to acknowledge his son is to confess to his disloyalty, his transgression. As such, one's loyalty to the race must be continually asserted, a loyalty fostered early on through subtle moments of training until the neophyte becomes a disciple, mature in her following. Writer and social critic Lillian Smith points to such formation in *Killers of the Dream*, where as a child she learns early the "lessons" concerning her body and the bodies of those around her. She writes: "I do not think our mothers were aware that they were teaching us lessons. It was as if they were revolving mirrors reflecting life outside the home, inside their memory, and we were spectators entranced by the bright and terrible images we saw there."[37] One of the first lessons she learned concerned the meaning of her own body in relationship to other bodies and to God. Smith is clear that the shape of these lessons centered upon the meaning of her race and how it was to structure her everyday life.

> We were taught in this way to love God, to love our white skin, and to believe in the sanctity of both. We learned at the same time to fear God and to think of Him as having complete power over our lives . . . we were learning also to fear a power that was in our body and to fear dark people who were everywhere around us, though the one who came into our home we were taught to love.[38]

Her life becomes one of discerning the boundaries of loyalty and disloyalty, learning who to look at and who not to look at, who to love and who not to love, who you can treat poorly and who you cannot.

Such lessons take place under the auspice of something that is present yet profoundly distant. Somehow white bodies represent it, but this is never enough, for within this society there is a proximity to darker bodies that poses a threat. This proximity is one wherein the presence of light and dark bodies are gauging the other and negotiating the terms of involvement and appropriate distances. Formation is the process of learning how to negotiate these lines, but it is more so the process of learning what these lines and practices of negotiation mean for one's life and people's lives together. This is a system that inculcates white bodies into itself, while drawing all difference into an order to assert an ethos among the people of the Western world.

The demand for loyalty marks the adherents of whiteness and the boundaries of exclusion. In this way the dark bodies of America are not excluded from participation or loyalty, rather they are forced into a participation from beneath, where their glances, desires, and daily lives are now enveloped within the terms of demand for loyalty and surrender. For dark bodies, these rules serve as the condition of an exclusionary participation. Their bodies and their loyalty are still necessary to uphold the system of belief for white fullness, but their participation is one that requires distance.

Such demands are seen clearly in American anti-miscegenation laws. Such legislation against interracial sexual relations remained intact even until the 1970s in some southern states, and remained as de facto law throughout the United States for some time after. These laws evidence how American legal code outlines the conditions of participation, not merely as a means of control or instantiation of power, but as a claim to white purity. The Virginia "Act to Preserve Racial Integrity" of 1924 concludes with the following provision: "It shall hereafter be unlawful for any white person in this state to marry any save a white person, or a person with no other admixture of blood other than white and American Indian."[39] Historians Leon Higginbotham Jr. and Barbara Kopytoff note the importance of antebellum legal codes in maintaining clear racial boundaries; whites were charged with maintaining racial purity, but the law supposedly protected white women from black men.[40] Analogous to the levitical laws of ancient Israel, American law subtly preserved a certain notion of purity while maintaining order. The law made clear the shape of participation in the racial order while providing the means to persecute and beat back that which would defile the hope of white flesh.[41] Such laws served both as a means of control and as mechanisms to discipline and shape the desires of its adherents. The laws effectively deepened and shaped a distrust of black flesh as heathen, overtly passionate and sexual, and lacking in rationality, while emphasis upon white maintenance of purity reinstantiated a vision of white self-control and innocence epitomized in the white female body.[42] This not only provided order, but inscribed a religious ideal that outlined the shape of white life and hope.

While the legal codes also performed an important function of maintaining the purity of the "nation," these laws first governed the appropriate relation among peoples. The purity of the nation was not constituted by the purity of the people themselves. Historian Matthew Frye Jacobson in *Whiteness of a Different Color* notes such racial lines were drawn and redrawn as European immigrants flooded the United States. Yet these laws did work to govern sexual intimacy among peoples so as to inscribe and reinscribe the proper relationship between light and dark, citizens and aliens. It is this relationship that constituted purity, for purity could not be established ontologically or through biological claims or any other claims concerning one's essential nature (although this was certainly attempted.) Rather, the necessity of the legal codes (and their enforcement) indicate a much deeper awareness that it was the clear establishment of a borderland that made the interior intelligible. That is, the legal codes served to demarcate what constituted citizenship, whiteness, or civilization. These boundaries could not be drawn through positive accounts of white life alone. They had to be drawn by demonizing black flesh. The legal codes instantiated these ideals concerning white and black flesh by using black bodies to inscribe an outline whose sole means were intended to highlight a center.

Amidst this demarcation the tragedy of mulatto/a existence visibly emerges. Mulatto/a bodies are those that reveal the boundary and the center to be permeable. Further, mulatto/a bodies reveal the presence of the center in the boundaries and the presence of the boundary in the center. The mulatto/a body is not merely a momentary tour into the promised land or a foray into the exotic, but is the very product of these two polarities. Yet mulatto/a life is incomprehensible within the concrete imagination of racialized lives. It at once interrupts and is summarily crushed even as its body speaks. The mulatto/a is sacrificed upon the altar of race in order to maintain the illusion of walls and frontiers. The mulatto/a disrupts the notion of proper relations that the law so fiercely guards, for the mulatto/a body represents both sides of the transgression. It is the inner and the outer bound together in one person. Its life is tragic because it is deemed from one vantage point to be an impossibility, from another a degradation.

While American legislation served to discipline desire and outline a certain telos for striving adherents, they also marked the points of transgression. Such transgressions within this racial space must be accounted for; they must be atoned. Again, Hughes' allusion to the "falling pillar" of the temple points to the way purity becomes religiously bound to white identity, as well as how the presence of mixed-race bodies threaten such a claim. In the face of the possible transgression of the pure with the impure, there must be a sacrifice that might render such impurities pure again. In the face of the law and the hope of white purity, transgression must be met with sacrifice and death. Here it is not the exclusion or death of the transgressor that renders atonement, rather the sacrifice of a mediating body. The death bound to all dark bodies becomes complicated in the mulatto/a as they negotiate either an "escape" from dark life or an ascendency into the promise of white life. The mulatto/a mediates these boundaries even as he or she resists or lives into the inevitable death of his or her daily possibilities. These lives enact the ritual of all racialized life as they either abandon themselves to perpetual slavery, despite and because of their white fathers, or live as children lost, "passed" into the white world, becoming dead to their mothers, sisters, and brothers.

Between 1889 and 1932 over 2,900 African Americans were lynched.[43] The rhetoric justifying the vast majority of these sacrifices surrounded a

black man's sexual advances toward a white woman. Ida B. Wells pointed
to the great disparity in this rhetoric and the actual circumstances sur-
rounding lynching, critically noting exactly *how* the rhetoric functioned.[44]
Here the desire to protect white female bodies represented a deeper desire
to protect all white flesh from the impurity of black bodies. White female
bodies represented the rational and the beautiful, a veritable repository of
the image of God that must be protected from the savage aggression of
dark bodies (who cannot control their own sexual desires), who assuredly
desire the goodness they do not inherently possess. A particularly stark
example of how the rhetoric of the legal codes was bound to the myth
of purity is found in the 1915 film *The Birth of a Nation*. A subtext of
this film clearly pronounces a "higher law" while depicting the heroism
of individuals who can uphold said laws to protect against the threat of
"heathens." But what is actually protected here is the deification of white
bodies, in particular the purity of the white female body that carries with
it the promise of the nation.[45] Her corruption at the hands of the darker
race not only represents a threat to her safety, but a threat to a larger ideal
of what it means to be a member of this nation.[46]

In the face of such transgressions these dark bodies were summarily beaten, hung, and burned, often with the extremities cut and given as
remembrances of the moment. The exclusion that functions here threatens the dark outline, not the white adherent. Sacrifice was a means to
atone and demarcate one's faithfulness to their identity. The necessity of
death on the part of another upheld the myth of whiteness and further
demarcated what whiteness was, simultaneously seeking to punish those
who had transgressed the conditions of participation set for them. This
system of sacrifice, which yielded the "strange fruit" of the South, served
to instantiate a racial imagination of white goodness while reinforcing the
consequences of transgressing this goodness. The material of this sacrifice
was not white flesh, but a ritual of atonement where the black body was
given over to death in order to reinscribe whiteness. While not all white
people participated in these rituals of sacrifice, they did participate nonetheless in the conditions that made it possible, and through their daily
interactions with one another and with darker peoples, continued reiterating the necessity and reliance upon such sacrifices. The legal codes served
to mark the conditions of participation within American racial religiosity
while lynching cleansed its adherents of sins real and imagined, rendering
all "clean."

The religious nature of racial performance enveloped the lives of its adherents as well as their practices. In particular, Christianity became co-opted into a larger narrative of race and was performed in its service. Antebellum baptisms typify such a co-opting and highlight how Cobb's last aspect of ultimate concern—promise—becomes simultaneously injected with demand and threat. Through a process of initiation that undoubtedly began as children were small, slowly nursing on the gentle reminders of who was who, slaveholding Christianity and later a dominant white Christianity institutionalized these dogmas through its baptismal practices. By briefly outlining the deviations of the practice for slaves in South Carolina we also observe the formative power of the same practice for white Christians.

As recorded by Francis La Jau, Anglican bishop of colonial South Carolina, the demand for loyalty and surrender is most distinctly witnessed in the antebellum baptismal rite of confession for slaves.

> You declare in the Presence of God and before this Congregation that you do not ask for the holy baptism out of any design to free yourself from the Duty and Obedience you owe to your Master while you live, but merely for the good of Your Soul and to Partake of the Graces and Blessings promised to the Members of the Church of Jesus Christ.[47]

La Jau's confession exemplifies the manner in which the presence of God was invoked, not as an entrance into a new kind of community, but in order to concretize one's participation in a racialized community. In this way we see the baptismal moment as much more than a practice of spiritual initiation; it is a moment of profound cultural encounter where the meaning of blackness and whiteness are arbitrated through the language of baptism. At stake in La Jau's confession is the extent to which baptism rearranges the political and cultural realities which blackness and whiteness represent. Here the church, as well as the presence of God, are but tools that fortify a reality far deeper and more profound than God and the church—race.[48]

While this rite was intended for the initiation of black slaves into the church, we must attend to the way it also served to incorporate and instantiate whiteness in the world. The slave is baptized into a particular institution governed and sustained by racial logic over and against any gospel. The slaves themselves understood this reality, as numerous accounts of the "invisible institution" have shown.[49] In these moments such baptismal rites are less the binding of a confessor to their God, but the making sacred of a master's bond to a slave, confirming the primacy of white bodies over dark bodies. The slaves' surrender and loyalty are racially construed as their lives become bound to God *and* master. But here the inverse is also true: whiteness arches above this moment, making it sacred not as it relates to God and participation in the church, but as it further mediates the participation of black bodies in relation to white bodies. The master's dominance is baptized, legitimated, and divinized in this moment less through the aspects of the rite itself, but in the way that racialization has already established the bounds within which the rite might take place; the logic of race determines the efficacy of the rite and its transformative possibilities. The demand is both threat and promise. Even the explicitly religious has been co-opted by a reality that is understood to be prior and primary. Baptism became a rite of race where notions of fulfillment and promise were to be construed strictly through the materiality of white dominance.[50]

In the initiation of black bodies into the church the ritual of race serves to bind together black and white bodies within a certain framework of dominance and submission. However, this relationship is one that is perpetually contested, reimagined, and lived into. That is, the baptismal moment La Jau makes visible shows how black and white bodies are bound to one another in this "religious" moment. Black and white bodies rehearse religious laws and mores, making possible the telos of white life. Progress along this trajectory however, necessitated the incessant sacrifice of dark flesh.

Ultimately legal codes, sacrificial death, and racial rites formed a material reality in which all people in the United States would live. Connected to these material realities, which illumined how race shaped American (and Western) life as a religious imagination, is the function of religious symbols and myth. In Cobb's consideration of the various aspects of religion, religious symbols serve to point beyond themselves while still participating in that which they symbolize. They are not artificially produced, as they grow out of the religious identification of an aspect of the adherent's devotion. Religious myths, then, "work with symbols to guide in determining one's relationship to the world."[51] Myths are particularly important in that they help (a) make clear the connections and order of the world in which the adherents live, and (b) begin to dictate the patterns of relating to others and to the world around them. Cobb notes,

> Myths feed us our scripts. We imitate the quests and struggles of the
> dominant figures in the myths and rehearse our lives informed by myth

plots. We awaken to a set of sacred stories, and then proceed to appre-hend the world and to express ourselves in terms of these stories. They shape us secretly at a formative age and remain with us, informing the ongoing narrative constructions of our experience. They teach us how to perceive the world as we order our outlooks and choices in terms of their patterns and plots.[52]

The notion of myth described by Cobb highlights the performative char-acter of religious lives. It is the breadth of these mythic claims and the manner in which they envelop the entirety of a nation that begins to give it its religious character. The claims that whiteness make as an ultimate concern: the myth of white flesh, the practices of daily life in ceremony, law, and incorporation now drip with the claims of white bodies. These claims are not particular to white people but expand their reach, incor-porating all peoples into participation with its claims, even against their will. Again, *The Birth of a Nation* offers a vivid example of how such myths function to solidify political and social imagination. The myth of a nation's "birth" is tied to the violent suppression of darker bodies and the coupling (or breeding) of "good" families.[53] Thus the movie suggests a new historical narrative while engendering the vision of personhood and social participation in that it is eschatological. This is not to say that such a movie was widely accepted (although it was wildly popular), but such a film, released only ten years prior to the Hughes poem we have dis-cussed, does point to the necessary exclusion that American nationalism is built upon. These examples articulate how religion, not only explicitly religious syntax, comes to constitute a particular society's cultural fabric so that "cultural" moments remain deeply religious despite their lack of explicit religious self-understanding.

The religious structure of seemingly cultural or racial bias reflects how racialized lives are never sure or given, or even natural, as such lives must be *performed*. That is, while the rhetoric of race in modernity has pressed upon racial purity and its inherence or essential character within peoples, how such "natural" lives must be maintained begins to make apparent the way "natural" traits are, in fact, acts of strength, struggling to maintain something inherent. They are rather always contrived and thus performed in one's negotiation of daily life. Cultural theorist Judith Butler points to how such claims to one's essential nature becomes ultimately tied to bitter attempts to control.[54] She notes that we must attend to the various interconnections and textures of lives in order to see how each performs and articulates a certain notion of freedom.

In our previous examination of legal codes, sacrifice, and religious ritual we saw the way racial imagination provided the means of attaining to or participating in racial life. As Butler notes, essential aspects of life are not given. They are lived into. What we have seen in the various aspects of racialized cultic practices is not the maintenance of something that is prior, but that racialized life required adherents. It required those who would participate in the system and make its necessary sacrifices in order to maintain notions of their own purity and their own goodness. Racial life had less to do with biology and more to do with participation. Race in the West formed disciples who performed its ideal and in so doing reinscribed the system and enforced the obedience of others.

In this performance the ideality of whiteness was never fully attained, rather, it was to be maintained, protected, and hoped for. Throughout the West this ideal was but a specter never fully present, but vigilantly guarded and served. Here the claim regarding how a people seek to live into a reality that is always beyond them—the racial ideal—is a transcendent category that hovers above, ever present, but is difficult to locate. Yet this ideal is made visible through the lives of those who adhere to its possibilities via their desires, their hopes, their religion, and their vision of justice.

Conclusion

At the center of modernity's racial fidelity was the mulatto/a. The mulatto/a body rendered visible the ways racial lines were maintained and transgressed with regularity. Within a religious structure of law, sacrifice, and initiation notions of purity were legally (by law), sacrificially (by lynching), and ceremoniously (by baptism) maintained. These moments reflect a profound religiosity where striving for the ideal required the continual preservation of a perception of racial certainty. Such performances were engrained within the possibility of citizenship, meaning whiteness required a particular biology in conjunction with a kind of assent. Whiteness required faithfulness and proper participation in the modes of life that allowed these myths to maintain their intelligibility. Such lives are marked by the way in which its adherents are disciples of race. They are those who do more than participate; they work to maintain the pillars of the temple by monitoring the proper participation by their sons, daughters, neighbors, and friends under the threat of exclusion, all in hopes of the ideal of safety and "good" families.

The mulatto/a body creates precisely this participatory reality that mulatto/a existence unveils, for while nonwhite lives contest racial dogmas and claims, they are nevertheless relegated to a mythic underworld where their existence makes possible white life. Their darkness is shadowed by the broader racial myth struggling to uphold the temple of race. Yet, mulatto/a existence makes apparent the transgression of these seemingly disparate realities, and thus unmasks its faith and tears down the veil of its inner life, showing the presence of darker peoples *within* white lives. These lives unveil the idolatry of white religiosity and require us as Christians to begin to account for (a) the ways in which such religiosity is present among us and (b) whether or not we participate. We are challenged in this moment to reappraise whether we are saved or we are heathen.

The mere presence of mulatto/a bodies in the world frays an already unstable system, but these contestations, passing, and tenuous notions of racial fidelity are revelatory of either white assertions of dominance or dark refusals that consequently reassert an illusion of purity and adherence. Interpreted theologically, mulatto/a bodies display the way race is not merely a construction or performance, but a hope that orders the lives of its believers even in spite of themselves. In this way racialized religious performance is best seen not in its theoretical construct, but through the lens of discipleship.

Within a framework of discipleship, the articulations of racial imagination and performance suggested throughout this chapter might now be theologically interpreted in relationship to Christian articulations of entrance into Christian community. This religious character could be said to share certain marks of pagan ritual common in the culture that the early church had to confront as it invited and welcomed new members into its community. These churches were challenged not only politically, but had to reorient their members in relationship to the religious structure of the Roman Empire as well as the various pagan religions the Christians would come into contact with on a daily basis. Even after the "conversion" of Constantine, Christians would have to negotiate the remnants of Roman religious life embedded within everyday life.

One powerful example can be drawn from the catechetical orations of Cyril of Jerusalem and the renunciation that marked the beginning of the baptismal rite. Here the catechumens of fifth century Jerusalem rejected the devil, his pomp, his service, and his work.[55] Each of these marks of the evil one had explicit ties to the pagan culture in the Roman Empire. But Cyril's reflection points to the ways such religiosity is performed within the daily lives of its adherents. Marriage, games, meals, and shows (among other things) all become the ground of a religious identity where one is bound to a particular idea one must adhere and conform to. In the wake of a modern world that created bodies to be sold, that classified the world within pages, and forged economies of faith and hope upon race, the church and theology must begin to see its complicity in new ways. The church must confess its worship of an idol and renounce the evil one.

Hughes' poem has shown how racialized lives have become profoundly religious moments of unfaithfulness in the West. Almost every aspect of American daily cultural and political life was saturated with racial logic aimed toward the maintenance of certain notions of racial purity and hierarchy. Yet, in the midst of these strict assertions and policing of boundaries there were, in fact, voluntary and involuntary transgressions of these boundaries. Here mulatto/a bodies were witness to the illusiveness of such claims of purity and the way the aims of such claims are ultimately illusory. This visibility indeed renders the life of the mulatto/a tragic, and profoundly witnesses to the tragic in all racialized lives caught in such perpetual and perilous performances of race in contemporary society. These performances delimit the possibilities of personhood, becoming in themselves moments of deep idolatry, binding adherents into lives that cannot imagine their being in Christ outside of their own image. Discipleship is thus a profoundly inward distortion of racial and nationalistic hope. It is a religiosity of desires refracted through the discursive realities of racialized bodies.

Within these illusions all bodies and lives must navigate discerning truth from falsehood. It is this negotiation, this path of racial discipleship that we will turn to next. Looking to the literary portrayals of mulatto/a lives we see the performance of race and the attempts of these interstitial bodies to claim a real space within society. But as they do so we see the deepening of these claims upon their lives and the enclosing of race upon their various attempts to find hope in the world.

Chapter 2

NEITHER FISH NOR FOWL
Presence as Politics

Identities are, as it were, the positions which the subject is obliged to take up while always "knowing" that they are representations, that representation is always constructed across a "lack," across division, from the place of the Other, and thus can never be adequate—identical—to the subject processes which are invested in them.

—Stuart Hall[1]

INTRODUCTION

The mulatto/a is a peculiar creation. Mulatto/a existence cannot be described strictly in terms of what it is, but must also take into account the circumstances and the people that gave birth to it. In the years following slavery and Reconstruction the reality of the mulatto body would remain a perplexing presence among assertions of white and black.[2] And, while these interracial bodies were rendered neither/nor, they themselves sought to embody a wholeness in the space between black and white. The interracial life was a dissonant bodily performance wherein authenticity within the white world or black world was impossible but to occupy both spaces was heretical. Consequently, the interracial is rendered "neither/nor" and continues to occupy a nebulous space in between the claims of what is white and black. As children of the slave ship the interracial became subjected to the scrutiny of classification and

41

yet sought to assert a wholeness in the face of their neither/nor existence. Seeking to escape the power of classification bound to the slave ship, interracial lives resisted and capitulated to the New World's racial order. In their resistance and their capitulation mulatto lives made visible the illusory contours of racial life. The ways mulatto people represented themselves and were represented by others opens a way of seeing how interracial lives were (and can be) an interruption. These bodies bore, through their simple presence, the possibility of disorienting the claims concerning racialized life in the West and thus can be understood as inherently political. Through three particular literary moments we see how interracial lives themselves, created through transgressive desire and discursive refusals, negotiate racial life, at once disrupting its claims and norms yet also becoming subject to its claims and hopes. Resisting the legacies of slavery, interracial existence sought to claim the power of its own classification.

But how might bodies that have been born of lust and power, whose lives, thoughts, and possibilities have been delimited by a system of classification, live truthfully? Do these people envisage themselves as "a people," throwing off the vestiges of racial hegemony and the doctrines that seemingly participated in their enslavement? Or do they seek a higher ground, a higher knowledge, a *meta* narrative that can resist the circumscription of theological knowledge within the confines of history or religion? And what of the lives that must live into or out of these modes of formation and resistance?

The interruptions of the interracial body, however hopeful, ultimately fail within a logic of identity that calls adherents to resist the transformation such mulatto bodies indicate. Racialized life, even for persons who are interracial, becomes an inherent trap. The power of racial logic ceaselessly enfolds identities into moments of competing self-assertions. This negotiation of assertions becomes embodied in the mundane and the intimate as white, black, Latino/a, Asian/Asian American, and "inter" all discern and are disciplined to resist the implications of encounters with difference and their possibilities.

While the first chapter described the encounter and representation of interracial bodies, this chapter seeks to exegete these bodies and lives themselves. Making visible the process of identification explicit in interracial existence (as well as any formation of identity), interracial lives display the contours and impossibilities of racial discipleship. Moving from the formation of this identification or discipleship in chapter 1, I now turn to consider the rhythm or shape of interracial existence as the lines of racial identity shift in the United States, giving rise to the peculiar phenomenon of "passing."[3]

"Passing" as a means of contestation is most clearly seen in the early twentieth century as racial lines continued to be negotiated in the northern as well as the southern states.[4] In particular, literary depictions of life and longing begin to display the power of racial imagination and American citizenship. At the same time, these literary descriptions of American life reveal mulatto/a existence as disruptive and bound within the racial logic the writers so desperately want to escape. Three particular literary iterations of interracial or mulatto/a existence and passing display racial discipleship and its ultimate tragedy: Charles Chesnutt's *The House Behind the Cedars*, James Weldon Johnson's *Autobiography of an Ex-Coloured Man*, and Nella Larsen's *Passing*. These texts underscore how mulatto/a bodies and the performance of race through these bodies should be understood as intensely and inherently political. They disrupt because they *are*. Such accounts can be read as varying ways to account for their "whatness."[5] Chesnutt, Johnson, and Larsen each display various methods of negotiating racial life in the United States. While each writer examines the disruptive force of such lives and performances, each does so by highlighting a unique strategy of conformity or resistance while at the same time bearing the mark of tragic refusal and death.

Written within twenty-five years of one another, between 1902 and 1927, these three works reflect the deep ambiguity and struggle to interpret the interracial body. From Chesnutt's to Johnson's to Larsen's works we see the themes of alienation and loneliness that pervade the lives of their mulatto/a protagonists. Yet, these works also make varying interpretations of these bodies. These interpretations or representations of the mixed body indicate the possibilities and impossibilities of not only those mulatto/a bodies, but all bodies within the "crucible" of racial existence in America.[6] In each of these texts we see how interracial lives exhibit the discipling character of racial life while also destabilizing it.[7]

"Inter" Existence and Literary Performances of Identity

Before I explore these texts in particular it is important to first highlight the relationship between literary articulations of race and racial life in the United States in the nineteenth and twentieth centuries. The peril and fascination of the interracial was perhaps no less clear in the Western and American imaginations than in the question of "whatness" or racial classification of the early twentieth century. The seemingly never-ending system of names to describe the various intermixtures of races served to create a discourse through which the children of these interracial encounters might be incorporated into the larger racial polity of the colonial West. This process of classification served to not only define the names, but also discipline or structure their relations as well. That is, while much of the question and desire to name interracial bodies in the eighteenth and nineteenth centuries was centered upon biological questions, these biological realities were merely the face of a deeper cultural and political claim. In this regard we begin to see the birth and life of the mulatto/a (or interracial) child in deeply political terms. The bodies of these children indicate the possibility of something new, which must be perpetually resisted, contained, or sacrificed.

The very conception and birth of the mulatto/a child becomes the instantiation of a deep disruption within the religiosity of racial performance and life. The lives of these children who seek to articulate their lives in the midst of this disjuncture, which characterizes their life, points to the ways in which all bodies ultimately perform into racial claims. Yet for these mixed bodies the possibility of participation or personhood is bound between two impossibilities. In other words, they are neither/nor. Here mulatto/a bodies both point to the performative nature of such lives and at the same time begin to disrupt these performances through their presence and negotiation of racialized life.

Although ethnic and racial intermixture is not an unknown phenomenon in the history of peoples, such intermixture became a subject of profound interest in the West beginning in the eighteenth century. Such reflections upon racial intermixture became intensified in the United States during the nineteenth and twentieth centuries when the question concerning these hybrid bodies inherently challenged the economic, political, and social scaffolding upon which American society had been built. Judgments concerning the identity of these neither/nor bodies not only includes questions determining freedom or bondage, but also, as we examined in the previous chapter, the reality of intermixture and the children such encounters produced were moments that either threatened or disrupted the racial hierarchy that dominated American social and political realities. While notions concerning racial purity were varied, the reality of a radical racial polarity engendered not only a fear, but also a deep fascination, with the "hybrid" child.

At this point I should note that while racial themes were present in American fiction and other literary genres, the aim here is not to historically trace the development of how the interracial person was viewed or viewed himself during this time.[8] Rather, the aim here is to begin to ascertain the *meaning* of these bodies and lives. That is, the continual interpretation of these bodies indicates a profound reality regarding the power of racial formation in the West. The aim here is to begin to delineate a particular theological interpretation of these bodies and the realities of race they unveil for all of us. The understanding of these children as tragic is construed in a variety of ways by a variety of authors, and while these bodies fascinate the public we must also attend to the ways in which these bodies (real and literary) began to articulate, disrupt, and display the utter performativity of all racial subjects as well as point toward the ultimately tragic state of existence for all racialized lives.

The birth of the interracial child perpetually calls to us the refrain of the advent hymn of new birth, "What child is this?" With every birth of a mulatto/a child the system of classification exerts itself to narrate the child into a certain reality, policing its borders and continually reevaluating its own measure of inclusion. Through the rubric of race and the correlations of purity, whiteness, and being American the mulatto/a body is both created and disruptive. This disruption derives not from the mulatto/a's "hybrid" body as radically different, but rather the way in which this hybridity reverberates within the lives of those who assert their own purity. This refusal of the mulatto/a is the refusal of the hybridity of all identities. The nature of identity as fundamentally hybrid is, as literary and cultural theorist Samira Kawash notes, "a force utterly heterogeneous and unrecuperable . . . Hybridity in its most complex sense is in fact an impossibility; it is not something that one can be. . . ."[9] The mulatto/a body is a political presence that confronts all claims to a racially (or ethnically) grounded personhood that resists its own realities of mixture. These hybrid bodies thus display not only the subversion of racial knowledge but also the patterns of life born out of those assertions and assumptions. The mulatto/a body is created by the radical polarities of colored and white that serve to make possible notions of mixture.

The interracial body is disruptive because of what it indicates as well as the ways in which such bodies must perform through these realities, pointing back to the falsity of the claims concerning purity. Their lives are sheer performativity. Mulattos/as are constantly negotiating their relationships and realities because their lives are negotiating the lines (and practices) that constitute racial lives (either white or black), as well as seeking to live into racial space despite the impossibility. Attempts to live into such entrenched and powerful modes of identification are vital aspects of what is the inherently political body of the interracial person.

Through the mulatto/a's enactment of racial discipleship however, the impossibility of identification becomes apparent. Yet, these bodies and these lives must be accounted for. They are present in the world, just as they have been created by the world. Such lives are inherently *political* even in their passive or not so passive assertions of racial fidelity, insofar as they disrupt the claims of belonging and otherness by existing on both sides of the divide. In claiming a race they are requiring those members of "their" race to either accept or reject that performance. The necessity of reception or rejection that these lives interject into the modern world suggests their inherently political nature or their capacity to "deauthenticate community."[10] To fail to attend to these lives is to blur the line that gives national identities their power.

It is in the midst of the totalizing claims of race and the curious category of mulatto/a existence that we find the phenomenon of "passing." Passing, in the American context, was the practice of a person of African descent who could be perceived as white "passing" themselves off as white and thus "pass" into white society.[11] Such instances reveal the fantastic effort required to attain a "better" life as well as how such racial constructions bore concrete realities.[12] The mulatto/a body lives into the patterns of white life, disrupting it from within and inscribing white bodies themselves with the other. In the passing moment the white body becomes rewritten and interpretable as something that can be signified from within one who is "dark."

The patterns of life, tastes, education, language, desires, etc. become articulated through bodies rendered "dark" and thus the telos of white life itself. Such practices reveal the intense pressure of racial life and hope in America, underscoring that passing is not the exclusive mode of racial performance. The ability of some folks to pass implies how racial purity and notions of fixed identity require peoples to adhere or live into racial (and cultural) ideals. Practices of placidness do not constitute the entirety of their existence, but also cannot be easily extricated from the mundane choices of daily life. That some pass into certain societies only opens up the question to us concerning how we all pass for what we are as well as what actions or practices reveal us to be traitors. The disruption of racial knowledge upends the political processes of becoming that characterize the ontology of American citizenship. The policing of participation becomes subverted through the passing body. Passing fiction seeks to rearticulate bodies "long indicted as a symptom of middle class bias, racial self-hatred, and internalization of white values."[13] This rearticulation "in African American fiction of the New Negro Renaissance the trope of passing functions instead as an aggressive strategy to reinterpret race as a socio-cultural construct, rather than a biological destiny."[14] African American passing fiction of the early twentieth century reimagined these racial lines while also seeking to articulate themselves anew within them.

Theologically, interracial lives and the texts that expressed the significance of their bodies to us, begin to indicate both the promise and the tragic embedded in their "inter" lives. These lives indicate the anemia of Christian belief upon the people that exist in such profoundly racialized ways. They signify the intensification of the daily choices that confront our lives and the hopes we press ourselves into as well as the infidelities we resist. These lives, reverberating through the unfolding of white and black life alike in modern America, are representations of how Christian bodies are both living into and out of racial faithfulness and ultimately marking our lives incongruous to the lives baptism wrought upon us.

CHARLES CHESNUTT: DISRUPTION AND THE RECIPROCITY OF DESIRE

Writing in the late nineteenth and early twentieth centuries, Charles Chesnutt wrote a series of short stories and novels reflecting upon African American life. Central to most of these stories were mulatto/a or interracial characters whose identity as such was central to the arc of the story. His works were lauded for their realistic portrayal of black life and in particular a growing African American middle class that displayed mixed race men and women and African Americans more generally as intelligent and capable.[15] Chesnutt has been considered to be a significant precursor to what would become the Harlem Renaissance, but his reception among African Americans and the white community alike is a complicated one.[16] While depicting African Americans in ways that resisted the typical caricatures, Chesnutt's work was also read as implicitly suggesting the superiority of lighter skin. However, these readings tend to dismiss the ways Chesnutt's notion of racial amalgamation served to threaten the seemingly secure notions of whiteness.

Each of his novels as well as his essays, therefore, must be read not only through a lens of racial uplift, but also as one of racial contamination

or more profoundly, an "absolute rupture."[17] In arguing for a racial amalgamation, the possibility of transformation served to tear notions of what
was and what could be. Chesnutt's racial amalgamation disrupts in its
explicit assertion that whiteness might become dark.[18] This possibility of a
"darkening" of the white world becomes expressed through the negotiation of mulatto/a figures who seek to live into a white world yet find its
promises unfulfilling. However, Chesnutt does not stop here. Oftentimes
his novels, while following the forms of mulattic literature preceding him,
typically climax with the reversal of white desire and the refusal of a white
world. Ultimately, these gestures become muted, but they nonetheless
point to a radical modulation of hope in the mulatto/a figure that becomes
ultimately impossible within the American world.

Articulations of the tragic continued to be present, as did themes
revolving around the permeability of racial lives as well as themes concerning social uplift. But Chesnutt's novels are also marked by a peculiar
innovation that was not represented in the Harlem Renaissance literature
that would follow it: the transformation of white desire and thus a problematizing of white purity and the binary logic of race.[19]

His novels indicate a nascent, if aborted transformation of borders
and people where these lines become amorphous and permeable for both
black and white, while also remaining deadly. The presence of these figures among white and black lives alike becomes politically weighted with
the potential for transformation, but also with the possibility of death,
given the deep reality of racialized life. For Chesnutt, it seems, death is
still inevitable. Within the corpus of his work we see not only the movement of interracial lives into white lives, performing into white racial life,
but in several stunning moments we see this decision reversed as white
lives are drawn into black lives and hopes. This intermittent allusion to
the possibility of white hopes becoming bound to black bodies and black
lives becomes present in a variety of his works such as *Paul Marchand,
F.M.C.*, *The Colonel's Dream*, and *The Wife of His Youth*. While such
depictions of borders are certainly idealistic for their time (and perhaps
ours) they are a striking departure from the considerations of mulatto/a
life of Chesnutt's time. This reversal of white hopes into black life marks
Chesnutt's truly disruptive gesture. Recent scholarship has rightfully
attended to how these depictions destabilize the notions of racial certainty
that undergirded American social and political life. However, in my view,
the depiction of exchange or living into dark life unveils the deepest disruptive force of these bodies.

Chesnutt had a difficult time getting his work initially published, and some suggest the hesitancy of publishers was the display of black lives as capable and intelligent, but it could also be suggested that the permeability of the racial lines is what made these works so threatening. That black life was something that could be "chosen" or desired, that somehow white identity could be given up in favor of identification with dark bodies was a revolutionary concept in early twentieth-century writing. The radical inversion of the passing narrative scores these texts as particularly unique and threatening in a time when the lines of racial logic were becoming more strongly demarcated. This is not to suggest that Chesnutt's work is idealistic or overly romantic, for even in these works the tragedy of interracial lives is still pronounced, for such transformation is equally impossible and equally dangerous for all parties involved. For the purposes of this work I will attend to Chesnutt's 1901 work *The House Behind the Cedars*. It exhibits the themes I have discussed previously (the performativity of race and the tragedy of racial discipleship) but also inverts these tragedies and reverberates them within white lives and bodies, binding the tragedy of racial life within both black and white people in profound ways, ultimately gesturing to the necessity of an utter transformation engendered through interracial bodies.

The novel takes place in North Carolina and centers upon Rena, a quadroon,[20] whose mulatta mother, Molly, lives in relative isolation, intentionally distanced from African Americans, but not fully white and thus excluded from white life. Molly was in love with and had been supported by a wealthy white man until his death. Upon his death the estate would be given entirely to the white man's wife, leaving Molly and her two children Rena and John with only a small home and a bit of land. John, determined to inherit his birthright, secretly apprentices for a local lawyer and when he is old enough leaves his mother and sister to practice law in a distant town as a white man. There, he becomes a prominent and respected member of the community. He returns to his hometown hoping to convince his mother to allow Rena to come back with him and pass into white society as well. Rena is initially overjoyed at the idea and Molly, while saddened, allows her daughter to go.

Rena quickly catches the eye of another prominent bachelor in her new town, is engaged, but begins to question the love of a man who does not truly know who she is. She also mourns for the mother she left. After an ill-advised visit to see her mother, Rena is discovered by her fiancé, Tryon. Tryon quickly dismisses her and Rena retreats to her mother. But in Rena's absence, Tryon comes to realize his true love for her and begins to pursue her once again. Yet this time Rena is torn between her life with her mother, her decision to teach "her people," and the love of Tryon. Eventually Tryon is willing to give up his position in society to be with Rena only to find her dead, torn between the psychic violence of these two worlds that she cannot fully inhabit.

The House Behind the Cedars takes place within the gap of certainty that constitutes white and black identity in America. The distance that marks Rena and John constitutes their existence in the world as black despite their appearance as white. This gap between classification and appearance renders them utterly in between these societies. Such distancing suggests the way mulatto/as' themselves tended to live into the "privilege" of their hue and thus exhibited themselves as also recapitulating the performance of race in problematic ways. This is why it is crucial to note that interracial bodies are themselves not a way out, but rather represent or perform a disruption they themselves do not fully understand or live into. Thus their presence is political even if they are not.

Narrating the middle life of this mulatto brother and sister, Rena and John, Chesnutt narrates the presumptions of mulatto/a existence as well as their perils. In each sibling the hopes of participation and a grander life are bound to a blindness regarding those who truly love them. Their presence in these worlds leaves them both tragically transformed and agents of transformation. This transformation offers only a glimmer of promise at the conclusion of the text, but outlines the deeply tragic nature of these lives, existing between the boundaries that are imposed both from without and within, suggesting that interracial love and desire and the fruits of those scandalous encounters are perpetually measured, sorted, and disciplined in order to maintain the certainty of the system. *The House Behind the Cedars* displays the negotiation and disruption of American racial life through three movements or thematic depictions of John and Rena's life: Departure and Return, Border Crossing and Death, and Death for All. In each of these moments the mulatto/a body is pregnant with the possibility of transformation, but becomes modulated through the differing desires of Rena and John and the particularly gendered negotiation of these bodies. Rena's and John's lives display the religious ethos of white life as well as the sacrificial nature of entering that life. In particular, Rena's life demonstrates how the female body is both subjected to these racial realities in particular ways, and because of this negotiates the pressures in ways that are distinctly different from John's strident entrance into white life. Through these three movements the reality of racial life is not only bound to Rena and John, but we see how their lives are intimately connected to the lives of dark and light alike.

DEPARTURE AND RETURN: THE PERFORMANCE AND POSSIBILITY OF RACE

Rena is reunited with her brother who has "returned from the dead"[21] after leaving his mother and his sister to pass into white life. In the ten years since he has left he has become a well-respected lawyer, married into a wealthy and established family, and become well known within white southern society. However, also during this time his wife has died, leaving him to raise his daughter alone. His return is a dangerous one, for if his true identity were found he would surely lose his place within this society, but he returns to take Rena with him. In part he seeks to provide a female caregiver for his child, but he also hopes that she might escape the life of stigma that marked their lives as children. He returns to ask her to cross over with him into a new world.

The return of John Warwick as one who entered fully into the life of promise is bound to a messianic call to lift his sister up from the darkness of her position "for he was not only a son—a brother—but he represented to them the world from which circumstances had shut them out, and to which distance lent even more than its usual enchantment; and they felt nearer to this far-off world because of the glory Warwick reflected from it."[22] However, the messianic imagery of John Warwick's return is muted by the cost of this salvation. For Rena to enter into a new life her old life must die. The baptism she must enter into upon immersing herself into white life requires the death of her old self and "henceforth she must be known as Miss Warwick, dropping the old name with the old life."[23] Here, entrance into redemption requires sacrifice and death.

Her life was, prior to entry into the white world, one where her darker brothers and sister were to be pitied for their distance from white life. But upon her own rejection from the white world "where once she had seemed able to escape from them, they were now, it appeared, her inalienable race." In seeing the ease with which white desire and love could be abandoned she returned to "her people" as "new-born [with a] desire to be of service to her re-discovered people."[24] Chesnutt's articulation of departure and return is an aspect of the passing phenomenon that we will find articulated differently in Johnson and Larsen as well. The power of differentiation serves to elevate, giving rise to a sense of departure from shackles and the consequence of departure indicates how classification is a process of association through which a people are subjugated. The departure of Rena and John indicate how escape from classification is indeed possible, thus ripping the fragile veil with the ease of a new name. But this possibility, this desire, also demonstrates how deeply such logic inhabits even those who can see the fallacy of such distinctions. The depictions of this moment also indicate the sacrifice of Rena and her mother. The isolation of Rena's life served to make the tie between them all the more important. Rena's departure into a life with no mother reveals slavery's distorted reach even in the lives of those who seem to "benefit" from its logic.

The notion of return, however, is not a simple one, for this return is continually marked by a fundamental difference. This is a difference that is not necessarily connected to superiority (in Rena's case), but a recognition of the way one's hue binds one to another people despite one's own desire. This binding becomes apparent in Rena's attachment to Tryon. In her entry into a white world of endless possibilities she, in fact, sees deep limitations. Her participation is always precipitated by an incoherence, an incoherence, who she knows herself to be and who she represents herself to be. Therefore, the desire for Tryon is a desire for recognition that cannot be expressed through economic participation, as in her brother's situation, but instead demands the full recognition of the one whom she loves and it is upon that basis that her participation in that world can be rendered full or blessed.

Rena's departure and the possibility of her return mark a crucial observation regarding the texture or rhythm of interracial existence—the necessity of departure and return marks these lives. Participation in one world forecloses the possibility of participation in another. Thus the neither/nor that constitutes the life of Rena and John is a life where the possibility of participation in white life is attainable. But this participation is always mitigated by the loss or death necessary to make it possible. John's return as one who represents the fullest possibilities of personhood returns to those to whom he was dead. His return is one of being confronted not only with the possibilities of entrance into a world forbidden, but also as a reminder of the limitations inherent in such promises.

This life of perpetual departure and arrival, where every place lies as a possibility but at a distance, is one of ontological exile. Such an exilic existence, characterized by this "habit of dissimulation" is, according to Edward Said, "both wearying and nerve wrecking. Exile is never the state of being satisfied, placid, or secure . . . a life of exile moves according to a different calendar, and is less seasonal and settled than life at home. Exile is life led outside habitual order. It is nomadic de-centered, contrapuntal; but no sooner does one get accustomed to it than its unsettling force erupts anew."[25] The exilic order of things pointed to in Said is bound to a certain geographical reorientation that must take place as one negotiates the daily disruptions of what is known and what is new. But the interracial body takes this decentering reality and locates it within one's very body. Their bodies become the location of this geographic dislocation. The possibility of departure and return latent in the lives of those who can pass reverberates back to the impossibility of a homeland. Rest and longing lay tragically beyond Rena and John as their bodies represent impossibility and incoherence in the union of difference that produced them.

It is this disjuncture of personhood and possibility that forms the difficulty of the choice before Rena to leave her mother and follow John into the "redemption" of white life. One temptation lies in the comfort of her life with her mother. But residing within the temptation of the white world is also the cause of the incoherence of her life with her mother. They are behind the cedars, veiled from being seen or revealing themselves fully to either world. Undoubtedly this quasi-exile from their darker brethren is self-imposed, for throughout the narrative the faithfulness of Frank, the darker friend of Rena, remains. She both resents and lives into the constitution of this racial reality. She is both its disciple and subject to its discipline.

Entrance into the redemption of white life is made possible not by the inherent supremacy of the mulatto/a's biological heritage, but how their hue allows for a faithful performance of white life. The possibility of becoming white is situated in the inherently performative character of racial existence that requires only a "passable" mark. Rena enters into such a performance even in the midst of her mother's deep sadness, for Molly realizes that this is not a momentary escape but a cutting off, a new death of her now only child.

The possibility of a new world that is before Rena is the horizon of becoming, a freedom situated not by the proscriptions of limitations of others, but by the seemingly endless expanse of opportunity that white life represents. John's final attempt to convince his mother to let Rena return with him is framed eschatologically. Within the confines of the house behind the cedars the lives of Rena and John were bound within the impossibility of being white and the refusal to be dark. Their lives were a nebulous interstitial space that was only perceivable through its negations. Yet the world beyond the cedars represented participation and possibility. Beyond the cedars was a life that could be lived without the fetters of limitation. John was calling Rena to a life without an end. It is the possibility of emerging out of the shadows of nonbeing, for in this world, in the world behind the cedars, "the [Civil] war has wrought great changes, has put the bottom rail on top, and all that—but it hasn't wiped *that* out. Nothing but death can remove that stain, if it does not follow us even beyond the grave. Here she must forever be nobody!"[26] The precipice between being and nonbeing, a body and a *no*-body, is the color line. The possibility of participation in the social and economic structures of the American dream bestow the possibility of becoming, the quintessential mark of Western personhood.[27]

The promise of moving from Rena to Rowena Warwick, the possibility of her entrance into the life of her brother's promise was not one of inheritance, but of training. She would attend boarding school where she would become refined in the manners of her new people. She would become white. Her subsequent life bears the burden of avoiding the marks of a person who does not belong. Her manners, her tone, her nods, her distance from those darker than she, and her embrace of her white "kin" now become pregnant with the possibility of betraying the "truth" of who she is. Becoming and loss are thus pressed into each moment of Rena's life and as she descends more deeply into this new personhood her dissimilitude becomes more marked. This descent into a life that is "foreign" to her perpetuates a life fraught with the loneliness of the exile discussed earlier. John expressed this exile as having "always been, in a figurative sense, a naturalized foreigner in the world of wide opportunity."[28] The loneliness of this perpetually in-between existence underscores the sheer performativity of the life that John and Rena enter into. They must "live into" this world. They must adopt its customs, its accents. Their daily decisions and refusals signify the necessity of a performance appropriate to the attestation of who they are.

Rena is confronted with the sheer performativity of her chosen life as she becomes the object of the most eligible bachelor in the city, George Tryon. They quickly fall in love, but at the same time Rena becomes aware of the consequences of her decision and the risk she enters into should she marry him. She becomes torn between this man she loves and the possibility of his discovery of her identity. Rena's living into this life is marked by the possibility of discovery and death. Upon Tryon's proposal, the reality of Rena's isolation and danger awoke.

> Stated baldly, it was the consciousness of her secret; the complexity arose out of the various ways in which it seemed to bear upon her future. . . . It had not been difficult for Rena to conform her speech, her manners, and in a measure her modes of thought, to those of the people around her; but when this readjustment went beyond mere externals and concerned vital issues of life, the secret that oppressed her took on a more serious aspect, with tragic possibilities.[29]

The possibility of binding her life to another now complicated the possibility of participation.

At this point it is important to consider the importance gender plays in Rena's negotiation of this racial life. The shape of her discipleship is different from John's.[30] Specifically, Rena's reception into the fullness of this social redemption requires recognition, the incorporation of one into another to be made whole. It is a life or a performance that must be received and acknowledged to make it "true." What makes her life and performance so precarious is that she has no means to redeem herself. Her life is intertwined with and subject to another. This necessary subjection of identity is contrasted by her brother John's performance, whose participation is precipitated by his assertion concerning who he is. The female body is rendered by Chesnutt as one whose existence and participation in society must be mitigated by male authority in order to be rendered visible or full. Through this lens Rena's ascendency into white life through the deception of passing exhibits a self-assertion present within masculine life. Rena's movement into this world deepens her in-betweenness as she seeks to assert, while simultaneously subjecting, her admission to male authorization.

Rena's inability to maintain the boundaries between the worlds of the racial and feminine would lead to an eventual psychic rather than physical death. Therefore, Chesnutt could be read as reinscribing a notion of weak femininity. But to do this would be to miss the subtle way that Chesnutt observes how both Rena's presence as mulatta (or mixed *and* female) disrupts the narration of male self-assertion and the ideality of participation in white life. While not victorious, Rena takes a couple of men down with her, testifying to the weakness of the masculine and racial edifice they all existed in.

This can first be seen in how Rena's participation becomes mitigated by her expectation of recognition that is not based upon her vocation or her own self-assertion, but by a certain reception of her full self. "Would he still love me?" is the question she asks of Tryon. Her hesitancy regarding

Tryon's proposal is not an economic concern or based upon its useful-ness as entrance into the fullness of a white telos. Rather, Rena's struggle is grounded upon the necessity of Tryon's full recognition of her. Ches-nutt himself seems to cast this desire both as one of great depth as well as a mark of a feminine nature where "the fact of human nature makes woman happiest when serving where she loves."[31] Despite Chesnutt's own seemingly chauvinistic characterization of Rena's desire he nonetheless conveys how the interracial body's presence begins to disrupt the disciple-ship of racial life.

Up to this point, John's mixed presence may disrupt certain assump-tions concerning what whiteness is, but this is more of what James Wel-don Johnson's narrator in *Autobiography of an Ex-Coloured Man* would describe as a great practical joke on the world. John's secret is not known and the disruption reverberates only within the loneliness of his own life and the satisfaction of his "place among men." However, Rena's perfor-mance disrupts more publicly, more profoundly as she seeks more than economic or social participation as a space for self-assertion. She wishes to be known—to be seen. In her reception of Tryon's proposal she under-stands that she is also receiving herself. That is, her personhood in this world is bound to another's reception of her. Yet she also recognizes the incoherence this giving and reception will mark within her and with her mother as well as in being bound to this man. The seemingly weak mark of Rena's femininity thus drives forward a powerful undercurrent of Ches-nutt's novel, the necessary interdependence of America's citizens. Rena's refusal to placidly participate in the deception of participation therefore becomes a radical assertion of mutual need, the refusal of exclusion or denial. Thus, it is not only Rena's interraciality but also her femininity that constitute an identity of wholeness within Chesnutt's narrative.

In her refusal she begins to disrupt the patterns of racial logic that promote assertion above reception and utility above a fullness of person-hood. Rena endeavors to fully exist within this confined space. She desires to be received fully. In so doing she begins to work against the discipling of racial logic and the internal decentering that has characterized her "redemption" thus far. In Rena's struggle with Tryon's proposal and her painful desire to see her mother again, Chesnutt delineates an interracial presence that disrupts the order of racialized life and resists its categories of pure appearance and necessary sacrifice. Desiring to be seen and loved fully, to be known and loved, Rena iterates her resistance to the mode of participation left open to those who might choose to pass. To exist within

this system Rena resists that internal bifurcation that the color line circumscribes. The possibility of becoming, of participating requires a certain fullness that will necessarily disrupt the very line she transgressed.
Thus her performance of white life is marked by a disruptive mode of
being that dares to be seen.

The disruptive arc of this resistance, of the politics of presence, is
marked not by a new assertion of in-betweenness or the seizing of a life
one is entitled to. Rather, the disruption of the interracial life enters and
asks to be received. This reception is bound to the one receiving. Rena
does not desire the life of one who "passes" and thus must implicitly fear
the world she inhabits. She does not want to be a stranger, but a citizen.
She wants to be embraced within this new homeland. Yet the fullness of
this personhood, Rena recognizes, is not bound to the perfection of her
performance, the attainment of her life (as is the case with her brother),
but is rather bound to the depth of desire of the one who is receiving her.
She is not whole without the love of Tryon. This love is not true without
his full reception of her.

The mark of Rena's arrival into the white world of promise and its
fulfillment as marriage was born with the necessity of death, the sacrifice
of her ties to her mother and those she had grown to know and love. In
her life of promise and fulfillment, with desire for a life with Tryon, comes
also the possibility of loss. For John, the means of recognition, and therefore participation, are iterated through the means of assertion, vocation,
and economic achievement. These means are undoubtedly subject to loss,
but they may also be reproduced, and thus at heart this endeavor remains
coherent with the underlying American value of self-making. This coherence may explain Tryon's hesitancy to reveal John's true identity to the
community while still initially distancing himself from Rena. But in Rena
the mulatta presence disrupts because it entangles the hopes and desire
into one another. Departure and return are now not so clearly recognizable. To return is gain and loss, to remain secluded is to die in order to
gain. She refuses (or cannot) acquiesce to the sacrifices necessary to keep
her "whole." This inability will ultimately psychically divide her, but its
reverberations will not distill quickly.

BORDER CROSSING AND DEATH

In tracing the patterns of departure and return, the transgression of
the color line is not one of promise. Chesnutt's rhythm of departure
and return is bound to accounts of death. Ultimately John's hope for

participation in the fullness of his "inheritance" is understood to be a delusion, for Rena's life testifies that one cannot be fully happy in a world where she cannot be fully known and loved. Chesnutt reminds us of the consequences of these transgressions. The danger Rena felt so keenly is realized as her true identity is discovered and Tryon rejects her in disappointment and shame. Rena returns to her mother and determines to use her gifts, her intellect, and her hue to work toward the uplift of "her people." She inverts the messianic promise of her brother's arrival to return to her mother and "be of service to her re-discovered people . . . where once she had seemed able to escape from them, they were now, it appeared, her inalienable race."[32] Her return to "her people" is rendered this time not as heroic, but as a descent. Though Chesnutt demonstrates the disruptive power of the mulatta body in this moment, he also displays the power with which the racial imagination still inflicts even those who may benefit (even partially) from their light position. Rena remains a disciple trapped by the illusion of her difference from the "colored" world and the refusal of her similarity by white society.

This desire, which Rena discovers, is apparently impossible for Tryon as he breaks off the marriage and disavows his former relationship with her. Again, Chesnutt makes the articulation of death visible. Tryon laments upon the discovery of Rena's true identity, "lost she was, as though she had never been, as she had indeed had no right to be."[33] The discovery of Rena's identity is rendered as a tragedy of death where the one whom he loved was now imaged not only as dead, but as nonbeing. The significance of this moment must be read theologically, participation within the white world has been construed by Tryon not only as the moment of freedom, but recognition by the white world is what is now constituted as true personhood.

The distortion of racial discipleship reverberates with the echo of Athanasius and the constitution of being and nonbeing. To recognize oneself as created and live into that form of salvation is to be, but to forget and besmirch the image of God within oneself is to fall into nonbeing. The trope of personhood within the dynamism between ontology and participation as constituted by white life betrays the religious or theological structure of racialized society. Participation and freedom are not social categories, but rather fulfillments of ontological hope. What is so unique to Chesnutt's work is the way this characterization of rejection and participation remains complicated. The complication Chesnutt inserts is the lament by the white male. Here there is no stoic anger or justified rage at the deception worked against him. Tryon laments at the "loss" of this love. It is this lament that begins the formation of something new in Tryon and in racial literature of the time. Chesnutt continues the description, "[Tryon] burst into tears—bitter tears, that strained his heartstrings. He was only a youth. She was worse than dead to him; for if he had seen her lying on a shroud before him, he could at least have cherished her memory; now even this consolation was denied him."[34] Tryon's lament, complicated by Rena's being rendered *not*, served to draw Tryon reluctantly into this world of neither/nor. To recognize his love for her would be to indict the authenticity of his claim to white citizenship and the benefits of participation that such status granted him.

While Rena's entrance into white society and eventual relationship with Tryon are marked by a dangerous flirtation with discovery and death, Chesnutt does not insulate white society (or Tryon) from this influence. While Rena will fall victim to the inevitable brutality of the color line, Tryon will also become subject to it, rather than be its arbiter. Tryon cannot discipline his growing desire to be with Rena. He cannot cease to forget her or leave her. He cannot cease to love her, and this leads him to begin to transgress the very boundaries that constituted his own life and identity. He began to enter into a dangerous land that tilted on the precipice of danger and exile. The presence of Rena within Tryon's life was one that was not without effect. That is, in Tryon's discovery of Rena's full identity and the subsequent lament over her "death" he ultimately recognized his own desire for her and his own resistance to the sacrifice necessary to be married to her. This is not to say that Tryon's "conversion" was complete. It was only a gesture, but a startling one given American racial politics in the early twentieth century. Because of this we must attend to Rena's presence within the white world as one that exerted itself and required this world to account for her through the particularity of her relationship with Tryon *and* her mother. Tryon could not move on. His own possibilities were now inextricably bound to Rena even if this desire would not be without tragedy.

That death seeps even into the lives of those who benefit from this system is a pervasive and unique claim in *The House Behind the Cedars*. Rena's presence in Tryon's life served to disrupt his own self-understanding and move him from a place of assertion to reception. His pursuit of Rena was no longer a pursuit of possession, to grab hold of and control, but rather his pursuit was one in which his own sacrifice would be necessary. His life would have to be bound to hers for him to be whole and this meant that he would have to leave the world he knew. In this way the tremor of interracial existence that marks Rena's entry into the white world has now reverberated within Tryon's own world in a way in which he cannot resist. He must become something new. This possibility requires a sacrifice which is now inverted upon the life of the white male who must receive himself from Rena, this "dark" woman.

But in Chesnutt's view this possibility is ultimately still enclosed within the tragic confines of the color line. The binding of these two worlds is an impossibility as Rena dies in the psychic sacrifice of her own soul and yearning. She has been torn in half by two possibilities rendered irreconcilable in this racial world. And yet her death is tragic not only for her mother and for her brother, but for Tryon as well, as his life is now stained by the love he refused.

Here Chesnutt draws out for us the ways in which nation and race have ordered desire and happiness. Freedom is now construed entirely through a lens of race where one can either pass and be happy and "free," or one can sacrificially begin the work of social uplift and thus participate in the attainment of freedom for one's people. These categories are inscribed with race. To participate in one's nation requires sacrifice and/or purity. Neither of these possibilities is true freedom, for each requires the refusal of the other, a delusion, public or private, that suggests these two peoples are impossibilities. This delusion of certainties and impossibilities render each invisible to the other and ultimately a slave to a racial world, a place of utter nonbeing.

DEATH FOR ALL: RACE DISRUPTED

Rena's foray into whiteness was one, from the beginning, marked by death. Her transgression into the white world, the ease with which she took the form of one who should inherit the promise of the kingdom, disrupted the notions of purity, race, and nation. With each step she took and each guest she welcomed, her life disrupted the very norms and assumptions which allowed Western society to function along its racial rails.

It was the knowledge of who Rena truly was that began to disrupt Tryon's conception of himself and the truthfulness of these racial lines. To know her as colored was to disrupt his own judgment and his capacity to see rightly the lines of color that had so long implicitly guided his life and his choices. To be confronted at once with this love of the Other, of the possibility of him binding himself to an Other was to grieve for a love for one who had died. Yet Chesnutt does not remain here. The progression of this fascination saw Tryon soon descend into death himself in order to pursue her. This possibility is one that is, again, unique and extraordinary in American literature, for at the end Tryon began to reimagine the lines of kinship and possibility.

Of course, even this nascent moment of transformation is marked with the tragic. Tryon could only imagine moving to a new town to resume the certainty of a white life. Nonetheless this moment of sacrifice gives view to the disruption wrought through Rena's presence. The possibility of trans-formation reverberates through each of the main figures of the story, yet each succumbs to the tragedy of racial existence and its borders. All of these figures were bound to its ethos, to its consequences. None can escape the certainty of its sentence because despite their transgression and their desire for transformation, they cannot escape the ways these possibilities are themselves racially circumscribed. Rena has become new and can no longer remain among her darker kin, John's life is marked by perpetual loneliness, Tryon has lost the one whom he loves and now knows himself to be one who has loved the impossible, the dark, a nonbeing.

The relationship between Tryon and Rena is marked by the tragic lines of desire and color that cannot tear themselves from the incoherence of race. Their encounter leaves them both marked and renders those reali-ties fixed, determining those whom they desire to love and those whom they cannot. Their love reveals the control and possession of Tryon and his race and the implicit but present distinction between mulatto and colored. Rena and Tryon cannot love because their loves and their lives are bound to race, "to the sins of their fathers."[35]

Yet their tragic affair leaves them both different. This is the unique-ness of Chesnutt's narrative. Within Tryon's legacy of possession and control he ends with sacrifice, with the possibility of being bound to one whom he knows to be dark. Whether this is an embrace of a wider people is not the question here. Chesnutt gestures toward the possibility of white transformation as Tryon subjects himself to the sacrificial economy of racial discipleship. Similarly in Rena we find the sacrificial desire to uplift her people. However, Chesnutt leaves her not as the exemplar of black selfhood, but as a more complicated tragedy of both her own estimation of those who she sought to serve and the complicated desire for true love which had made such a life so bitter. Here desire for one's people becomes obscured in Chesnutt's depiction of the love that tied Rena and Tryon.

Hers was not a love for a different people (like John's love) but rather love for a *particular* person. This distortion of kinship serves to underline the tragic in Chesnutt's depiction.

Chesnutt's groundbreaking narratives subtly co-opted the theme of the tragic mulatto/a but also sought to disrupt the very lines that created mulatto/a bodies and pressed themselves so violently into the lives of all bodies in America. This and his other works exemplified not the threat of such contamination, but the impossible, that whites lives could live into dark lives, and perhaps more profoundly, that such lines were less certain than we might think. This assertion was not mere speculation, but a rendering made visible by the already messy and hybrid reality that was American life. These renderings thus sought to put forward the radical claim of America's existence as an "inter" reality despite America's repeated and emphatic denials. Chesnutt's implicit appeal to the possibility of transformation and the necessity of integration were measured and sounded clear intonations of doubt regarding its possibility.

JAMES WELDON JOHNSON AND THE PERFORMANCE OF BLACK AMERICAN LIFE

Within ten years after Chesnutt's *The House Behind the Cedars*, representation of black life began a process of concretization in the burgeoning movement of the New Negro and the Harlem Renaissance. Against the haranguing racial degradation in the North as well as in the South, the Harlem Renaissance in particular would come to express a vision of black life grounded in the beauty of its people and their possibilities. In the midst of this shifting context of assertion and representation, the tale of racial transgression is one where the possibility of transformation is a profound temptation. And yet in the face of this deepening of the outlines of black cultural thought and representation, the child of interracial transgression is again poised upon a life of persistent choice and the possibility of alienation. In this respect, alienation is depicted not as an inherent status, but as a resistance to who she truly is. As we noted in Langston Hughes' poem, "Mulatto," the tragedy is his death and rejection by his father, but there is also an implicit commentary concerning his resistance to "his own people."[36]

Johnson's *Autobiography of an Ex-Coloured Man*, written just ten years after the publication of Chesnutt's *The House Behind the Cedars*, exemplifies the nationalism of the New Negro. In the midst of this coalescing of black identity, Johnson describes this negotiation through the mulatto's negotiation of dark life in America and the discovery of true "freedom." In this depiction, Johnson demonstrates again the departure and return, isolation, and ultimately death, but these are now reconceived within a nascent black nationalism that renders the life of the mulatto no less precarious or disruptive.[37] The mulatto/a body is now conscripted within a more pronounced decision, a calling to perform into black existence. Johnson's work here demonstrates not only the tragic performativity of light living into lighter but how the constitution of racial discipleship rearticulates itself within assertions of "black" identity and particularly the "New Negro" of the Harlem Renaissance. The work itself represents an attempt to resist the hope of amalgamation offered in Chesnutt by reiterating the costs of such blending, the loss of self, the loss of certain identities that can be offered to a cultural people for their uplift and hope. In this way we see how Johnson's assertion of identity becomes the inverse refusal of Langston Hughes' father in "Mulatto." Black identity must now assert itself in such a way as to refuse the refusals of those who desire to enter the white world, for those who enter the white world are refusing their own people.

James Weldon Johnson's *Autobiography of an Ex-Coloured Man* concludes with the haunting reflection, "It is difficult for me to analyze my feelings concerning my present position in the world. Sometimes it seems to me that I have never really been a Negro, that I have been only a privileged spectator of their inner life; at other times I feel I have been a coward, a deserter, and I am possessed by a strange longing for my mother's people."[38] These musings, of a widowed man living as a white man in France with two children, portray several important aspects of racialized life: the possibility of racial performance and its perpetually tragic consequences.

Published in 1912, *Autobiography* received widespread critical acclaim for its deep and seemingly intimate portrayal of black life. First published anonymously, it was received as the true confession of a black man who had "passed" into white life. The autobiography follows the life of a mixed-race child, born of a mulatto mother and prominent white, southern father. The mother and child move to Connecticut where he receives his formative education both intellectually and socially. The child exhibits exquisite musical talent and a keen intellect. In the midst of his schooling he is confronted with the reality that he is, in fact, a "dark" child. As the story unfolds he sets out to knit himself into "his mother's people" by attending school at a prominent southern university established for the "uplift of the Negro race." But through a series of unexpected events the narrator is drawn into a variety of experiences, from rolling cigars with Cubans in Jacksonville, Florida, to gambling and playing piano in Harlem, to playing privately for a wealthy white aristocrat whom he eventually accompanies to Europe. While in Europe he expands his linguistic and musical repertoire, immersing himself into the refined life of the social elite.

In Europe however, his desire to be reconnected with "his mother's people" is again rekindled and he sets off to the United States to immerse himself in the life and music of Negro people, with the hopes of accumulating the raw material of their soulful and spiritual songs. His hope is to marry to his own refined training to these spiritual songs, and thus create a new musical form. However, during his time in the South as a teacher the narrator is overwhelmed when he witnesses the lynching and burning of a black man in the community, and at that moment decides to "leave" the race.[39] He writes, "I had made up my mind that since I was not going to be a Negro I would avail myself of every opportunity to make a white man's success; and that, if it can be summed up in any words, means 'money.'"[40] The narrator eventually marries and has two children with his wife who dies in giving birth to the second. He finally moves to France to live as a white man to protect his children from the racial life of America. Yet this decision to live in exile is not an entirely happy one. The narrator laments,

> My love for my children makes me glad that I am what I am and keeps me from desiring to be otherwise: and yet, when I sometimes open a little box in which I still keep my fast yellowing manuscripts, the only tangible remains of a vanishing dream, a dead ambition, a sacrificed talent, I cannot repress the thought that, after all, I have chosen the lesser part, that I have sold my birthright for a mess of pottage.[41]

In these concluding lines we see Johnson's *Autobiography* display the passing figure's tragedy as his self-denial. Such a conception is a marked shift in the tragedy of mulatto/a existence as seen in other literary portrayals prior to the twentieth century, where the tragedy of the mulatto/a figure lies in its utter displacement.

Yet, here, Johnson suggests the tragedy lies less in an ontological displacement as it does in the narrator's refusal of his place among "his" people. Throughout the text Johnson highlights the profound adaptability of the narrator's musical and linguistic skill. Through the trope of music and language Johnson displays both the capacity and the refusal to perform as one of "his" race. Throughout the novel the decision for or against his people can be seen as a process of identification.[42] This process of identification or discipling as we have described it in the previous chapter is displayed through the trope of music and language, but is often explicitly stated as we saw in the narrator's decision to become white.

Johnson positions the narrator's adaptability to be read as either a gift or as a lack of character. His gift for learning languages and different musical styles is a critique of the way race could be construed as an illusion that is easily imitated. However, the narrator is also seen as one who has learned race. He is not seeking to imitate or manipulate, but as he learns to play a new tune he is also learning to fill out the possibilities that each situation presents to him. He is learning to be in the world in a variety of ways. Underlying this adaptability in identification or performance is a marked distance between the narrator and the darker people of the novel.[43] This negation is found even in the narrator's childhood. Growing up in Connecticut the narrator observes the difficult plight of the darker children in his class, but nonetheless considers his darker classmates as essentially different than himself. This belief is so deep that his being grouped with them one day in class is described as a tragic rebirth of sorts where "I did indeed pass into another world." He continues, "from that time I looked out at the world through other eyes, my thoughts were colored, my words dictated, my actions limited by one dominating, all pervading idea which constantly increased in force and weight until I finally realized in it a great tangible fact."[44]

Johnson's ex-colored man makes visible the rigidity with which racial lines were drawn. That is, the only possibility for the mulatto/a, quadroon, octoroon, and so on was a life that was either black or not black, colored or ex-colored. Regardless of the various hierarchies that developed within black social life there remained a perceived impenetrable boundary between what it meant to be white and black. These were constants that bound all of those who lived within these social boundaries. Johnson's depiction of the narrator's life displays how on the one hand such boundaries are permeable and porous, but on the other hand how such fluidity is never without consequence and a certain death.

While this new birth enlightened the narrator to the perils of his own existence his revelation served only to help clarify the object to be performed into. But this knowledge did not serve to overcome the deep distance exhibited even in the earliest days of his childhood. He continues to be one who watches and learns. In his life among "darker peoples" he displays a perpetual distance, a difference from those he counts himself among. Such moments are reiterated in his references to "his mother's people," but are also highlighted by the ease with which he adapts to new languages and new customs, whether it is learning Spanish in Jacksonville or the rhythms of ragtime in Harlem. These moments of adaptability serve to further outline the absence of a tension in his own life, a rhythm of departure upon entering into these new worlds. Every new world is a new song, a new performance the narrator can utter. For the narrator, racial life is a performance made possible by the congruence of a certain set of skills and the hue of his skin.[45]

Interestingly, Johnson's brother suggested the title for this work be "Chameleon," noting how easily the author could change his "skin" to suit his environment.[46] It is this adaptability that renders the narrator both perpetually distant and at the same time "at home" among various peoples. This distance is, at times, intentional as he seeks to avoid the perils and disgrace of black existence. In part, this distance is the result of self-preservation and a desire not to be classified among such a desperate lot. Yet, Johnson notes this distance not only in terms of self-preservation, but also as a deeper existential distance. Somehow the lives and hopes and pain of these people (even his mother) seem distant from him, something not immediately accessible to him. It is a reality that must be lived into. The mere fact that he feels he must enter into it highlights this distance that he will never be able to fully overcome. He exists in a space of neither/nor, where he possesses the possibility of entering fully into a variety of circumstances and by virtue of his own skill, "pick up the tune," but consequently because of his training and his history he is never fully "in." For he is continually hearing something slightly different in the tune and adding to it, seeking to reconcile it to his own varied strands of life and songs. But part of what is present in this difficulty is the tragedy of his racialized life, which allows him to hear but prevents him from learning. These strands of life which he brings into each circumstance cannot be fully reconciled with his present moment. The songs fall victim to the radical polarity of racialized life in America so that ultimately ragtime and jazz can only be fetishes, or momentary oddities, or classical music displayed as the music of a "higher white society" with nothing to say concerning black life. The narrator's grand hope of reconciling two musical forms become crushed under the impossibility of the task given the reality of black bodies that are hung and burned. The narrator would ultimately have to choose. He could not occupy this space of multiplicity because the polarities of race resisted, and ultimately he could not bridge a gap between him and "his mother's people."

The inevitability of this decision attests to the rigidity of the color line compared to its permeability in fact. Yet in Johnson's depiction its permeability is not one of hybridity or mutual transformation (as I explored in Chesnutt previously), but rather utter loyalty and complete assimilation. In this way, even in the lives of interracial figures, we see the absolute claims that rendered racial purity as tragic, continuing to be modulated through these mixed lives. As the narrator laments his own weakness and willingness to squander his gifts he seems also to lament the sheer impossibility of the task. Given the structure of racial life one cannot live on both sides, and consequently the possibility of wholeness is an impossibility for the narrator, despite the ease with which he seemingly lives into each life.[47]

The implicit commentary about the narrator can be seen more clearly in the relationship between the depiction of the ex-colored man as a figure without a people and the implicit refusal of this possibility as Johnson's own life. The relationship of the text to Johnson's life is thus not one of autobiographical description, but that of a responsive performance. Johnson's rootedness within the African American community is thus reciprocated inversely as displacement through the figure of the narrator, despite his capacity to live into his race if he would so choose. This distance and ease thus betrays both the specter of the racializing line, but also the assumptions that can be made regarding it. The narrator's life displays a final tragic performance where the tales of his youth and the love of his mother's people must remain a distant and bitter memory. In light of the previous chapter we begin to see how the mulatto/a body becomes both articulated *by*, and an articulation *of*, deeply racialized lives that require one to perpetually adapt to its demands, but in a way that is not transformative but reifying and consequently always subject to the tragic. In exploring the life of the author we see this text not only as an indictment or cautionary tale, but also as itself a text of discursive racial imagination.

The depiction of the narrator as a "chameleon" of sorts suggests not only the way in which racial lives must be performed, for those whose visuality does not clearly indicate their allegiance or place, but rather Johnson's own life indicates the antithesis of his narrator. Namely, that racial life, life as a black man, is a radical performance that must be embraced, declared, and lived into boldly and without reservation. Johnson's life was one adorned by varying levels of public service, but always service to the African American community. He notes in his reflections on Fisk University that their preparation was not for their own prosperity or well-being, but it was always clear that their education was a training for service.[48] One cannot help but recall that in the *Autobiography*, the narrator's failure to attend Atlanta University was in no small part a contributing factor to his moral failure to resist the temptations of white life and service to "his" people.

To see the importance of Johnson's racial performance we must attend briefly to his contribution to the larger contextual moment of the Harlem Renaissance and the racial performativity it displays. The Harlem Renaissance (approximately 1915–1935) was an artistic movement where creative expression centered upon the celebration and careful/truthful depiction of black life. These expressions were poetic, visual, and musical. This unique moment saw a coalescing of intellectual and artistic assertions of identity and black possibility. These assertions were, according to African American Literature scholar Houston Baker, instances of a unique African American modernism characterized by strategies of "mastery of form and the deformation of mastery."[49] Through these practices, artists and intellectuals of the New Negro movement signified themselves uniquely within the American project, but in so doing rearticulated the meaning and status of American citizenship. The Harlem Renaissance was a celebration of black life and freedom. Johnson's contemporary, Alain Locke, acclaimed writer, philosopher, theorist, and mentor to many Renaissance poets and writers would note:

> Proscription and prejudice have thrown these dissimilar elements into a common area of contact and interactions. Within this area, race sympathy and unity have determined a further fusing of sentimental experience. So what began in terms of segregation becomes more and more as its elements mix and react, the laboratory of a great race-welding.[50]

For Locke the Harlem Renaissance was serving to coalesce the varying expressions of black life in the United States. The Renaissance represented a gathering of stories, resources, and sentiments, but more than that it was the articulation of a new people, thus the term New Negro is not necessarily a description, but the aim of these writers in many respects. This aim was not the reconstruction of a prototype, but in many ways the New Negro was a re-creation or a performance of a people which not only represented the past, but served to coalesce black lives into a wider black national identity and thus into a higher possibility. Johnson as a poet, songwriter, and playwright was a central figure at the inception of this movement, giving voice to the tragedy and triumphs of black life. But his life exhibited also a deeper ideal embedded within the Harlem Renaissance, a deep dedication to his people. This service led him to significant involvement with the National Association for the Advancement of Colored People, The Crisis, and public service in politics, culminating in his serving as ambassador to Nicaragua, Venezuela, and the Azore Islands.

To examine Johnson's life is to, again, look at the antithesis of the ex-colored man. Johnson's life exemplified the display of the "best within himself." We see this deep connection and service in giving voice to his people explicitly in his writing of "Lift Every Voice" or what would become known as "The Negro National Anthem." Written in 1900, the song became widely sung throughout the African American community as a testament to the strength and hope of the people as well as a rallying cry to work for greater freedom and equity.

Thus Johnson's own life points not only to a tremendous dedication to the defense and utterance of black hope, but interpreted alongside the life of the ex-colored man we see his own life as a certain performance of black life. In this regard racial performance and adaptability is not a task peculiar to those whose physicality allows them to "pass" but rather, for Johnson, is a task at the heart of black life (and perhaps all lives in a racialized world.) The prominence of his life and service exemplified in the inspiring melody of "Lift Every Voice and Sing" stands in stark contrast to the narrator's yellowing manuscripts laying untouched in France. Johnson displays in his own life what is absent in the narrator's life, but in doing so also demonstrates that all racial life is performative and thus must be chosen, embraced, and lived into just as all racial lives can live in self-denial, and for Johnson this denial is the true tragedy.

NELLA LARSEN AND THE DISRUPTION OF IDENTITY

Johnson's account of passing displayed the shape of racial performance as well as its costs. Within this depiction of racial performance was an implicit indictment of those who refused the realities of racial lines. *Autobiography* could be read not only as an example of how racial lives can be expressed but as itself a policing of these boundaries in a cautionary tale about the perils of passing. Written in 1929, seventeen years after Johnson's *Autobiography*, Nella Larsen provided her own novel centered upon the phenomenon entitled *Passing*. This critically acclaimed novel narrated themes that were also found in *Autobiography* and *House Behind the Cedars* such as the permeability of racial lines, the ease with which certain people pass from one racial site to another, the way such movement and existence is marked by a certain distance or isolation, as well as how racial life is ultimately lived into and asserted. Yet, in this work Larsen narrated a set of performances that are more complicated than the narrative of exit offered by Johnson. By "exit" I am suggesting that Johnson's account of passing depicted a trajectory of departure from the racial reality as a colored man. This notion of exit bears within it a stark dualism of being either in or out. It seeks to negotiate the reality of racial life in America and its binary logic of white and nonwhite or colored and noncolored.

In Larsen's work the interracial body and the performance of passing is transgressive on both sides of the binary structure, unsettling the social realities built upon these assumptions. The lives that are distinguished by passing and not passing are seen as simultaneously bound to one another and yet are tragically distant. In the midst of these complicated interrelationships the reality of passing and interracial life indicates the way in which such lives are not easily demarcated within the notions of purity that are conceived as "black" or "white." Rather, we see how such lives are continually seeking to live into the reality of racial hope in complicated ways that ultimately either instantiate or disrupt the racial and social order.

Larsen, herself the child of a Danish mother and a Danish Virgin Island father, problematizes the lines of race and transgression depicted in other fictive accounts of passing and their real life counterparts. In *Passing*, the disruptive presence of these interracial or passing bodies intensifies the revelation of the performative and beguiling nature of race in the lives of those around them. The story follows the encounter between Clare Kendry and Irene Redfield. The women are childhood friends who grew up on the south side of Chicago in an African American neighborhood. Clare, a child of a mixed father, is sent to live with her distant white relatives after her father's death. In her time there she was repeatedly reminded of her inferior status and relegated to little more than a house servant. When she was nineteen Clare married a white man and passed into white life, keeping her identity as a colored woman hidden from her racist husband.

Irene remained in the neighborhood and married an accomplished doctor, becoming well established within the burgeoning black middle class. She too is light enough to pass, but does so only occasionally. It was on one of these occasions, in a restaurant in downtown Chicago, that Clare and Irene meet again, at first failing to recognize one another. The encounter begins a series of meetings as Clare seeks to reestablish, albeit secretly, ties with her old acquaintance and her old life. This encounter is not entirely welcome by Irene, as Clare's presence begins to disrupt the uneasy social arrangements that constitute Irene's life. As Clare becomes more present in Irene's life a deep suspicion arises regarding Clare and her husband. But more profoundly, the ease and lack of care with which Clare moves in and out of these worlds seems to unravel Irene, though little is displayed outwardly toward Clare or her husband. Larsen biographer George Hutchison observes, "Clare is irritating in large part because she does not have the proper feelings about racial difference: she flouts the protocols of race."[51] This unease and disruption ultimately concludes with Clare's death. She has jumped/fallen/been pushed out of a third story window with Irene nearby and Clare's husband entering the apartment upon his discovery of her true identity from an anonymous letter. The book ends with little clarity or indication regarding why or how Clare died, only with her body surrounded by questions and the fragmented lives of those she knew, but who knew so little about her.

As is the case in *Autobiography* and *The House Behind the Cedars*, Clare's very presence is disruptive and so perpetually displaces racial identity. The depiction of explicit disruption serves to highlight the way refusals of racial amalgamation or assertions of belonging become similarly bound within this mode of racial discipleship. Larsen's depiction of Clare and Irene expresses how the articulations of white and black identity become mutually necessary, sustaining themselves through the relation of one over the other, and ultimately attempting to create lives of stability and certainty. Clare, one who refuses these limitations and their myth of stability, binds herself to both worlds in ways that can only be resolved in death. To acquiesce to their presence is to begin to acknowledge the impurity of one's claims to purity. In the world of American racial life it is to become *no-one*. Clare seeks to assert a personhood that is without division or confusion. She seeks to exist in the world in such a way as to be full, and yet this possibility is closed to her because within the confines of racial discipleship personhood is understood only within the confines of a particular people, despite their actual "interpenetration."

Through Clare, Larsen narrates the politics of one who refuses the claims of national identities yet does not ghettoize such an identity. Rather she is one whose identity or very presence is political, ironically challenging her racist husband's delusion of purity or directly confronting the middle-class notions of black provincialism that had derided one who was once poor and black, and was now willing to "cross over" despite her mistreatment among "her own."

In *Passing*, Larsen displays the complicated interconnections between distance and belonging, devotion and betrayal. It is through the passing figure that such incongruities and tensions are unveiled. Here it is the presence of Clare that makes such tensions rise to the surface, becoming apparent in the lives of those who carry them. Clare's entrance into Irene's life serves to introduce Irene to herself. Through this encounter Irene must begin to account for herself and her life and the choices that she has made or refuses to make. After her chance meeting with Clare in the hotel restaurant, as one who is temporarily passing, she must confront the ways her own life is not essential or natural to her, but in fact, requires a succession of choices and an exertion of force in order to maintain its appearances.

The first instance of this inner conflict and her own resistance to any further relationship with the one who "crossed over" is seen in Irene's first encounter with Clare and her resistance to any further relationship with the one who "crossed over." Regretting her invitation to Clare to come on a trip with her where many from the old neighborhood had gathered, Irene reflects,

> It wasn't, she assured herself, that she was a snob, that she cared greatly for the petty restrictions and distinctions with which what called itself a Negro society chose to hedge itself about; but that she had a natural and deeply rooted aversion to the kind of notoriety that Clare Kendry's presence in Idyllwild, as her guest, would expose her to. And here she was, perversely and against all reason inviting her.[52]

The conflict that rises within Irene at this moment is both deeply personal and communal. Clare's passing into another world was met with derision, in part for her apparent refusal of black life, but also for the ways in which it was perceived as a misuse of her body.

Irene's resistance to Clare is a resistance to the association of Clare, but also a resistance to the way Clare's presence creates certain questions about her own life and choices. In the midst of a tea in Chicago with Clare and another woman who is "passing," Irene notes her own annoyance, admitting "that it arose from a feeling of being outnumbered, a sense of aloneness, in her adherence to her own class and kind; not merely in the great thing of marriage, but in the whole pattern of her life as well."[53] Irene's feelings toward Clare are fraught with disgust for her choices as well as fear for Clare's own life and choices. And yet in this very moment, to three women passing for white, the racist husband rants against black folk, and he himself becomes deformed into the ridiculous. But Larsen is clear to indicate that Irene's own life is implicated and unveiled in her encounter with Clare. The feeling of adherence and loyalty is displayed throughout the novel as something more than an innate belonging. Loyalty and race is lived into, chosen, and protected. It is protected from Clare or from her husband's desire for a "raceless" South America.[54] Irene's desire for her people and begrudging acknowledgement of Clare as numbering herself among them (despite her refusal to do so completely) is placed in tension with the difficulty she lives into as a woman or an individual. These aspects of her life are never resolved within the novel or collapsed into one another. Larsen refuses to subject the characters either to a racial fidelity or individual desire. But in the deep complications of each figure these tensions are present and being negotiated in each meeting and with each thought of future meetings.

The perpetual presence of conflict, inner and external, is born out through Irene's negotiation of Clare's interruption. The grand weight of the racial life is narrated not in terms of social uplift or devotion to the race versus personal fulfillment, but in a complex interrelation of each. As much as Clare Kendry's choices disturb Irene, Clare represents a life untethered by the burdens of race that seem to entrap and comfort Irene. But this burden is also a source of compassion for this poor creature who does not seem to know herself and places herself in so much danger due to her own ignorance.

But through the disruption, the destruction that is Clare Kendry, Clare herself admits that "she is not safe."[55] Clare's position highlights a cognizance of the danger and a refusal to abide by these lines. Clare's honesty about her position, her willful occupation of this space, and her refusal to acquiesce to the claims, all bind her to and distance her from each community, thus representing the substance of her transgression. It is her desire to exist *in* this space that disrupts. As we saw in Rena of *The House Behind the Cedars*, Clare aims for an authenticity that is neither/nor, resisting the totalizing claims that might enclose her within one world or the other. To the lives she has transgressed, Clare's assertions reveal the precarious nature of racial performance on either side. She reveals inauthenticity as not residing within her but within the lives of those outside of her who so desperately seek to circumscribe her life. Clare is not safe for herself or for those to whom she has attached herself, for the lives she

seeks to seep in and out of are not as permeable as she might think. The
lines have been drawn hard and fast and must be maintained and sacrificed for. It is here that the politics of presence, as it were, becomes deeply
imbedded not within Clare's betrayal of her identity, as was the case in
Johnson's *Autobiography*, but rather it is Clare's refusal to perform into a
specific identity that unveils Irene's negotiation of black life as inherently
performed. Hutchinson observes how the very structure of the text serves
to image this disruption as one internal to Irene.

> By funneling our perceptions of Clare and nearly all of the action of
> the novel through Irene as the center of consciousness, Larsen makes
> Irene's defense against the psychic disturbance Clare generates insepa-
> rable from our understanding. Irene must do away with Clare, and this
> erasure, to maintain the order of her world while forgetting her own
> role in this North American ritual.[56]

The political danger of Clare's life and a disavowal of the danger her
presence in the old neighborhood represents is one that touches not only
Clare's life, but also the life of Irene and the standard of black life that
Irene must work so doggedly to maintain—not only against Clare, but
also against her husband's repeated desire to leave the racially charged
life of America for Brazil.

In the midst of these negotiations both Irene and Clare demonstrate
a deep connection with one another but also a profound separation. But
each inhabits these paradoxes differently. For Irene the connection to
Clare is one of racial consciousness. This consciousness is for one of "her
people" despite Clare's apparent betrayal of the choices necessary to live
into such a life. Irene's connection to Clare is one that continues to rise up
within her, despite herself and the personal costs it will entail. Yet it is the
very difference concerning these choices and the patterns of life each has
chosen that represents the most significant chasm for Irene. After Irene's
return to New York this chasm is described not only in terms of differing
patterns of life, but these patterns come together to image an ontological
difference. She recalls,

> Most likely she and Clare would never meet again. Well, she, for one,
> could endure that. Since childhood their lives had never really touched.
> Actually, they were strangers. Strangers in their ways and means of liv-
> ing. Strangers in their desires and ambitions. Strangers in their racial
> consciousness. Between them the barrier was just as high, just as broad,
> and just as firm as if in Clare did not run that strain of black blood. In

truth it was higher, broader, and firmer; because for her there were no perils, not known or imagined, by those others who had no such secrets to alarm or endanger them.[57]

In her initial sentiments toward Clare two important elements of this distance become apparent. First, the difference regarding choices and ambitions grows not out of an essential racial nature, but is lived into. The contrary desires of Irene for her people and Clare for herself (in Irene's view) give each person's identity its trajectory, its telos.[58] These choices derive not from an inherent connection, but rather a sense of belonging that must be continually confirmed through patterns of life. The divergence of these performances, in Irene's view, is the construction of a barrier, of a difference that borders upon natural, rendering each woman on contrary sides of the color line.

The second aspect of Clare's life Irene observes is the danger inherent in it. The danger for Clare is one of personal safety, for her husband is clearly racist and for her to be put out of her home (or worse) would be to be left without anyone in the world. But here Larsen also puts forth a certain foreshadowing of the peril that Clare would enter into not only from her husband, but also from Irene. Irene seems to see the lack of knowledge as a profound difference in terms of how one understands himself, although it is clear throughout the novel that she is, in fact, deeply aware of the danger yet refuses to succumb to it, which is itself another source of envy and consternation for Irene. Irene understood the boundaries and had no such secrets, and Clare's presence constituted peril for Irene's life as Irene conceived it.

These deepening inner conflicts and contestations over space and race ultimately conclude in Clare's death, or sacrifice. Earlier in the novel Irene had contemplated sending (or perhaps sent) a letter to Clare's husband, John Bellew, regarding Clare's life among colored folk and he has unexpectedly arrived at the party Clare was attending with Irene, her husband, and others.

> Clare stood at the window, as composed as if everyone were not staring at her in curiosity and wonder, as if the whole structure of her life were not lying in fragments before her. She seemed unaware of any danger or uncaring. There was even a faint smile on her full, red lips, and in her shining eyes.
>
> It was that smile that maddened Irene. She ran across the room, her terror tinged with ferocity, and laid a hand on Clare's bare arm. One thought possessed her. She couldn't have her free.

Before them stood John Bellew, speechless now in his hurt and anger. Beyond them the little huddle of other people, and Brian stepping out from among them.

What happened next, Irene Redfield never afterwards allowed herself to remember. Never clearly.

One moment Clare had been there, a vital glowing thing, like a flame of red and gold. The next she was gone.[59]

Whether Clare, confronted by the tragedy and the impossibility of her life, jumped; or was pushed due to John's hurt and betrayal; or was pushed due to Irene's desire to protect herself and her life, is left unclear. Yet in this confrontation we see the gathering assertions of race and life centering upon one who seemed to refuse to participate in these categories perfectly. Clare longed for lives that she could not want, could not desire. Her death came as these lives and worlds she inserted and reinserted herself into began to resist her presence at the same time.

Through Larsen's account of passing we begin to see the interracial body and the politics of passing as first inherently political, disrupting the assertions of race and life that are built upon or negotiated within the binary system of colored and noncolored or white and nonwhite, that are upheld by implicit notions of purity and essentialism. Yet Larsen also portrays how such lives are fraught with danger and death. This is bound not only to the possibility of death for Clare, which is first described as a kind of social death upon her leaving the African American neighborhood (as well as her perpetual distance while she was in it), but also the reality of death that her presence opens up for the lives that are predicated upon the denial of such possibilities.

For Irene Redfield and John Bellew, Clare's presence in each of their lives opened up the possibility that their racial identity was not as fixed and certain as they had thought. For Irene her life as a black woman must now be protected and asserted over against one who would seemingly enter and exit without a sense of its costs or its requirements. For John Bellews lay the possibility that he is the father of a colored child, that he desired a dark woman, and that his own whiteness is therefore much less certain. Here it is not Clare's life that is tragic but, rather, her life reveals the tragedy of Irene's certainty and Clare's husband's certainty regarding their lives and the fear that an unveiling and disruption might cost them. This transgression results in the death of the mulatta as the one who passes into a world that is not for them, yet seems unfazed by boundaries such as race. The complication of both Irene and Clare's capacity to pass, their representation as mulatta thus more sharply highlights what is being disciplined in this moment. It is not the body alone but its performance that is refused. Irene seeks to maintain her position, but in order to do so the mulatta must be black. Clare's refusal highlights this deep transgression. As with the depiction of Rena in *The House Behind the Cedars*, the disruption of the passing figure is modulated by a contrary performance of one who could pass but refuses to do so fully. Both Chesnutt and Larsen highlight the binding effect of racial discipleship and the refusal of their own bodies and the transgressions they signify.

The worlds that Clare entered into and that were so disrupted by her presence would ultimately sacrifice her so that their falsities might live. While *Passing* serves to unveil the fictions and complicated interrelations between racial life and self-assertion, it ultimately cedes to its impossibility given the structure of race in the United States. Clare cannot live this life. Neither Irene nor John Bellews will allow her. It is in these "mixed" bodies that such "certain" lives are unveiled as assertions, as modes of racial discipleship and allegiance and family that are negotiated and renegotiated in the midst of competing and overlapping loyalties. As in *Autobiography* the life of racial discipleship does not allow for mixture. One who exists or can exist in both worlds must ultimately betray one (Johnson) or hold an untenable schizophrenia shifting between one and the other, because to allow the two to meet one another would surely mean death. Thus the tragic nature of race is again reiterated here, not through the social death of racial self-exile, but through the refusal of the one who passes and her eventual sacrifice.

PRESENCE AS POLITICS

Each author, bound in his or her life by the constraints of color, sought to resist or renegotiate the means of participation—the ultimate aim of this unfolding drama. Writing in the shadow of race they understood the claims, the fallacies, and the rules of the system in which they operated. Yet through the lives of their mixed-race characters, these authors each sought to represent the shape, style, and significance of these disruptions quite differently. To exist within the racialized world was to disrupt it, but how? To what end? These are the questions of racial discipleship.

Chesnutt seeks to highlight the permeability of these lines where the life of the one who passes into white life and the white life that is passed into carries with it the possibility of mutual transformation. The desire for a racial amalgamation disrupts the claims that construe purities on either side yet still renders the dark body (particularly the female body) lost or dead. Johnson will similarly highlight the ease with which white existence (or any cultural mode of life) can be adapted, learned, and performed. Yet Johnson's tale serves to show how such performances must be ultimately rendered for a people, for *your* people. The death of Johnson's adaptation is a death of exile, exclusion, or a denial of one's "true" self. Here Johnson expressed a refusal of a "middle existence" where one must embrace his or her "true" self and live into the promise of one's dark existence for the uplift of all darker peoples. Lastly, Larsen's passing narrative diverges from both of these accounts in its sheer disruptive force. Larsen's mulatta figure defiantly chooses to live in both worlds. In this refusal of the divide Larsen neither hopes for an amalgamation exemplified in Chesnutt's work nor an either/or of Johnson's work. Rather, Larsen indicates an existence in both places *at once*. In the process Larsen unveils the lies held in both the white and black worlds but also the impossibility of this defiance. Ultimately both sides refuse her interruption, her mutual occupation and the work concludes with the mulatta lying dead on the street beneath the third-story window.

These novels and the lives of those who wrote them indicate the way in which the requirements of race required a response of them. Such accounting is not a strictly intellectual exercise. Their writing pronounces a deeper attempt to struggle with the adherence to racial discipleship in the midst of their "inter" existence and the seemingly authentic lives of those who dwelled in this world. While interracial existence itself serves to interrupt or interrogate claims of racial certainty, "passing" serves to again subvert this structure by transgressing the lines that demarcate white/nonwhite, participation/exclusion. Thus the act of "passing" as white or into white life could be understood as the deepest instantiation of this political embodiment. This reverberates through all mulatto/a and interracial literature, marked by continually present notions of participation and alienation.[60] It is my hope to suggest that the disruption of the mulatto/a body and its enactment through the act of passing highlighted by many authors prior to me is a disruption that highlights the articulations of race within a nation, but also indicates a limitation of "becoming" as the telos of identity.[61]

These various figures indicated varying observations about how race is performed: transformation (Chesnutt), adaptability (Johnson), and contestation or interruption (Larsen). Given the hardened lines of racial logic, such lives were not only fascinating in their peculiarity, but required the observer or reader to account for themselves in the encounter between the citizen and the "alien." Such accounting was bound to a refusal, a hiding, or a reluctant acceptance of something new. Yet what is also clear in each of these moments is the way racial logic pressed itself upon these performances so that death became inevitable. The pressure could not be alleviated by a transformation of the structures or form, but only through an exorcism of the alien. It is not incidental therefore that what dies in each of these novels is a female character—the one through whom such an anomaly might continue to be born—the vessel which represents the receptivity and the production of such disruption.[62]

Such bodies represented a disruption in their "performance," but in their presence modulated a particular performance of race that resounded a dissonance through all of the competing claims made upon them. Their lives constituted a reality that had to be accounted for and either resisted or destroyed. It could not be allowed to be maintained within the hardened binary system of colored and white. Yet its existence as that which resembled, as that which spoke like, as those who were not, could not be ignored. But such lives also required a response on the part of black bodies and lives, particularly in the north where interracial bodies would drift in and out of these white and black lives.

In the novels of Chesnutt and Larsen, the body of a woman becomes the locus of these political realities or is the significant catalyst of the events within the novels. But in particular these novels themselves become deeply political because their movement from involuntary to voluntary sexual encounters serves as the subtext of these lives. Professor of English Suzanne Bost notes the centrality of mulattas as revolving around the scandal of sexual desire. She suggests, "Throughout popular culture and literature, debates about the nature of mixed-race identity are mapped out on a body of a woman because thinking about racial mixture inevitably leads to questions of sex and reproduction."[63] Through the bodies of women, mulatto/a existence is born. Thus the disruption becomes intensified in the man's desire and the woman's assent and recapitulating desire—this existence of mutual desire now intensifies the threat to racial existence. The presence of mulatto/a bodies are no longer primarily fruits of power or economic interest, or even an obscured and rare fetish or deviancy—but possibly an intimate desire or even an expression of love.

The presence of these bodies disrupts the idolatry of racial performance, yet still cannot ultimately escape it. They cannot exist between the

enormities of this fiction and its structure that their bodies and lives challenge and must negotiate:

> Rena is torn asunder between mulatto lust and white desire.
>
> The ex-colored man lives "exiled" in France.
>
> Clare lies dead in the snow beneath the window.

They share a similar death to that which befell Hughes' tragic mulatto—
they defied and died. Thus racial performance of mulatto/a and interracial bodies make visible two crucial observations regarding racialized
life in the West—it is both illusory and tragic. Its illusions lie in the
necessity to "perform" into it and negotiate the ways we might conform
and be mindful of the outlines, the borders of what it is to be "this" or
"that." Interracial bodies indicate varying negotiations, how pigmenta-
tion requires the confirmation of a certain form of life, which points to
the illusion of race as well as its permeability and enduring marks.

In recent scholarship the disruption signified by these bodies has
been thought to be a space of hopefulness as they disrupt the problematic
assertions of purity and their refusal of dark bodies within the social and
political structures of society. Kawash, whose profound work has been
particularly helpful in this regard, understands the culmination of these
figures' disrupting work to point toward a certain political engagement
with the world where certainties of identity are continually subverted.
Cultural theorist and Professor of English Katya Gibel Azoulay similarly
interprets the interracial body as one which typifies the possibility of a
profound "becoming," centered upon the biracial body that is "a cogni-
tive and physical process of being in the world—in, and as a result of, a
race conscious society, is to be an interruption, to represent a contestation,
and to undermine the authority of classification."[64] The power of these
bodies and lives—the hybridity and passing phenomenon—serve to resist
the limitations of racial (and gendered) tropes that secure bodies within
certain classificatory moments.

Rather, the sheer hybridity of these bodies confound the logic of such
constructions making a space where all are free to "become." Professor of
English Elaine Ginsberg describes these practices of passing as having
the "potential to create a space for creative self-determination and agency:
the opportunity to construct new identities, to experiment with multiple
subject positions and to cross social and economic boundaries that exclude
or oppress."[65] For each of these theorists the telos of "becoming" is itself an

end, a political way of being in the world. Yet the tragedies of such trans-gressions seem to become muted in their conception of a way forward. To "become" necessitates a certain departure and a certain arrival. While the interracial bodies described in the work of Chesnutt, Johnson, and Larsen exhibit a disruption of racial logic, they also demonstrate how becoming is also inhibited by the problematic ways these bodies themselves inhabit the constraints of racial certainty. The possibility of becoming is thus not only delineated externally, but inhabited internally. That is, all bodies, even in their hybridity, must undergo a certain transformation, a kind of tragic death in order to live into the possibility of anything. The life of becoming, if construed as pure freedom, is thus a life that constricts through its mul-tiplicity . . . it is seeking to live into a certain myth of self-creation which itself gave birth to the myth of racial discipleship.

Lost in the recent assessments of interracial existence is that the disrup-tion of these bodies derives from a certain performance of race that makes their neither/nor status a public statement. It is this declarative refusal asserted socially or interpersonally that begins the gears of sacrifice. The possibility of becoming and tearing loose from the binds of reifying social logic is surely necessary, but we must always ask in the possibility of becom-ing, the ontology of interruption, what are we to become? The interracial body, its mere presence and more profoundly its peculiar inhabiting of racial life, is political. It subverts the assumptions of identity that allow the structures of everyday existence to function. The mulatto/a reveals how the aims of these identities do not escape the consequences of these transgres-sions or living into a certain mode of racially discipling existence.

Racialized lives are never fixed but always asserted and made, but these assertions and creations always require communities to make them coherent—to verify the lives of its participants. Intermixture is more of a fact than is purity, for all people's lives are marked by a variety of loyalties, particularities, etc. That race is illusory is not its present power. The pres-ence of mulatto/a bodies indicates the depth to which all lives, stories, and cultures are bound up into one another in complicated webs of desire and loathing. Intermixture as a biological category is only the visual indicator of a deeper binding of peoples and desires, which as yet does not know how to account for those individuals who "overlap," or the ways these indi-viduals reveal their own "impurities."

Interracial bodies begin to unveil the intricacies of Western identity and the difficulty that always arises in such genealogies—that we all are born of a woman who transgressed or was transgressed. The presence of these children is a difference that utterly disrupts simply by its presence among us. But such lives further reverberate within the racial substructure when they, even in small ways, refuse to abide by the dictums of racial discipleship, even as they are tragically faithful to it. Such lives also indicate the deep tragedy of all lives that are marked by the refusal of such impurities, and thus are bound to absurdly assert their own purity.

Conclusion

Part 1 sought to examine the peculiar phenomenon of the mulatto/a or "mixed-race" body born of the encounter between Europe and the New Worlds. The birth of these lives and their subsequent negotiation of this precarious world opens up for us important questions regarding identity, and in particular the character of Christian personhood. Identity is articulated in the midst of the encounters of difference. In this encounter identity is both expressed and impressed. The notion of personhood is thus not a static moment but becomes visible through the centrifugal force of encounter and difference. The relationship between identity, difference, and encounter cannot be neatly ordered one way or another. Rather, identity and encounter are bound in a relationship of reciprocal amplification. The realities of mulatto/a birth and life point not only to a particular form of life in modernity, but more broadly the drama of identity and identification in the modern West that all participate in. I have suggested this drama of identity becomes apparent through the bodies of mixed-race peoples and their negotiation of this world, and that these lives make visible racialized society as a religious phenomenon. Also, these bodies become subject to religio-racial ideals, seeking to perform, exist, and thrive within them. However, ultimately the mulatto/as die upon the altar of racial assertion. Theologically interpreted mixed-race bodies unveil the challenge of racial discipleship.

Despite the seeming impossibility of existing within the spaces of neither/nor, mulatto/a bodies also open up a way to reenvision Christian lives in the midst of this drama. First, mixed race bodies allow for a wider interpretive matrix of identity or personhood. Personhood is the reception of a name and its possibilities and the performance into these or against these possibilities. In the midst of these articulations and encounters the mixed race, mulatto/a, or hybrid body is born. It is born out of the encounter, out of two sides expressing and resisting one's presence in the other. In this way the peculiarity of the mulatto/a body is the peculiarity of all difference. It is the difficulty of human identity and difference that can be viewed in the very "identification" of culture itself. These bodies/lives of transgression mark all identities, mark all bodies—even the very creation of humanity.

In examining the creation of interracial bodies and the religious structures that uphold the dichotomies of race, as well as how the lives of those rendered in between sought to exist in that space, we see both a wider possibility of what it means to be human and the conditions of our fall. In this way difference and "inter" existence is not being imported into Christian thought, but rather is amplifying observations made within the biblical and theological witness of the church, which lacked sufficient language to describe the shape of its presence. Even within Israel's own life the *ger* or "resident alien" served to demarcate Israel's own promise and limitations. Israel's promise was bound to the incorporation of strangers, to encounters with the nations that amplified their own calling and demarcated those encountered. This interpretive matrix of the mulatto/a is not one where he or she seeks to exercise an inclusion or participation of mixed-race people.[66] This is to misunderstand the point. The examination of mulatto/a bodies makes visible the participation of all bodies within modernity's interpretive racial gaze. Identities are formed within this matrix of encounter and articulation.

Interracial lives cannot be simply observed but resonate in our own failed performances, identifications, and illusions of racial certainty that mark personhood in modernity. Mixed-race bodies bring before us the many instances in our lives, in our societies where race was more determinative of our lives than faith. Yet such a disruption, such an unveiling cannot save us from the tragedy of our own failed assertions, our delusions concerning our lives together, nor can these realities be untangled from the claims we have made regarding our lives in Christ. It is here that mulatto/a bodies allow us to look upon the life of Christ anew and grasp the depth of his work more profoundly. Through the fissures of discourse that render "mixed bodies" possible we can see Christ's own life as the ground of this peculiar personhood, even as he is its salvation.

Part II

Confession
Christ, the Tragic Mulatto

Chapter 3

UNTO US A CHILD IS BORN *OR*
"HOW CAN THIS BE?"
The Mulatto Christ

> Christ is a nigger,
> Beaten and black:
> Oh, bare your back!
> Mary is His mother: Mammy of the South,
> Silence your mouth.
> God is his father:
> White master above
> Grant Him your love.
> Most holy bastard
> Of the bleeding mouth,
> Nigger Christ
> On the cross
> Of the South.
>
> —Langston Hughes[1]

The angel said to her, "The Holy Spirit will come upon you, and the power of the Most High will overshadow you; therefore the child to be born will be holy; he will be called Son of God. (Luke 1:35)

INTRODUCTION

The possibility of imagining discipleship in a racial world must begin with Jesus. To imagine a life of discipleship, a way of being in the world that disrupts racial logic and formation, the church must begin to look

anew at the center of our faith. The conception of Jesus is undoubtedly tied to the conception of humanity that we imagine for ourselves.
Whether Jesus is a liberator, or the perfection of thought and action, or
the most profound example of humanity in its limitations, conceptions
of Jesus have been bound to humanity's self-understanding.[2] These conceptions are tied to the building of slave ships and the accumulation of
knowledge within encyclopedias. Jesus is tied to the responses of faithful
Christians to the profound problems of human trafficking and human
classification.

In this way the nineteenth-century puzzle concerning the impossibility of a black woman giving birth to a white child is not too distant from
the question of whether a woman (much less a virgin) could be the mother
of God. It is in the intimacy of these transgressions and the puzzle of
their fruit where we begin to identify personhood, or as cultural theorist Homi Bhabha suggests, the "location of culture."[3] In the midst of this
intimacy, Bhabha suggests, "the recesses of the domestic space become
sites for history's most intricate invasions. In that displacement, the borders
between home and world become confused; and, uncannily, the private
and the public become part of each other, forcing upon us a vision that
is as divided as it is disorienting."[4] For Bhabha the location of culture is
the encounter of these contestations. Importantly, they are not only grand
structural battles, but are more deeply felt and displayed in the minutiae
of daily existence. The possibilities of humanity are the fruit of this "intricate invasion," the birth of a child to a young woman. It is this encounter
which must be understood, for this claim takes place in the midst of an
encounter, but also breaks open the possibility of lives to encounter and be
encountered in a radically new way, disrupting the rhythms of daily life
and collective aspirations.

To imagine a way forward in the modern world, in a world imbued
with racial logic and desire we must begin to be confronted once again
with the mystery and difficulty of Jesus' body and life. Rather than aban-
doning the creedal descriptions of Christ or becoming buried in them,
theology and the church must be confronted again with the mystery of
the incarnation, of Christ's body for us. Ignatius' exhortation to the Trallians, "Jesus . . . of Mary, who was really born, ate, and drank; was really
persecuted under Pontius Pilate; was really crucified and died" is a claim
of liberation that is only possible within the concurrent claim that Jesus
was God.[5] In Jesus we are confronted with God enfleshed who encounters
us with a humanity we can neither classify nor ignore. In this encounter

we can no longer grasp Jesus as a means of enclosing ourselves against the possibilities of entrapment, but we begin to see the radical transformation Jesus' presence gives birth to. The mystery of Jesus' incarnation must consume us.

In turning to Jesus the question of discipleship turns on our response to Jesus' question to us, "Who do you say I am?" The possibility of our renunciation of a discipleship inflected by race only becomes possible by entering into the body and life of another. Imagining a way forward requires us to reconceive who Christ is, and relatedly the nature of Christ's work not as the establishment of certain bodies or the perfection of a tradition. While mulatto/a bodies have made visible the contours of racial fidelity, interracial bodies have also rendered intelligible the ways identity becomes contested between what is possible and what is impossible, what is pure and what is impure. This process of limitation is both a social and a theological process that gives rise to further modes of enclosure or classification. Reproducing itself through religious fidelity, these bastions of racial (or ethnic, or sexual, or other demarcation of difference) identity rely on enclosure and exclusion in order to be maintained.

To reexamine the creedal confessions and thus the person and work of Christ through the matrix of mulatto/a bodies disrupts notions of human personhood that would later enclose Jesus (and humanity) within static expressions of personhood. In the incarnation notions of personhood become conflated and reimagined in their relation with one another. Consequently mulatto/a bodies mark participation with the life of Christ inexorably bound to a mulatto/a existence, similarly fusing and fragmenting markers of identity in new and "impossible" ways, creating a new humanity which beckons the world to ask, "How can this be?" The reciprocity of identity thus has a particular economy in Christ. It is a personhood that does not successively and tragically fail to identify, but radically identifies so that identification with God (our deification) becomes possible. To claim Christ is mulatto is to interpret humanity christologically.

CREEDAL CONFESSION AND THE DISCOURSE OF IDENTITY

The attempt to work out this "impossible possibility," this question, "How can this be?" could be said to be the posture of theological reflection. The various creedal responses to seemingly ill-conceived notions of Christ or the Godhead are themselves attempts to express life in the midst of this question—this call posited by God's promise and presence to us. In this chapter I will focus on one particular creedal confession, the Definition of Chalcedon (451). The Definition of Chalcedon is representative of a series of attempts to testify to the pattern of God's relation to the world and the identity of relations of the Son to the Father and the Spirit. The definition of Chalcedon is unique in that it seeks to describe an identity through both its assertions and its negations. Chalcedon utters a paradoxical identity wherein personhood is established through a negation while articulating a body that nevertheless occupies space.[6] Such a formula can be understood as having a distinctly "mulattic" character.

The formula of Chalcedon was not the first word nor was it the last word concerning Jesus, but in many respects it represents the sheer complexity of any assertion regarding Christ's person. Chalcedon's formula and Christ's confession of himself displays a fundamentally mulatto character. That is, it displays Jesus' nature as "neither/nor—but" and in doing so we see the tragic nature of mulatto/a existence prefigured, but now interpretable not as a theoretical or social challenge, but itself echoing a profound (though distorted) christological moment. The neither/nor that gives birth to and inheres within the interracial body in the modern West is but an iteration of the deeply "inter" character of all human lives. These lives are established in creation and reinscribed upon humanity through the incarnation, yet become distorted within in a racial telos that leads only to the tragic in its ever failing attempt to negotiate the claims of racial purity and cultural essentialism.

"How can this be?" Mary's confession upon the angel's annunciation marked the first question of Christ's identity. Within Mary's question reverberates the call and response of her people. Inhabiting her confession is the echo of Israel's birth and Abram's similar response to the promise of the Lord, "How can this be for I am far in years?" Israel's own life was born in the midst of this call and response. They are a people whose lives are constituted by a question and whose lives witness to this encounter. Their existence is the transgression of God into the world marking the boundaries of their possibility within this impossibility. The unfolding of Israel's life is the bending into this promise despite its own impossibility. Its life is marked by miraculous births that defy expectation and mark these people as born of expectation. As Abram's life exists in the gap between YHWH's pronouncement to him and the birth of Isaac to Sarai, the lives of Israel reverberate between this call and response between the impossibility and the possibility of the promise. They exist within the dissonance of what cannot be, yet is.

In the continual unfolding of Israel, its moments of redemption are marked by the reinscribing of this moment through the birth of children in whom God's promise becomes present in the world. The birth of Isaac becomes reiterated in the birth of Moses. Moses, born of Israel yet raised within the house of Egypt, leads "his" people into a promise, birthing Israel through the waters of the Red Sea. Within Mary's confession resounds this melody of salvation. The annunciation to Mary is the fulfillment of a promise of the nation of Israel.[7] The shape of this promise permeates Mary's confession—it is a confession of her own limitation and God's possibility. These two poles of Israel's identity become enfleshed in Mary's womb. In this encounter of limitation and possibility a child will be conceived. It is in Mary's assent that we see creatureliness not asserted or built, but received. Creation is birthed through the impossible, through an incarnation of the promise, the Word, first uttered to Abraham. The promise was the possibility of bearing God within one's own body so that all might be reborn through God's own body. Jesus' person is the call and response to creation. He is the remaking of humanity through this union of flesh and Spirit fulfilling God's promise to those peculiar people and enfolding humanity itself into this peculiar existence.

From the moment of his conception, through his birth, his ministry, and in his death and resurrection, Christ's identity, his person, has confounded description. The Gospels and Epistles of the New Testament are an attempt to witness to the nature of this impossibility and its meaning for creation. The subsequent councils and doctrinal claims concerning Christ's person continue to seek to somehow grasp this "impossible possibility." In the incarnation the very limits of possibility become transgressed. Again, Mary's confusion, "How can this be?" is our perpetual confusion as we seek to reflect on the meaning and the implications of the claims that Christ makes concerning himself and concerning us.

In the midst of these attempts to interpret and discern the meaning of Christ's body and his claims about himself, what has been often overlooked or underinterpreted is the fundamentally "mulattic" or transgressive claims the biblical witness and ecclesial councils give us concerning the nature of Christ's person. There has undoubtedly been deep disagreement regarding these attempts to discern Christ's personhood and my intention here is not to trace the historical development of these claims.[8] Chalcedon's claim seems rather nonsensical at first in light of his rather explicit denial of an ontological mixture. But as I have suggested in Part 1, mulatto/a identity is grounded in the presumptions of purity that give rise to the space that is articulated as "mixture," as well as the intimate encounters of "difference" that conceive mulatto children. In this way mulatto/a identity is both discursive and embodied. The mulatto/a is not a positive identity, but rather a tragic identity of negation wherein its existence is marked by a "neither/nor," left to negotiate and perform itself into an illusion of purity, thereby participating within a wider vision of national or racial hope. Notions of mixture within embodied existence are not displayed in people as dilutions of their mother or their father. Rather mulatto/a existence displays a complication of personhood insofar as it asserts the interracial person as full, whole, complete. The language of racial, ethnic, or cultural purity delimits the possibilities of personhood and thus limits how we envisage Christ's personhood, and consequently his salvific work. It is through the complicating language of mulatto/a that we can begin to reexamine both the discursive and embodied disruption that is Jesus Christ, the Son of God.

THE CHALCEDONIAN CHRIST: NEITHER/NOR—BUT

The ecumenical councils beginning with Nicaea and leading to Chalcedon are widely understood to have created the primary boundaries of conversation concerning the person and work of Christ or Christ's relationship to the Father. These councils represent a continual conversation or reflection upon the person of Christ. As such this progression served to highlight more emphatically not necessarily who Christ was, but what Christ was not. The central addition of the Chalcedonian Definition reads:

> We also teach that we apprehend this one and only Christ-Son, Lord, only-begotten—in two natures; and we do this without confusing the two natures, without transmuting one nature into the other, without dividing them into two separate categories, without contrasting them according to area or function. The distinctiveness ·of each nature is not nullified by the union. Instead, the "properties" of each nature are conserved and both natures concur in one "person" and in one reality <hypostasis>. They are not divided or cut into two persons, but are together the one and only and only-begotten Word <Logos> of God, the Lord Jesus Christ. Thus have the prophets of old testified; thus the Lord Jesus Christ himself taught us; thus the Symbol of Fathers <the Nicene Creed> has handed down to us.[9]

The agreement here regarding the teaching concerning the person of Christ is an addition to the affirmation of Christ asserted at Nicaea. But the agreement centers more upon what or who Christ is not, rather than who Christ is. The intermingling of positive and negative assertions highlights the possibility of Christ's mulattic nature. In this passage of the definition Christ's identity is rendered in the midst of several negations or boundaries (without confusion, without transmutation, without division, and without contrast). In the midst of the prior statement of Christ's unity the following claims seem improbable, if not impossible. In this regard Chalcedon begins to suggest an apophatic identity that transgresses our notions of pure and impure, division and unity, and thus any identity grounded upon these assertions that seeks to press one away from difference. Sarah Coakley suggests this complexity must be understood not in terms of assertion but rather through the category of the apophatic. In her view "Chalcedon is strictly speaking, neither end nor beginning, but rather a transitional (though still normative) 'horizon' to which we constantly return, but with equal forays backwards and forwards."[10] This framework of Chalcedon's definition as apophatic is crucial in that it offers a way of inhabiting the language of the creed. That is, the definition itself witnesses to a possibility that itself cannot contain. But here I want to push Coakley's point a bit further to suggest that in the definition's apophatic framework it does in fact begin to assert the shape of Christ's presence in the world and that this shape is not unrelated to Christ's work.

In these negations or boundaries the definition puts forth a certain "neither/nor" as an aspect intrinsic to the identity of Christ. What makes this "neither/nor" so paradoxical, however, is the way in which it is bound to the unity of Christ. While the seeming impossibility of conceiving of an identity in the midst of such contradictory claims seems difficult, this contradiction in fact marks all identities and thus every identity itself an inflection of "hybridity." What the definition of Chalcedon presses us toward is that the apophaticism does not resist a possible conception of hybridity within the God-man. He is and he is not. The apophatic speech serves to clarify the center in such a way as to obscure the mystery of the internal workings of the wills, but nevertheless presses this internal moment as central to the person. Christ is a full and complete person. The mystery of his lineage, his "biology" can only be sorted out within the confession of Christ's undivided personhood.

The dynamism Christ's inextricable twoness exhibits is both the difficulty and the possibility "inter" bodies pose in contemporary society. As we have seen in Part 1 the interracial body's very existence points to a transgression, an impossibility which requires those who adhere to race to confess the paradoxes of these relations. The white mother and her black child, the white father who's colored children are not sons and daughters—these interracial children are rendered neither/nor not through the union of a essential difference, but are rather born of the structure of race and discourse that gives birth to half-breed bodies. Their bodies are not rendered mixed, hybrid, or impure because of their biology, but because of the discourse that seeks to make sense of the sexual desires that led to the conception these bodies. As in chapter 2, the lives of interracial folk inhabit an impossibility. The tragedy of their existence is the way the space they inhabit is at once disrupted by their presence yet co-opts them into a certain distorted participation. Mulatto/a lives exist within this space that has rendered them nothing, nonbeing. In this dissonance their bodies and lives are sacrificed through death or exile.

In the apophatacism of Chalcedon we see this gap of mulatto/a lives as an echo of Christ's own entrance into the world. The space that Christ inhabits, interpreted through the definition of Chalcedon, can be understood spatially. Homi Bhabha, while not invoking a Chalcedonian logic, nonetheless suggests culture as a hybrid phenomenon that structures identities through negations that are nonetheless bound to one another and thus hybrid. Bhabha poses hybrid identity through a spatial language of interstitiality. For Bhabha identities are found not necessarily within "pure" national, racial, or ethnic notions of identity but rather within the spaces that such claims create and the performances of identity that make those spaces possible. Identities are found in a "third space, though unrepresentable in itself, which constitutes the discursive conditions of enunciation that ensure that the meaning and symbols of culture have no primordial unity or fixity; that even the same signs can be appropriated, translated, re-historicized and read anew."[11] For Bhabha, identities are articulated within these various spaces of contestation. While some may understand themselves to occupy a certain position, they are, in fact, imbedded within a larger network of interconnections that are destabilizing their very claims of identity. When a person begins to see themselves in the gaps of such an identity they begin to occupy a truer self-understanding.

In locating personhood within these interstitial spaces personhood then becomes a disruptive identity in relation to the claims of purity that constitutes its borders. The presence of the one who refuses to be absorbed or represent a particular group becomes itself a disruptive force within each of these articulations of identity. Such a conception of identity can be interpreted within Chalcedon's formulation.[12] Bhabha's claim concerning the destabilizing contentions of cultural space is what marks Chalcedon's rhetorical power. Chalcedon represents Christ both as an assertion and a refusal. The definition seeks to suggest how Christ is and is not, thus problematizing notions that bind Christ to a particular way of being in the world that is static.

The identity here is one that is not bound within the particularity of one claim or in its genealogical purity, but rather the identity is constituted in its occupation of multiple spaces *at one time* and *in one person*. Maximus the Confessor, clarifying the position of Chalcedon, later described Christ's personhood as "a union that realizes one person composite of both natures, inasmuch as it in no way diminishes the essential difference between those natures. . . . For it is fitting for the Creator of the universe, who by the economy of his incarnation became what by nature he was not, to preserve without change both what he himself was by nature and what he became in his incarnation."[13] What is crucial to note in Maximus' description of Christ's person and work is the inherent tension in seeking to express the duality and the unity of Christ's personhood. Christ's identity is bound between these two claims, yet in this tension humanity becomes interpretable only within this tension.[14] To refuse the tension within Christ's own life is to misinterpret the nature of the new humanity being created in his birth, life, death, and resurrection.

Such claims concerning the identity of Christ could be read as attempting to simply create the borders by which faithful explication of identity might be drawn. The space that the definition creates is not a vacuous space, but rather one that is inhabited. Jesus' incarnation occupies a space that defies possibility and in so doing breaks open all lives and the claims they make of themselves. Humanity, as constituted by its being bound (implicitly or explicitly) to others, is now bound to the divine creating, an interstitial reality that is marked not only by contested claims of culture, but also now by a transgression of human and divine possibility. In this regard Chalcedon is an articulation of the incarnation's reconception of humanity within a seemingly impossible multiplicity.

The person of Christ in Chalcedon then becomes reconceived as the binding of assertion and negation.[15] It is within this moment of simultaneous assertion and negation concerning Christ's person as one and many—one without confusion, one without transmutation, one without division or contrast—that both the "high" and the "low" become bound within one person in such a way as to disrupt not only our notions of what is possible within creaturely personhood, but within divine personhood.

Chalcedon's struggle to name Christ's personhood adequately was one driven by an understanding of the relation between his person and his work as necessary. However, the formulation ultimately put forward in fact describes more powerfully the reality of all human identities. While the claims concerning the constituent aspects of this identity were different than ours, the process of identification and differentiation are what constitute all conceptions of personhood. The hybridity or mulatto existence that constitutes Christ's person is thus grounded upon an identity that is "neither/nor." This interstitial space is thus a mark not of Christ in particular, but of the particularity of humanity that Christ takes on fully. This mulattic rhythm of personhood is a mark of humanity universally, while humanity's history is an unfolding drama of refusals and transgressions.

This drama becomes reiterated in the varying attempts to classify (and therefore subjugate) interracial offspring. The mulatto/a of the nineteenth and twentieth centuries arose from the certainty of the identities that gave birth to him or her. Mulatto/a is not a positive identity. By this I mean it is not an identity that can posit what it is. Within the binary poles of colored or white interracial bodies could only posit what they were not. Despite the attempts of these mulattos to perform into a kind of whiteness this performance was only an approximation of the purity of their (typically) fathers. Consequently they were colored, but they were not, for in their white oppressors they saw the face of their father. Claims concerning mulatto/a identity were negotiated between assertions concerning biology and the negations such biology implied. They were neither/nor. But in the midst of this negotiation interracial lives also posed a challenge to the very system of black and nonblack, colored and noncolored, and all those that get lost in between these polarities that pervade American social and political realities. Mixed bodies posed a challenge to the presumptions of intimate encounters that must inevitably be violent or a disgraceful fetish. Their lives displayed the very blurring of the lines of certainty upon which this structure is built.

It is within this negotiation of assertions and impossibilities that we again enter into the controversies regarding Christ's body. He was, but he was not. To Mary's inquiry, "How can this be?" Chalcedon echoes the constitution of Israel's existence and prefigures the disruption of the interracial child. The incarnation is not the instantiation of neither/nor existence, but rather the reinscription that perplexes the structures established upon claims of purity. Here the incarnation resists the power of self-assertion and idolatry that began with Adam and Eve and matured in Babel and would ultimately grind down upon the darker inhabitants of the world.

Here we must return again to the claim concerning Abram's and Sarai's response and the people born of this encounter. Such a confounding is again not initiated in the incarnation, but is rather the culmination of the calling of Abram in the empty space of tribal self-assertion. God called out Abram and made a people out of nothing.[16] These were a people whose lives and loyalties confounded the demands and the identities of those around them. They would welcome the alien among their number in some moments and at other moments throw them out. They would worship a God without a name and yet proclaim God's presence among them. Israel was not a people who created their gods, but a people whose very existence was only intelligible inside the God whose name they could not utter.

The very creation of Israel begins the process of assertion and negation, and is ultimately fulfilled in Mary's assent and the birth of Jesus. Thus Mary's question, "How can this be?" is only a recapitulation of Abram's bewilderment when told by an angel that through him a people would be made. He replied to the angel, "How can this be for I am far along in years?" We return again to these two moments because these questions now press us more deeply into the mulattic character of Jesus' person as bound to a mulattic humanity. Jesus' personhood arises out of a people who confound the world. Thus, "How can this be?" is a question that not only frames Jesus' neither/nor existence, but also always reflects back upon the humanity Jesus enters into and remakes. Humanity is now confronted with the puzzle of its own creation, its own inter-existence, and its own mulattic life.

This nameless God would now enter into this space betwixt and between. Through the people who were created only out of a word and one whose lineage, whose heritage was questionable, the fullness of God's presence would enter. Jesus was, and he was not. He was not a mixture of human and divine, nor was he two separable entities trapped in one body, nor was he a communion of human and divine switching internally within. He was and he was not. He was fully God and fully man. In these boundaries we see an identity constituted through the limitations of language, a discursive identity which we can only struggle with to grasp the power of his presence and the possibility of his flesh for humanity. Jesus' life and presence reflect a radical unity of possibility and impossibility that presses itself into humanity in such a way as to refuse its refusal. He was mulatto not solely because he was "mixture," but because his very body confounds the boundaries of purity/impurity and humanity/divinity that seemed necessary for us to imagine who we thought we should be. The creed suggests what Jesus is with only minimal clarity, but suggests what he is not, unequivocally.

This reconfiguration of humanity is thus reconstituted as conceived in Chalcedon through a neither/nor—*but*. Chalcedon helps us to see the way in which the neither/nor is not merely a method of clearing space and establishing the rules of faithful reflection but is a positive assertion regarding Christ's personhood. But what must also be noted about Chalcedon is that while it seems to explicitly resist a formula regarding the composition of "mixture," it nonetheless outlines a necessary presence of humanity and divinity that does not resist mixture broadly speaking, but seeks to present the form of this "inter-penetration." It does so less through the explicit or formulaic articulation of what Christ's mixture is constituted by, but more in the articulation of the varying negations' significance. One is left with a multiplicity of assertions about the nature of this man that abide within one person.

"Mixture" or "hybridity" or "mulatto," are thus all confessions of the reality of a personhood born of two realities, yet it is a personhood without division. It is a personhood that refuses any attempt to distill the constitutive parts of one's person as though we could attribute Mary's laugh to her mother and her nose to her father. Mary's personhood is certainly bound to these facts concerning her life, yet they are also bound to the interconnections that constitute Mary's uniqueness, her "Maryness." We do not call Mary a "mixture" because we assume a purity in her parents. The constellation of traits that Mary receives constitute her, but also do not distinguish her significantly enough. Yet Christ confronts us with a personhood born of utter "difference." It is a personhood that displays realities that are not of us. These essential differences thus require a qualification in order to understand Christ's relation to us. In what ways is he like us, in what ways is he not. The language of mixture helps us to make sense of this for it seeks to acclimate his personhood more to an understanding of who we imagine ourselves to be. This economy of identification and differentiation only becomes visible in the moments of transgression, when those that do not belong produce something that is contrary to what we thought possible for ourselves. This economy produced the mulatto/a, mestizo/a, the quadroon.

Christ's body and life inhabit the neither/nor that marks all human lives, but that is particularly resonant in mulatto/a bodies. Yet Jesus inhabits this space in a different way. His presence as mulatto recreates the space around him. He is neither/nor—*but*. Bound to this negation is an assertion that both creates mulattic life and lifts it from its tragic circumstance. In this regard what Chalcedon describes is not entirely apophatic. Its continuity with Nicaea serves to perpetually establish that Jesus is divine and one with the Father. This assertion is bound in a deep and complex relationship with the boundaries that delimit the possibilities of this claim. Yet the definition also puts forth something that must be said positively concerning this person.

Inherent within this positive assertion of who Jesus is in relation to its accompanying negations is the possibility of asserting Jesus' mixture or hybridity. In this way, my claim that Jesus is mulatto is not a rhetorical or theoretical argument that allows broader participation in his identity through a contextual approximation because he now essentially "looks like" mixed people. Rather, I am suggesting that the claim that Jesus is mulatto is an ontological claim that does not confirm or stabilize mulatto identity by seeking to deify it, but rather reconfigures what we must consider to be mulatto/a or interracial existence and thereby all poles that make "inter" intelligible. This reconfiguration is a christological moment that opens up the possibility of transformation into an "inter" existence that is established within the pneumatologically grounded humanity Christ's incarnation reveals to us.

Jesus is mulatto is an ontological claim that suggests the union of flesh and Spirit is a fact of Jesus' personhood. As I will examine in the following section, Cyril of Alexandria refuses the stability of personhood. For him Christ's life must always be fully constituted by these two realities of his birth: his "father" and his "mother." Yet, this claim regarding Christ as mulatto does not stabilize mixed-race identity. While mixed-race identity and the discourse that produces it illumines Christ's personhood, the radical difference of this mulattic life lies in what constitutes these bodies and how these constitutive marks operate in different ways.

The mulatto/a body's mixture is the product of an empowered refusal of the very encounter that gave birth to it. These lives are left to live into an impossibility, to "pass" or to abide in the refusal of a parent's people. The claim concerning Christ's mulattic life does not seek to include these refused people nor lift their bodies into an identity of stability and rest by remaking Christ in their image. Rather, the constitution of Christ's "hybridity" reconfigures the very notion of humanity that discursively creates "mixed-race" bodies. That is, in the Creator becoming the Created One, humanity's claims concerning purity and possibility only become intelligible within Christ's body. In subjecting himself to the discursive limitations of human language regarding themselves or God, Christ renders such poles incoherent through his birth, life, death, and resurrection. He recreates humanity and renders "inter" existence no longer through poles of race (or ethnicity) that are tragic in their impossibility. Rather "inter" or mulattic existence is laid before humanity as the possibility of new life in the Spirit, as being born of flesh and Spirit, and whose fulfillment is not impossible, but an ever present "already but not yet."

While not suggested in Chalcedon I believe that the beginning of such an articulation is found in the first accounts regarding Christ's birth. Mary is told, "The Holy Spirit will come upon you . . . " (Luke 1:35). Here the text suggests that the child is born both of Mary and the Spirit. The fruit of this encounter is thus the infant Jesus. Born of the word of God and flesh and pressed into life through Mary. The way in which divinity and humanity interact within the person Jesus is certainly a mystery and beyond the scope of this reflection, but what I want to highlight in this moment is the way in which this encounter itself transgresses the assumptions of Israel regarding their God and God's possibilities and impossibilities.

For in this claim concerning Jesus' birth is a confession of who Jesus is. Jesus is the contamination of the "purity" of God with the "impurity" of flesh. He is the presence of what cannot be contained within the limitation of a body. He is the one who is before all and yet became a child. In these moments the conventional language of boundaries and identities and assertions could no longer be adequately applied to this man. Jesus' very presence in the world transformed the boundaries of identity and thus the possibilities of how identities might be configured in the world, but especially within his own body.

The power and the threat of this claim is displayed powerfully in Jesus' invocation of the Tetragrammaton in John 8:58. Following a protracted discussion concerning forgiveness and judgment Jesus reiterates the authority by which he is offering forgiveness and judgment, telling the Pharisees, "Truly, Truly I say unto you before Abraham was, I am." To this the Pharisees responded with the threat of stones. In this interaction we see first the claim concerning the perception of some Jews at the time regarding the possibility of divinity dwelling among them. While this is the most explicit of encounters, even the disciples' own difficulty in comprehending the claim Jesus was making about himself again suggests the inherent dichotomy that was envisioned between the Creator and creation. God was the one who sent or who spoke through creatures but did not abide with them . . . God could not look like them. Yet in Jesus' claim regarding his own beginninglessness such notions of purity and impurity would become disrupted and overcome.[17]

Jesus Is Mulatto

The conception of Jesus points to the possibility of an intermixture of divine and human that was conceived as impossible, as that which could not be. Yet this claim is implicitly bound up within the boundaries established by Chalcedon as well as throughout the reflections upon Christ's person in the church's early reflections upon Christ. The next section will examine this claim regarding the ontological identity of Jesus as mulatto by briefly examining Nestorious' challenge to Nicaea as well as Cyril's response that were initially contested at the Council of Ephesus, but ultimately challenged and refuted in Chalcedon's definition. In examining Cyril's refutation of Nestorious as well as his implicit resistance to Apollinarianism I will show how Chalcedon's assertion regarding Christ's person is not only a rhetorical boundary, but also an ontological claim that is best interpreted within a notion of mulattic hybridity. To be sure, notions of mixture as conceived in Apollinaris are to be vigorously resisted; yet the notion of hybridity or mixture need not follow a similar pattern. Further such a conception of Christ's person as "hybrid" is necessary to discern, for the addendums to Nicaea were not merely additions of political import, but of pastoral and ecclesial significance. That is, the refutation of Nestorius, Apollinaris, Arius, and their teachings highlight the way in which the early bishops understood the theological and pastoral implications of problematic teaching. Specifically, living into the promise of Christ's birth and life necessitated a faithful articulation of his body and life. Christological formulations were not matters of logic, but were always implicitly or explicitly tied to anthropological claims. A consideration of Christ's identity was always bound to an implication concerning what humanity could become and how humanity entered into this possibility. In examining Cyril we will attend not only to the necessity of a certain ontological "inter" existence in Christ's person, but also the implications of problematic notions for the body of Christ, those who would seek to participate in his grace and love.

In *Against Nestorius* Cyril makes his most substantial refutation of Nestorius' teachings. This refutation centers upon perhaps the most egregious of Nestorius' errors, his refusal to call Mary the "mother of God" or *Theotokos*. Outlining his positive affirmation of Christ's person he writes, ". . . having made his own body which was from a woman, and having been born from her according to the flesh, he recapitulated human birth in himself, he who was with the Father before all ages having come to be with us according to the flesh."[18] For Cyril, humanity becomes subsumed or incorporated into divinity through the incarnation's inhabiting of a deep, seemingly contradictory, reality. Christ is the one who fashions for himself a body and comes forth through the womb of a woman. The conception and birth are real moments in the unfolding of the Word made flesh. The incarnation is thus the recapitulation of birth itself opening up the possibility of redemption for bodily life. But Christ's birth is itself a conception. For Cyril,

> The Only-begotten has shined on us from the very substance of God the Father; having in his own nature the fullness of the one who begat him, he became flesh . . . and mixed himself as it were with our nature by virtue of an inexpressible conjunction and union with this earthly body. So he who is God by nature was called—indeed actually became—a heavenly man (not a god-bearing man as he was called by some who do not correctly understand the profundity of this mystery) so was God and man in one. He made a sort of union in himself of two things which are utterly distinct and remote from one another in nature, and thereby made man to share and participate in divine nature.[19]

The incarnation binds divinity to humanity in such a way as to conceive humanity anew. The conjunction is what cannot be expressed perfectly (it is inexpressible), yet is nonetheless a definitive union of the two. Jesus' personhood is wrought between these "two things which are utterly distinct and remote." The presence of Jesus in this "neither/nor—but" is the constitution of who he is. But in this moment Jesus' body overturns the impossibility of neither/nor by welcoming the other into his own body just as Mary welcomes the other into her own body. In this reciprocity the Creator and the created encounter one another so as to conceive new lives that will burst forth from the womb that will be Jesus' tomb.

The mystery of the incarnation that Chalcedon utters so paradoxically must be understood within the trajectory of the work its object serves to accomplish. The definition of Chalcedon thus lays the foundation of human possibility. The confession of Christ's twoness is to confess the possibility of humanity's becoming. To resist the essential unity of Christ's personhood as holding divine and human within himself is to not only claim a limitation of God, but also a limitation of human life and longing.

Nestorius sought to resist this essential presence suggesting that Christ was not born but "passed through" Mary's womb.[20] This resistance arose from a concern that divinity could change or suffer. The unified conjunction of Nestorious' christological reflection sought to account for this unity while maintaining the central claim of Christ as human. The maintenance of Christ's unity as divine and human was, for Nestorious, a soteriological question for "the body is the temple of the Son's deity, and a temple united to it by a complete and divine conjunction, so that the nature of the deity associates itself with the things belonging to the body, and the body is acknowledged to be noble and worthy of the wonders related in the Gospels."[21] Nestorius' "conjunction" was one that suggested that the body and soul of Christ were distinct. Somehow in this union each aspect of the divine and human were incised. The body was thus a biological reality, which, infused with divinity, made possible the redemption of all bodies. The attributes of Nestorius' christological person characterized Christ's life and works within a profound bifurcation which preserved the Word's divinity and humanity's limitation.

Yet in Cyril's view Nestorius' understanding of conjunction exhibited a certain resistance to the radical claim that Christ was fully human and fully divine in such a way that was inseparable, suggesting "that Christ is a God-bearing man and not truly God, a man conjoined with God as if possessing equal status."[22] As with any conjunction, such as *don't*, it is a unity of utility, and when that utility meets its need it can be disjoined and each part still serve its purpose and be recognizable on its own, thus *do not*.

Cyril responds to this problem with an emphasis upon the essential unity of the two within the person of Christ who, "Being God by nature, became man, not simply by a conjunction, as he himself says, that is conceived of as external or incidental, but by a true union that is ineffable and transcends understanding."[23] The difference between how Cyril and Nestorious conceive Christ's unity relates, in part, to how Cyril is also seeking to avoid an Apollinarian mixture that was contested in previous years.

As with Cyril, Apollinaris also expressed the paradoxical nature of Christ's person, noting that Christ, the one who sanctified and was sanctified, was one person.[24] Yet Apollinaris sought to resolve the paradox based on a certain anthropological limitation. He suggested the nature of the one whom the divine intellect indwells is fully human, but merely flesh and thus:

> [I]t is inconceivable that the same person should be both God and an *entire* man. Rather, he exists in the singleness of an incarnate divine nature which is commingled [with flesh], with the result that worshipers bend their attention to God inseparable from his flesh and not to one who is worshiped and one who is not.[25]

This is an assertion that Christ's unity is made possible through an anthropological limitation. This delimiting of human possibility serves to de-emphasize the flesh in such a way as to render humanity merely a body or flesh, and thus asserts Christ as a kind of mixture where certain elements coalesce so as to become something new. Christ is thus a new kind of human whose difference is constituted in the mystery of his union with us, that he still sustains us even while he inhabits our vulnerability. Apollinaris' christological formula is bound to a problematic anthropological vision that becomes the ground of his soteriological description. The humanity Christ saves becomes enfleshed and thus the transformation made possible is one that is limited to one's ordering of the flesh. This ordering is merely the stabilization of the person's own works, rather than the transformation of the person.

Both Apollinaris' and Nestorius' descriptions of Christ and, implicitly, humanity, departed from some of the earliest christological assertions that themselves presented a certain anthropological vision as well. In particular Athanasius' resistance to Arius clearly maintained the restoration of humanity's rationality as embedded within Christ' incarnational work. This deep impression of the Word upon and into humanity brought forth the possible transformation of those who would gaze upon Christ.[26] Such transformation was more explicit in Athanasius where in reflecting upon the Word one's rationality became transformed, thus suggesting a wider interpretation of personhood and consequently the possibilities of truly becoming like Christ.

Cyril maintains a certain tension concerning Christ's unity, being sure to avoid the implication of Apollinaris.[27] First, Cyril's conception of human nature displays a significant dissimilarity from Apollinaris. Cyril writes concerning humanity:

> for a human being is truly one compounded of dissimilar elements, by which I mean soul and body. But it is necessary to note here that we say that the body united to the Word is endowed with a rational soul. And it will also be useful to add the following: the flesh, by principle of its own nature of the Word is essentially different from the flesh. Yet even though the elements just names are conceived of as different and separated into a dissimilarity of natures, Christ is nevertheless conceived of as one from both, the divinity and humanity having come together in a true union.[28]

Cyril's assertion regarding human nature describes a compound or hybrid creature whose wholeness is constituted through the union of its parts. To suggest a mixture which requires the replacement or emptying of one aspect distorts the identity or the unity of the person. The importance here is crucial for Cyril. In his commentary on John he suggests that an interpretation of John 1:14, "and the word became flesh," suggests flesh to mean humanity or a human being. The assertion that the word of God became a human being with a rational soul is an important distinction that implicitly addresses the Apollinarian tendency, but also underscores the assumption that would lie at the heart of Cyril's eventual opposition to Nestorius. What is problematic with Apollinaris' conception of mixture is that it reduces humanity to flesh in order to assert the unity of Christ's person as divine soul or intellect with his human flesh. This resistance to contamination of the divine served to both limit divinity and human possibility. Cyril's assertion of the paradox sought to express the incarnation and human possibility as more than mere chemistry.[29]

Cyril's resistance to Apollinaris helps us then to also frame his resistance to Nestorius. On one side there is an assertion of mixture that is a problematic rendering of the body as bifurcated from its soul and intellect, thus rendering redemptive transformation as solely within one's flesh, thus rendering the intellect or soul unaffected. On the other side Cyril recognizes the difficulty of a language of conjunction that on its face describes a certain unity, but when pressed suggests a fundamental division, as seen most explicitly in the contestation over Mary as *Theotokos*. Cyril's conception of Christ as two-in-one hypostasis thus serves to press against two assertions of bodily or creaturely possibility or limitation.

The threat of Nestorius is the possibility of human nature being rendered static and implies an embodied existence that cannot escape its creatureliness even in divinity's assumption of it. Mary cannot be the "mother of God." Human persons are limited even in the midst of the incarnation's redemptive work. This deep bifurcation is one that we cannot see explicitly in terms of purity and impurity within these conversations, but a similar pattern can be seen as a language or distinction between creativity and creatureliness. The emphatic defense of *Theotokos* is the attempt to preserve the mystery and the tension such a word claims. *Theotokos* engenders a certain paradox of creativity and creatureliness abiding within the same moment or person. It is this paradox that Nestorius resisted so vigorously in hopes of preserving a certain perception of divinity that he deemed necessary to save us. In doing so he utterly limited the transformative possibilities implicit in the incarnate union of the Word and body.

Apollinaris' conception of hybridity was one that resisted radical notions of change or transformation on the part of the Godhead, but his notion of mixture ("O new creation and divine mixture! God and flesh completed one and the same nature!"[30]) redacted aspects of each to constitute the whole. This redaction of humanity and divinity served to reify or harden bodily possibilities and thus the mixture he imagines is not for the transformation of human nature or a human person, but for a certain purification of human action. In this way Apollinaris resists the hope of the incarnation, the redemption of humanity's redemption being grounded in its being taken up by God in its fullness. While Nestorius seeks to portray this unity in a slightly different way there is similarly a certain hardening of human possibilities.

The tenuous and mysterious unity Cyril articulates is a neither/nor that is eventually exhibited in Chalcedon's language, understood in relation to his conception of the incarnation and transformation of the human person. In his commentary on John 1 Cyril observes that such a life enters the world for humanity, so that we might "ascend to a dignity that transcends our nature on account of Christ, but we shall not also be sons of God ourselves in exactly the same way as he is, only in relation to him through graces by imitation."[31] The possibility of human participation in Christ is grounded upon a fundamental transformation of our lives beyond what is natural to us. Though humanity is still essentially different from Christ in terms of our origin, the very notion of redemption, for Cyril, is bound to an entrance into a life, or a nature that is neither us, but which we participate in and thus is intrinsic to who we are.

Christ joins to humanity in such a way as to refuse any claim of a human identity without him. In his own person Christ is the paradoxical neither/nor—*but* wherein his humanity is now bound to his divinity. Our imitation of Christ is located not to our likeness in essence, but our entrance into this neither/nor—but instantiated through his miraculous conception and birth. His life now becomes bound to us in such a way that humanity cannot be understood apart from him and the mysterious union that constitutes his life. Thus mulatto/a existence is born not only out of this encounter, but also within the disruption of discourse that suggests we can be understood in terms that are apart from another. For the Christian this discourse is construed in terms of only one other, Christ. In this regard we are not—but we are in our imitation, in our living into the space of disruption created for us in us. This possibility of transformation is reiterated throughout Cyril's letter against Nestorius as the implications of Nestorius' error and Cyril's response are narrated through the implications regarding embodied life, where Jesus "being life in virtue of being God, he rendered the body life and life-giving."[32]

Such implications for the necessarily transformative nature of Christ's person are again seen in Cyril's explication of the analogy of coal and fire laying on an altar where Christ "is compared to a coal because he is conceived of as being from two things which are unlike each other and yet by a real combination are all but bound together into a unity. For when fire has entered into wood, it transforms it by some means into its own glory and power, while remaining what it was."[33] The incarnation is bound inherently to the possibility of transformation of human personhood so that it might take on the form of humanity that has been given through Mary's womb. Cyril's resistance to Nestorius is not one of poor logic or bad chemistry, but one of pastoral concern that binds together Christ's personhood and the personhood of the faithful who gather to partake in his body and blood. This partaking draws the believer into the transformation initiated in baptism and binds them to the "neither/nor—but" existence of Christ's person.

This "neither/nor—but" existence is a "mulattic" existence, drawn in the midst of negations which continually assert what it is not, but in the midst of embodying and making those boundaries apparent. This christological claim also bears witness to the assertion of an identity within bodily space that draws the boundaries into itself, transforming the conceptions of in and out, high and low, and thus blurring the ways in which we assert what bodies will and will not be and what they might be transformed

into and what they cannot be transformed into. The body of Christ is
further a mulatto/a body in that it is itself a mysterious union of God and
humanity. It is the fullness of each bound to one another, but without division or confusion or dilution. The mulatto/a bodies of the nineteenth and
twentieth centuries were repeatedly conceived of as infertile, effeminate,
neither/nor people who neither exhibited the physical strength or virility
of their darker lineage nor the moral or intellectual prowess of their lighter
lineage. Their mixture was conceived of as dilution and impurity.

CONCLUSION

Christ's existence is the mulattic assertion of utter difference inhered
within one person. In Christ this inherence, this hybridity, is not tragic,
but rather the tragic is overcome. Its union, its identity is not the negative
space between illusory assertions of purity or stability, but rather it is the
utter union of the Creator with the creature that confounds the notions
of purity and impurity, in and out. The tragic nature of the mulatto/a of
the nineteenth and twentieth centuries lay in the impossibility of its reso-
lution. Its life was bound to a performance of betrayal or return. These
lives were repeatedly marked by the utter discontinuity of the violence
of their conception or boundaries of death that constituted their personhood. They existed within a world and within classifications that served
to perpetually resist their presence in the world.

Yet in Christ, the tragic mulatto's identity is not bound to our descriptions, but rather utterly confounds the claims of possibility and impossibility through his very birth. His conception and birth reconceives difference,
disrupting the rubrics of race and ethnicity, drawing those who can claim
his name into a difference wrought through the fire of the Spirit. Jesus'
birth reinscribes creation as Adam was formed through the breath of the
Spirit and fell asleep to have Eve drawn out of him. Humanity is conceived
through the inherence of dirt and and flesh Spirit and becomes bound to
an identity of participation with the one who breathed upon them.

In Mary's assent the possibility of human redemption was pressed into
existence in her hope and her pain. Christ, the tragic mulatto, came into
this world not through the violence of the master and slave in the night nor
through the ill-fated love of a man of color and a white woman, but through
the assent of the creature to an encounter with the Creator. The tragic in
this moment is overturned not through the destruction of hybridity or the
assertion of racial purity, but through the radicality of that hybrid moment
through which all assertions of purity must now be rendered. Creation

through flesh and spirit, high and low renders the transformation of the low and the inexorable binding of the high to that which it created. Thus intermixture is no longer construed as tragic, for it is a performance of human lives and thus transforms the meaning of purity recreating true humanity through a hybridity of flesh and spirit. Thus the tragic is no longer construed in biological impossibility, but rather in the idolatrous assertions of purity which deny the possibility of transformation that lies in the incarnation. Imbuing all human personhood with the Spirit, the incarnation, bound to baptism renders all who confess mulatto/a.

Chapter 4

I AM THE WAY
Mulatto/a Redemption and the Politics of Identification

> In every case; the mulatto always moves beyond, not by being alter but
> by being ultra. Indeed in a curious antidote to conquest and reduction,
> the mulatto subject describes a movement of reverse colonization of the
> Ideal that is always more and not less, always additive and forever seem-
> ingly shifting. The mulatto subject is the true plus ultra of the Atlantic
> world.
>
> —José F. Buscaglia-Salgado[1]

INTRODUCTION

The mulatto/a bodies of the modern world, children born of the slave
ship and whose lives resisted the power of knowledge and classification
bore witness to the ambiguity of modern racial classification. Caught
between the seemingly endless claims of white or black and everything
in between we can neither find Jesus in ourselves, nor can we more
accurately theorize his person within the confines of creedal confession.
Jesus is a body that confronts us and the assumptions we make about
ourselves, each other, and the world. Neither a black Jesus nor a Jesus
of the tradition can save us, for these images are but mirrors of our own
hopes and possibilities. We must look to Jesus again and be confronted
with his own impossibility and the possibilities he creates out of our
lives and for our lives. We must see this mulatto Jesus as not only for a

particular people, but we must begin to see how the mulatto Jesus stands before us to remake all people.

In the space of Jesus' body, God with us, humanity is performed out of the assertions concerning itself and is welcomed into Jesus' own life. To say Jesus is mulatto is to make a claim concerning the possibility of our own humanity as something with a reality, an identity beyond itself. It is to speak of our lives as necessarily full only in the life of another. This mulattic re-creation is not a synthesis of ideas, a mixture of parts that mitigate two contrary poles. Rather, Jesus' body is a body that renders the idea of dichotomous poles incoherent. Christ's personhood and life does not synthesize but disrupts through his radical unity with humanity. Jesus' complete identification with humanity does not submit to the "contamination" of human limitation, but submits humanity to Christ's radical space of personhood, God with us.

This process of identification, of radical presence, is political. The incarnation displays a politics of identification. Jesus' life is a presence that makes apparent humanity's refusal of Christ's kinship. Christ's life is a demand upon the disorientation of our lives that we have so long presumed to be oriented. To name Christ as mulatto is to not only name his person but to express his work. The Word became that which he created. To take this claim seriously we must examine not only the "content" of his personhood, but how this personhood itself performs humanity into God's life. Christ gives birth to a mulattic people.

In Christ the tragedy of identities circumscribed by a racial, national, or cultural telos becomes overturned by rendering the neither/nor, the negation, no longer as the basis of exclusion, but now as the entry into participation. Christ welcomes participants into the impossibility of their own lives with Christ and the neighbor. He welcomes humanity into life where a mother, sister, father, brother will be lost and mothers, sisters, fathers, brothers will be added. This exchange is not without pain or difficulty but it is also not without joy or belonging. To enter into the life of Christ is to depart and to enter. To follow is to enter into Christ's alienation and rise with his acceptance. Christ's mulattic work is the creation of a mulattic community, a new people who are born and live in the Holy Spirit.

Christ is mulatto. He is the mysterious union of God and humanity born of the Spirit and Mary. As Irenaeus reminds us, "why would Christ have come down into her if he was to receive nothing from her?"[2] To fail to account for this "mixture" within Christ's own body is to obscure the disruption and promise of his life. To resist Christ as mulatto is to resist the possibility of our own transformation and the politics of that personhood.[3] Christ enters into our lives to perform us into new creatures and a new way of being in the world. This speech, this word of prayer articulates humanity into a new thing, resisting and disrupting the formations of identity that sought to establish personhood within the confines of race, nation, and culture. Christ's identity as mulatto becomes essential at this point not for his identity, but for ours. To confess Christ's identity as mulatto is to begin to perceive the reality of racial and ethnic formation constitutive of our lives together and of our lives as disciples of Christ. Confessing Christ as mulatto is to faithfully confess our location in a world remade by racial logic.

This chapter will examine the claim that Jesus is mulatto through an examination of Christ's incarnation and life as a politics of performance. That is, bound to an articulation of Christ's body as "mixture," is an explicit claim concerning the bodies recreated in the enfleshment of the word of God. These reborn lives display not only new bodies, but a negotiation of life that Christ's presence inaugurates. But before I consider this anthropological re-creation and corresponding politics, I will attend more closely to the shape of Christ's enactment of humanity. More specifically, I will outline how the claim regarding Christ's mulatto existence is an ontological claim that corresponds to a disruptive mulatto, pneumatic personhood.

GOD WITH US: THE PRESENCE OF REDEMPTIVE DISRUPTION

Christ's work takes upon our unlikeness so that we may take on Christ's likeness.[4] This radical unity or identification draws us into the life of one who is and is not us, who is us, but is more than us so that we may become more than ourselves. This transformation is one not only of an inner spiritual union but is a transformation of our whole persons, such that our lives now call and respond, depart and enter within the rhythm of Christ's life. Our lives become mulattic disruptions as flesh and Spirit, our very wills must now struggle with the presence of another will within. This correspondence engenders a shift, for the claim to be "in Christ" is an inherent identity rendering our lives presences of disruption amidst illusions of certainty.

As we saw in Part 1, the reality of transgressive bodies performed or negotiated racial life in such a way as to render claims to race and nation incoherent. Christ's life exhibits a disruption bound not only to his assertions but also to his person. Through these enactments Christ both refuses the idea of personhood as pure assertion, but also performs humanity's own life through the Spirit. While the bodies rendered mulatto/a in the nineteenth and twentieth centuries would ultimately be bound to a tragic impossibility, Christ's presence explodes these tragic assertions from within, culminating with his own resurrection in the tomb so that even death itself could not be understood apart from life. In this way Christ's mulattic existence does not succumb to an ideal purity, but rather "purifies" all through a holy contamination.

This overturning remodulates the tragic as no longer an oppressive impossibility that renders persons nonbeings who are external to its patterns of purity. Rather Christ's body creates a space of perpetual interpenetration, an ecclesial womb through which humanity becomes intermingled with the Spirit, becoming new creatures. This life is not without tragedy for this new birth is the reordering of lives, the loss of mother and father, but it is not unto loneliness or exclusion. To be reborn in Christ is to be sutured into the community of God. God is with us so that we may be with God and that we might be a new people.

Theological reflection has resisted articulating the divinity and humanity of Christ in terms of mixture or hybridity. But as I have sought to show thus far the exclusion of a certain construct of hybridity limits a consideration of Christ's work upon and in humanity. Theological reflection must struggle to articulate not only Christ's hybridity but the significance of his personhood reflected in Scripture and the lives of those who would follow him. The unity of Jesus' person is bound to a vision of Jesus' soteriological work, to the type of people Jesus re-creates through his birth, life, death, and resurrection.

Perhaps the most prominent among twentieth-century-Protestant theologians, Karl Barth does not consider Christ in terms of mixture or hybridity explicitly, but given a structure of hybridity as neither/nor I believe Barth's work can be read as articulating the mystery of Christ's person in such a way as to point to Christ's fundamentally mulattic character. For Barth,

> Jesus of the New Testament is supremely true man in the very fact that He does not conform to the later definition, and far from existing as the union of two parts or two 'substances,' He is one whole man, embodied soul and besouled body: the one in the other and never merely beside it; the one never without the other but only with it, and in it present, active and significant. . . . [5]

Christ's personhood as whole, as two parts irrevocably present constituting the wholeness of a person is the claim of mulattic personhood. Jesus' personhood establishes true humanity. The mulatto/a of the nineteenth century as a "mixture" was the refusal of a profound unity. The implication of Christ's radical personhood can be understood as an intermixture or transgression. In Christ's taking on humanity's "no," "our unholy human existence assumed and adopted by the Word of God is hallowed and therefore a sinless human existence; in our unholy human existence the eternal Word draws near to us. In the hallowing of our unholy human existence he draws supremely and helpfully near to us."[6] The character of Christ's healing is constitutive of Christ's presence of holiness in the midst of humanity's unholiness. As such, unfaithfulness becomes apparent in the assertions of purity or attainment of virtue rather than in a radical reception of Christ's presence.

It is Jesus' presence in the world that heals. The healing presence, the salvific personhood for Barth is summarized in the refrain concerning Christ, "God with us."[7] Contained within this name is the substance and trajectory of Christ's personhood. The claim concerning who Christ is points to what he has done (and is doing). Thus the refrain "God with us" also contains the claim "we with God."[8] Christ's personhood is an enactment of those contained within him so that "although our believing, loving, and hoping themselves and as such are in us, they are not of us, but of their object, basis and content, of God who in that one man not only answers for us with Him but answers for Himself with us, who gives it to us in freedom that we may believe, love and hope"[9] This rhythm of faith, hope, and love that is Christ and the shape of his life opens up a particular shape of Christian life, a pneumatic life.

Christ *as* faith, hope, and love creates faith, hope, and love. His personhood is his work insofar as his work creates our personhood. The power of this presence thus *speaks* humanity into a new mode of being in the world where, as Barth suggests, "to be man is to be with God."[10] This presence of identification is one that is not only bound to Christ's conception but penetrates the unfolding of Christ's life. For just as Jesus' birth "births" humanity, so too Jesus' living, speaking, mourning, lives and speaks humanity back into Jesus' own conception and life. As Irenaeus reminds us, "for what has been tied cannot be loosed unless one reverses the ties of the knot so that the first ties are undone by the second, and the second free the first."[11] In this way Christ's identification with us is not only classificatory, but performative. Identity or personhood as a process is an identifying with (or from) a particular people so as to declare or "suture"[12] one's personhood in relationship to others.[13] In Christ there is a radical unity of personhood that both repairs the breach between humanity and God, but also explodes the grammar of humanity that is from within.

Returning to cultural theorist Stuart Hall's description of the process of articulating identity serves to highlight two important observations regarding the creative power of discourse and its corresponding reception in the formation of identity within realities of difference and power. Such theoretical tools can be (and perhaps already are) observable within theology's claims concerning the person and work of Christ as I am conceiving them here. First, the creative power of discourse is the use of words and description to *create* peoples. The creation of *mulatto/a* people was an example of this examined in Part 1. These descriptions served to referentially maintain whiteness through a classificatory system of descent. Through the erection of social and legal codes these bodies were continuously created by the refusals that constituted their bodies. Yet these discursive spaces were also inhabited, lived into by so-called mixed bodies in an attempt to correspond to the world of whiteness. Thus, speech both created bodies and bodies sought to perform into or articulate themselves within these discursive spaces.

The claims concerning Christ's person and work can be understood powerfully within this interplay of the Word and reception. Here Christ *is* the Word. His enfleshment is the creative speech that first spoke humanity into existence and in so doing uttered not only humanity's difference, but also its similarity. In Christ, this speech itself becomes enfleshed, present in the world, and as it does so the very discursive space of Christ's body serves to describe the limits and possibilities of human bodies. But what is crucial to see here is the way in which such a difference is not maintained in this speech, but is rather transgressed. The speech takes the Other into himself so as to eradicate the difference. Yet in this radical unity, this mulattic personhood, Christ also becomes humanity's response. He becomes humanity's reception of God's Word and corresponds humanity into this Word of promise spoken to it. In this way his reception is the *articulation* of humanity; his life is the spoken, lived response of this call. His articulation of humanity is the performance of humanity, the re-creation of humanity that humanity must now itself live into. Performance then refers to the mode of human enactment that takes place through the *identification* of the Word to humanity.[14] The incarnation is an identification that takes humanity's difference and its self-induced exclusion into God's own very life so that identities are now articulated through a radical unity that splinters the "dividing wall of hostility." This incorporates humanity into God's own life as God's incorporation into us incorporates us into the loves of one another. The process of identification leads to an in-breaking or unveiling of a "new reality," wherein Christ reorders the problematically performed tension between finite and infinite freedom and humanity's efforts to resist this tension. Here humanity lives out these tensions in problematic ways on a number of fronts such as between man and woman, body and spirit, and the individual and community.

The connection between who Jesus is and the nature of his work can be seen in late twentieth-century Catholic theologian, Hans Urs von Balthasar's clarification of Karl Barth. Balthasar describes the connection between Christ's person and Christ's work as the transformation of persons and lives.[15] For Balthasar, the person of Christ illumines human possibility. This is not to say that absolute likeness is possible for individuals, but rather that Christ's personhood ushers in a new possibility for created personhood, namely a pneumatic existence in which the body of Christ participates in the life of God. Balthasar reminds us that "this purely human subject cannot surmise and seize his mission, or God's will for him, or the idea God has of him through his own autonomous power; man must open up to something that is infused into him from above, something that is laid upon him as a task."[16] The relationship between the person and mission of Christ and human personhood are not to be confused as identical possibilities. Rather, Christ's person and mission breaks open the frontier of possibility for individuals and, through the Holy Spirit, makes participation possible—although only participation in the sense that what was created can commune with its Creator in the fullest way it was created to do so.

Christ's person and mission reflect not only a radical self-giving, but also a radical receptivity to the Father's will. Thus, the personhood that is opened up expresses a perichoretic economy wherein each person is radically receiving and giving to the other. To confess Christ as mulatto is to confess Jesus' mission and personhood as bound to another. Christ is the one who is not us, but in us in such a way as to recreate humanity within him (though we are not him). Christ's mission adheres humanity to himself in such a way that our lives can only be uttered within his own life. To suggest Christ is mulatto is on the one hand to make a claim concerning Christ's own "hybridity." But on the other hand, this claim also implies the inhering of Christ to humanity. Christ's personhood is a radical union of divinity and humanity that must be construed within the difficult language of hybridity in order to faithfully discern the shape of Christ's salvific work and the re-creation of humanity that Christ's incarnation makes possible. Through such a mulattic framework personhood and mission can be seen as a mutual adherence and transgression of humanity and divinity, divinity and humanity. This reciprocity marks human lives that participate in Christ's person and work as mulatto/a, as participating in the life of the mulatto Christ.

In the person of Christ the human possibility of participation in the Triune life is expressed through a radical receptivity and self-giving (to God and to the community) of the individual in response to the unique call of God through the unique person of Christ. The mission of Christ was not merely to make a way for creation to know God and recognize God, but to share in God's life, to recreate humanity as a "holy mixture." As such, to become a "person" in this sense is to accept Christ's call, when "finite conscious subjects identify themselves with the qualitatively unique mission that has been designed for them and that lies within the mission of Christ."[17] This mission derives from the eternal love of the Father for the creature.

The reciprocity of love constitutes the basis of this new reality or new rhythm of human life constituted in and by Christ's life. It is through his presence and his life that humanity is loved and through whom this love is offered back to God. Christ's conception and presence ushers humanity into a life of the Spirit, a pneumatic existence which is bound through its continual reception with and correspondence to a life of the Spirit. (We will explore this more in Part 3.) At this point it must be clear that this rhythm is bound to Christ's very body conceived in this rhythm of call and response, and Christ's mode of life performs humanity in its identification, in the Word enfleshed.

This communion does not constitute a purely intellectual posture of rationality, nor a set of practices that are properly ordered. It may begin through these practices or in the midst of deep contemplation, but this does not constitute the fullness of the call or the shape of discipleship. To love and be loved is to be encountered by the eternal one. It is to be transgressed and in this union be reborn. Through this encounter the child can no longer be accounted for as within or without, but neither/nor, for they are in Christ but they are not Christ. The lives of God's adopted children are measured by a presence within the very life of God, but are also marked by the attenuation of this life to the one into whom and out of whom they are born.

Christ's person not only breaks open the possibility of participation with God, but also displays the shape of this participation. Through love the "theological" person participates in the life of God and in this way the individual and community become radically joined in mutual service to each other. In Christ the one incorporates the many. The lives of the many are now measured in their relationship to the one through their mutual incorporation into Christ's own life. Christ's work serves to break open identities that were once enclosed, but now are marked by a rhythm of redemption that reiterates an identity of love and procreation through the transgression of incorporation. To participate in Christ's life is to welcome the many and the transformation of practices, lives, and culture that such mutual incorporation requires. The mulattic life is one that welcomes people into a pattern of transformation and unfolding. In Christ the neither/nor, the abnegation of mixed bodies opens up and incorporates, conjugates Christ and humanity into a *both/and*. Here hybridity is not only the negation of personhood but the radical incorporation of distinctions which create something new, something beyond. Buscaglia-Salgado's description of mulatto/a life that opened this chapter is worth repeating here.

> In every case; the mulatto always moves beyond, not by being alter but by being ultra. Indeed in a curious antidote to conquest and reduction, the mulatto subject describes a movement of reverse colonization of the Ideal that is always more and not less, always additive and forever seemingly shifting. The mulatto subject is the true plus ultra of the Atlantic world.[18]

The mulatto/a life, while rendered visible through the negation of possibilities, in fact inhabits all possibilities within the mulatto/a performance of life. Christ's performance of mulattic existence overturns the tragic negation of personhood and the illusions of certain identities so as to incorporate all peoples into Christ's own body. Through this identification Christ expands the possibilities of identity of those who live into him. This process of incorporation is not a loss of identity but its reorganization, identity's rearticulation. Christ's personhood as mulatto is bound to his mission incorporating humanity into himself, articulating human lives in his own, performing humanity into the very life of God through the Spirit, and bearing new creatures in his womb. These new

creatures are not only creatures of a spiritual birth, but display bodies
that no longer indicate the normativity of whiteness or must declare the
absolute beauty of dark bodies. But rather, to be in Christ is to embody
a refusal of these structures. Christ gives birth to mixed-race children
whose very presence and whose lives declare a different possibility.

Christ's Person as Pneumatic Performance

Christ's conception and life fragments the structures within which
humanity has ordered its life in the modern world. This fragmentation
does not leave people or culture dead, but opens up the possibility of
humanity's own reconception and a new life together. The interconnec-
tion between Christ's person and work make it difficult to speak clearly
of one without the other. If it is not only Christ's person that redeems,
but his life that performs us into redemption, the shape and rhythm of
his life discloses a mode of being in the world that is bound to the kind
of people we become. Christ's mulattic life is bound to the creation of
mulattic people. These people are not only those born of flesh and Spirit,
but a mulattic Christian personhood bears witness to this conjugation
of Christ and humanity through a particular politics, through a way of
inhabiting the world. These children of God disrupt the claims of modernity's citizens and ultimately overcome the tragic articulations of human
longing, racially and nationally construed, through a peculiar death and
rebirth of familial hope and life. To begin to see the shape of our own
lives we must therefore attend to the conception and arc of Christ the
tragic mulatto.

Christ's mulattic personhood occupies a space that performs the lives
of those who follow Jesus into Christ's own life. Christ's mulattic personhood, his neither/nor—but existence creates humanity even as society's
refusal of this claim seeks to subject him to death. Mulatto/a existence
refers to lives bound to a peculiar existence rendered neither/nor and consequently gives rise to a particular negotiation of daily realities that iterate
a deeper claim of identity.

In Matthew 1–3 there is a constellation of three claims regarding
Christ that expresses the connection between the identity or person
of Christ and the work of Christ. The centrality of Jesus' genealogy as
well as the discussion of Jesus' conception make for clear markers of identity that, in modernity, have constituted the basis of classification, exclusion, and oppression. Such markers in the United States would become
the basis of anti-miscegenation legislation as well as the way to determine

whether a person was colored or white, thus determining the mode of participation within American political and social structures. Relatedly, the way Jesus' personhood is established both disrupts notions of Jewish ethnic identity and theological presuppositions regarding the possibility of creaturely existence and divine presence in the world. Matthew 1–3 displays the outlines of what came to be understood in modernity as an interracial identity, and yet challenges the structures of identity that rely on concretizing bodies within discourses of certainty.

In chapter 3, I examined the significance of the incarnation as the Word of God entering into the world and creating a discursive space which itself rearticulates human possibility. Mary's question "How can this be?" both confesses the reality of the human condition as limited and finite, yet also points to the impossible possibility that this transgression will inaugurate. But here I want to attend to the way such a scandalous birth itself overturns the tragedy of self-assertion while Christ's peculiar birth also begins to iterate a different mode of being in the world.

Matthew describes not only the annunciation of the angel to Mary, but also the revelation of this promise to Joseph in a dream. Mary's scandalous revelation could only mean the transgression of her own purity either on her own part or on the part of another. Mary's body was one that was not a body that could be joined to another. Yet in Joseph's "redemption" of Mary it is not his "redeeming" of Mary that is so interesting, but rather the way Joseph's reception of God's call joins him in a life of following his wife. Joseph's "redemption" of Mary is thus not manifest through Joseph's power or his means to protect, but now through his posture of reception. Joseph must listen to the one "who has heard." It is Mary who has been spoken to. It is Mary who has encountered God. It is Mary who will be the "mother of God." Joseph's marriage to Mary is not one of redemption, but one of living into God. Joseph's very life, his fleeing for Egypt, returning to Bethlehem, now become circumscribed within the promise spoken to his young wife. The shape of Joseph's life is now bent around and toward the words spoken and birthed in Mary. As a husband and as a man, Joseph can no longer be imaged around notions of certainty, power, or the "salvation" of his scandalized wife. Joseph's manhood is now predicated upon his submission to a word of God spoken to his wife.

But within the reordering of this marital relationship the "impurity" of Jesus' genealogy, highlighted in Matthew 1, serves to punctuate how Jesus' mission as Messiah is not bound within articulations of national purity, but rather arises out of the contamination that faithfulness engenders. As one "having heard," Ruth would bind herself to Naomi, her people, and her God and thus come to participate in the redemption of the very world.[19] Through the faith of one outside, the purity of Israel's faithfulness was maintained.

Matthew 1–3 provides an important progression of events that highlights the way in which the previous claims concerning Jesus' genealogy and conception, typically essential markers of identity that are thereby employed in the process of identification, become explicitly bound to what would come to be understood as the nature of Jesus' work. Jesus descended from Abraham and David, as one who "would save his people from their sins" (Matt 1:21), as seen in the initiation of Jesus' ministry and his baptism by John.

John's confession concerning the one who would follow him was that he would be the one who "will baptize you with the Holy Spirit and with fire" (Matt 3:11). Upon Jesus' own baptism "heavens were opened to him and [Jesus] saw the Spirit of God descending like a dove and alighting on him. And a voice from heaven said, "This is my Son, the Beloved, with whom I am well pleased" (Matt 3:16-17). The initiation of Jesus' work was thus marked by two important realities that are bound to the reconfiguration of personhood found in his body.

First, Jesus' identity is not one that is asserted or declared by him. Rather, his identity is given to him, first through the reception of the name his parents were to give him and his assent to being formed not only in the womb, but also to being reared and named by his parents.[20] Here personhood is not asserted or constructed, but rather received. Such a reception would be later highlighted in Jesus' characterization of himself as being sent. The humanity Christ performs or enters into is not the triumph of a self-made man, but rather it is a humanity that is seeking to be conformed into the will of God, being impressed upon with a name and the hope attached to that name.

Second, Jesus' ministry would be imbued with the Holy Spirit. Such a continual presence of the Spirit in Jesus' conception, initiation, and ministry can simply not be ignored. Yet, what is important to note here is the way in which the Spirit is essential, not as a tool to be wielded by Christ, but rather as that through which Christ's very presence enters the world as well as that which participates in Christ's work and ministry. In this regard the work of Christ is bound to the work of the Spirit and is at the same time preparing for the coming of the Spirit. The person of Christ is intimately bound to a claim concerning the movement of the Spirit and the Spirit is bound to the claims regarding Christ's work. Throughout his ministry of healing and preaching, his words and his actions form the basis of his personhood as conceived in Mary through the Holy Spirit. This claim regarding his identity, his personhood, must serve as the hermeneutic through which his life and actions are interpreted. In this way Christ's work and person are seen not as two aspects or two separate modes of inquiry, but are bound together; Christ's presence is his work and his works are his person. Each claim is pointing to the other claim where a description of his person refers to his works and a reflection upon his works indicates his person.

The relationship between personhood and works or practices, in some regards, is not isolated to a christological inquiry. As we saw in chapter 2, mulatto/a lives echo between these claims of personhood made upon them and asserted by them. These assertions are signified by practices or performances of identity that serve to either deny or confirm the identities they desire or are resisting. The lives of Rena, John, the Ex-Colored Man, Clare, and Irene are identities articulated through practices or works of race. Each decision, departure or return, cadence or adaptation serves to resist the disorientation of their bodies and lives. Their works or practices of life are a work of "redemption," of "reconciliation" and of their "true" selves to the world's discourse concerning them. These lives, despite their resistance, cannot escape the tragic because the horizon of this self-creation is itself illusory and impossible. Refusing the hybridity or the conjugation of Christ's person thus does not threaten a certain conception of God, but rather circumscribes human possibilities that have been particularly framed by race in the modern world.

In Christ the reciprocity between person and work, Spirit and flesh are not moments of self-creation and thus trapped within the tragedy of an illusory horizon. Christ's work is an invitation. It is an outpouring that recreates as it offers. Christ's identity is *pro me*.[21] This reciprocity is necessarily pneumatological wherein Christ's person is born through the Spirit, and his ministry is the process of incorporating creation into the life of God through the Spirit. Thus Christ's presence is a participatory presence that must be pneumatologically interpreted and must be seen as pneumatologically creating. We see the ontological claims concerning Jesus as mulatto not as incidental to his ministry of atonement and redemption, but as central to the promise of redemption, his work. The work of Christ flows out of the claim of Jesus' identity as a mulattic identity that disrupts the idolatry of creatures and the self-assertions built upon such claims.

From this constellation of markers concerning Jesus' identity we will be able to examine the ways in which salvation is construed not only through his work, but through the particularity of his person as mulatto or "inter." Such a claim then also points to the means by which humanity participates or receives Christ's redemptive work. Christ's preaching and his ministry now exhibit this disruptive character unveiling the nature of human redemption as the incorporation into Christ's transgressive body, thus creating bodies and lives that transgress racial and ethnic stipulations in order to enter into and be conformed into the will of the Father.

The transformation from individual to a "theological person"[22] or one living a pneumatic existence is the ground of Christ's encompassing person. The identity of Christ as one born of Spirit and flesh is the work of Christ whose identity opens up humanity's identity as theological persons. This work of transformation becomes clearly evident in the gospel narratives immediately following Jesus' baptism by John in Matthew 5 with the Sermon on the Mount. Through these teachings we are given the way in which Jesus' person not only exemplifies and opens up human birth and participation, but also the way such births open onto a way of life that disrupts notions of personhood that have become bound within self-assertion. Jesus' preaching exemplifies the disruption or transgressive nature of his person while his subsequent ministry demonstrates how this disruption reverberates the transgression of Word and body. The intersection of Jesus' person and life open the means by which humanity might be incorporated into Christ's person and into God's own life.

The Sermon on the Mount's apparent dichotomies (the poor will inherit the kingdom, those who mourn will be comforted, the meek shall inherit the earth) point to the first important aspect of Jesus' ministry and person. The kingdom of God is that in which notions of power and entitlement become inverted through a certain conflation of high and low. Thus poverty and inheritance, weakness and power become bound to one another in Christ's person, and through him those who dwell in the "lower" are bound to the "higher." Such a binding of higher to lower is not a transformative reality where low and high are blended so as to create a redemptive middle. Rather Jesus becomes the space in which high and low are present and presently bound to one another. This confession of God's presence on both sides in Christ is not a discourse that requires the rendering of one to make another intelligible. Both are present, and in this moment Christ's peculiar presence draws humanity itself into this disruptive mode of being in the world as those seemingly disparate peoples are drawn into one another. While much has been made of these verses to suggest Christ is overturning the economic structures of poverty and class, what must also be attended to is Jesus' incorporation of all people into himself. The poor, the destitute are not only economically or ethnically identified. As Christ encounters the poor and the destitute, the poverty and delusion of those who are rich and lacking nothing is laid bare. Christ's presence makes known the varied ways humanity has sought to establish itself and thus robbed themselves and one another. Christ incorporates all of these people into his body while each becomes fragmented and broken in differing ways.

As chapter 1 noted, the assertion of purity is the actual illusion. Thus what the Sermon on the Mount begins to unveil is the way in which the high and the low are intrinsically bound together. Such a binding is not merely a social description, but rather is made intelligible in Christ's own body. The position of the poor in the kingdom, the comforting of those who mourn, the inheritance of the meek are modes of life, as well as descriptions of Christ's own person—his action of taking the Word as divine and eternal, fully taking on the reality of human striving and yearning. In this regard the message indicates the mode of participation, but also the means by which such participation is possible—Christ's own body as a transgression of those possibilities which seemed foreign to one another.

Christ's transgression unveils a second important aspect concerning these promises. Not only are the high and the low bound to one another, now their relationship is fundamentally inverted. As echoed in the Christ hymn of Philippians, "He did not, but emptied himself, taking on the . . . " Christ's preaching is here a confession of his own person, as well as the prophetic declaration of how such relationships of power, high and low, with and without, become fused. These "poles," perpetually deployed in order to include and exclude, determine the boundaries of inclusion and exclusion that were now being disrupted, utterly distorting and confusing the way these dichotomies could be inflected. In Christ's person the high and the low flowed together in a fundamental unity so as to make it impossible to distinguish whether the high or the low was primary in a particular moment.

This confusion is exhibited clearly in the early church's initial attempts to name which aspect of Christ was active during various moments of weakness or strength. When he performed miracles it was his divinity and when he mourned we saw his flesh, they would speculate.[23] Yet, in the Sermon on the Mount the declarations regarding the high and the low, the dispossessed and those who would inherit the promise were now utterly confused. The confusion and reorientation of identity becomes more explicit as Jesus explicated the law, setting forth the means by which Israel might participate with their God. In so doing he did not abolish the law but intensified its possibilities. These intensifications display how Christ's presence in the world becomes modulated through a different inhabitation of the law. This mode of life reveals the distortion of the law which had turned faithfulness into a performance of religious assertion rather than faithful reception.

Four such clarifications or intensifications can be found in Matthew, whose couplet structure can be read as forming a baseline or rhythm of this pneumatic existence that disrupts and opens up the follower into the life of the other:

- vv. 21-22: "You shall not murder" . . . but I say to you that if you are angry with a brother or sister, you will be liable to judgment.

- vv. 27-28: You have heard that it was said, "You shall not commit adultery." But I say to you that everyone who looks at a woman with lust has already committed adultery with her in his heart.

- vv. 38-39: You have heard that it was said, "An eye for an eye and a tooth for a tooth." But I say to you, Do not resist an evildoer. But if any one strikes you on the right cheek, turn to the other also . . .

- vv. 43-45a: You have heard that it was said, "You shall love your neighbor and hate your enemy." But I say to you, Love your enemies and pray for those who persecute you, so that you may be children of your Father who is in heaven.

These four intensifications are then followed by a injunction against public piety (Matt 6:1), the ostentatious prayer of hypocrites in public (Matt 6:5), and the accumulation of treasures and desire for status and wealth (Matt 6:19). Read with these injunctions, Jesus' words indicate not only a conflation of the high and low, but also an exposition of how religious identity can become the grounds for assertion wherein identity and personhood is asserted through one's accomplishment and religious performance. Such performance highlights not one's createdness, that is always implicit in the confession of one's descent from Abraham, but rather outlines one's own justification.

The structure of these intensifications bears witness to how the law requires one to be subject to and reflect the glory of God. These intensifications or reversals do not constitute an abolition of the law, but rather must be understood confessionally as the institution of the law that is now Christ's person. Insofar as Christ inhabits these intensifications his presence also uncovers the distortion of the law that thwarted the fulfillment of Israel's presence in the world as God's elect.

In Christ the possibility of the law is now seen more clearly, not in the public piety of strict observance, but in the deepest recesses of one's being bound to and seeking the Father. Here Christ points to the law not as codes for fulfillment, but means of participation.[24] Insofar as these laws indicate the possibility of participation, they necessarily require and call those who hear to a new way of being in the world where they "seek first his kingdom and his righteousness" (Matt 6:33). The transformation of the law is a confession of Jesus' own identity and personhood, thus calling the people of Israel (and ultimately the world) to the possibility of its own transformation and its own possibilities through their participation with God in Christ through the Spirit.

Such confession regarding Christ's own person and his declaration of Israel's participation with God *as* their identity, however, is only further intensified in Jesus' subsequent ministry pointing to the profundity of Christ's healing. In so doing the divine encounters the sick and in this proximity the ill are awakened to the possibility of new life. Christ's body and presence in the world clarifies and bears witness to the embodiment of the Sermon on the Mount in such a way as to impress itself upon Israel. Impressing himself upon all humanity, Christ incorporates into himself such utter differences that all people become reconfigured individually and corporately within Christ. His presence among Israel incorporated lepers, the blind, the poor, tax collectors, and the prominent and in this incorporation each became present to one another in radically different ways. Each partook in Jesus' healing, or his forgiveness, or his mercy, and in doing so became enveloped within his mission, his acts, and thus his very person. The dispossessed received Christ and as they did their desperation and dependence softened them to the transformation Jesus' presence calls for and makes possible.

The incorporation of these disparate figures into Jesus' own life serves to disrupt the notions of purity upon which religious self-assertion was predicated. Overturning the presumptions of purity, the account of Jesus and his disciples plucking grain on the Sabbath (Matt 12:1-8), displays the threat that Jesus' presence and teaching posed to these assertions. The question regarding whether healing (or plucking grains to eat) was permissible on the Sabbath was posed to Jesus. These objections were raised, undoubtedly, to undermine Jesus, but the objections also betray an understanding of the law as that which can be fulfilled unto purity and that which can be wielded to determine the conditions of exclusion. The accusation seeks to reveal Jesus' own impurity in his disobedience of the law. Yet Jesus' response again indicates the deeper significance of the law, redemption. Jesus' healing of the leper at the synagogue only serves to reiterate his confession earlier that "something greater than the temple is here" (Matt 12:6) "and that mercy not sacrifice is desired" (Matt 12:7). Taken together, Jesus' healing and eating indicate Jesus' person to be *the* healing and thus further deepens the apparent intermixture of perfection and imperfection that is Jesus' body.

Reading Christ's life and ministry through this lens of a transgressive holiness we see Christ's presence among the people on the Sabbath as disrupting notions of work or healing on the day of rest. Rather, Christ's very body, his very presence *is* his work, his healing. Jesus cannot *not* work on the holy day. Jesus' person is the presence of utter holiness in the midst of Israel and the nation's destitute condition. Purity now becomes reconfigured in his body. Purity here is constituted or performed through his work as purity becomes, not an assertion or a sacrifice, but that which distinguishes the one who can participate from the one who cannot, into a love—into mercy which makes one subject to another and displays a love which incorporates disparate peoples into itself.

This reconfiguration must be understood not as a new way of understanding or a new set of ethical precepts that must be enacted through love, but as calling those who hear to a transformation of life and desire. This reconfiguration is seen most explicitly in the conclusion of Matthew 12:46–50:

> While he was still speaking to the people, behold, his mother and his brothers stood outside, asking to speak to him. But he replied to the man who told him, "Who is my mother, and who are my brothers?" And stretching out his hand toward his disciples, he said, "Here are my mother and my brothers! For whoever does the will of my Father in heaven is my brother, and sister, and mother."

The transformation made possible through Jesus' body and life is a transformation that culminates in the reordering of familial bonds. This transformation is not only a reordering of commitments along lines of obedience or ethical obligation, but rather a fundamental or, one might say, an ontological rebirth.

Through this examination of Jesus' mulattic character, his reordering of desire culminating in the questioning of the family, one can begin to see the reciprocal interpretation begun in Hughes' "Mulatto" discussed in chapter 1. Kinship and familial identity become disrupted in the presence and disruptive assertions of these mulatto/a children. Yet in their assertions and disruptions we see the timbre of mulattic presence in Christ resonating differently than in that of Hughes' "Mulatto." Hughes' mulatto is bound within a rhythm of assertion and denial, "You are my father . . . you are my brothe" while his father and kin deny "Hell no, You are not my son"; "ain't no nigger our brother." The mulatto/a of America is engulfed within his or her own refusals and the refusals of the world. The modern mulatto/a is present within white and black peoples while the structures that create these people articulate the mulatto/a into a space in between. For the mulatto, to seek his white father is to refuse his black mother, to seek his black mother is to refuse the truth of his own paternity and acquiesce to a system predicated upon his own internal division.

Hughes' mulatto is bound between these assertions and refusals, revealing the continual delusion of white purity. Christ's presence poses the question he states so boldly in Matthew 12, "Who is my mother and my brother?" The question of Christ's presence creates a refusal by opening up the neither/nor of his body and life to those who will believe, to those who do the will of the Father. Jesus' mulattic presence disrupts the delusion of purity and calls those who hear into a life of pneumatic contamination, a life sullied by the will of the Father. This contamination renders the participant neither/nor and calls them into a space where they may now be refused, their personhood denied. In this way Jesus calls hearers into the life of the tragic mulatto/a, to be hated by their father and their brother. Yet, Jesus occupies or *becomes* this space so as to create a communion of neither/nor where those who are refused are refused because they have become new creatures, members of a new family. They are crushed beneath the weight of exclusion but incorporated into a truthful existence. This existence is marked not by the leaving of mothers and brothers, but by the adding of mothers and brothers. The mulattic life then becomes a life of multiplication, a community of those outside. Jesus' presence invites the believer into a space where their own family might become strangers and strangers become family. In Jesus the mulattic life is one that opens up the possibilities of lives bound together while Hughes' mulatto of modernity is marked by the tragic refusal of the white father and the mulatto's own refusal of black life, all of which render the modern mulatto/a without a people, a nonbeing in a world of color.

In Christ this tragedy is overturned by rendering the neither/nor the
basis of participation, not exclusion, and he welcomes participants into
the impossibility of their own lives with Christ or the neighbor. He welcomes them into life where a mother, sister, father, brother will be lost
and mothers, sisters, fathers, brothers will be added. This exchange is not
without pain or difficulty but nor is it without joy or belonging. To enter
into the life of Christ is to depart and to enter, to follow is to enter into
Christ's alienation and rise with his acceptance.

Such a radical rebirth into this new family is one wherein adoption is
performed through entrance into the will of the "Father." It is here that
we return to Balthasar's pneumatic life of love, but we can express this
creative interaction more particularly through a consideration of Augustine's Trinitarian reflection upon the Father, Son, and Holy Spirit as lover,
loved, and love. Interpreted through this Trinitarian lens the will of the
Father is the desire for or movement toward that which the Father loves.
Entrance into the will of the Father becomes the rhythm or shape of this
mulattic existence. Augustine's reflection upon the Trinity suggests that
such movement toward, or the love of the lover for, the loved is not a tool
of the lover, but rather the fullest expression, the hypostasis of the lover's
desire for the loved. This love, Augustine suggests, is the Spirit.

The Spirit is a person insofar as it exists within the eternal relations
of the one who loves and the one who is loved. Augustine suggests, "And
while love is referred to the mind loving, whose love it is, nonetheless it is
also love with reference to itself, so that it is also in itself, because love too
is loved, not can it be loved with anything but love, that is with itself."[25]
This Trinitarian reflection is bound to a particular form of life wherein
"brotherly love . . . is proclaimed on the highest authority not only to be
from God but also simply to be God. When we therefore love our brother
out of love, we love out of God; and it is impossible that we should not
love especially the love that we love our brothers with."[26] The connection
between God as love and the love of neighbor is participatory. To love is
to enter into the activity of the Trinitarian life. It is to participate, through
the Spirit, in a communion "foreign" to us, yet naturalizes us in its own
extension of word and love to us. This participation then not only allows
us participation as strangers, but as family ("that they may be one, as we
are one" John 17:22).

The lover sees another and offers, adores, reaches out to the other while the one loved acknowledges the love and adoration that is offered, reciprocates, and in each moment love is offered and returned. For humanity, as creatures, this exchange must unfold in time. It requires an encounter with the other, a "getting to know," an acknowledgment, and so forth. Each of these moments requires the completion of another moment in order to unfold. But within Augustine's conception of the eternality of the relations this exchange simply *is*. The persons *are* in relation and the shape of this relation is eternal, without time, without progression or unfolding. Yet it is this implicit willing, desire, movement toward that, in Augustine's work, bears the mark or the work of the Spirit.

Christ's presence and person articulates that Trinitarian rhythm within humanity *as* humanity. To do the will of the Father is to participate, receive, and follow. The patterns of kinship revealed in Christ's life and work instantiate this rhythm within the very structure of human life and longing. Intensifying the participatory nature of the law given to Israel, Christ's birth and life ushers this participation of God with man (God with us) as the God-man. Christ's life makes possible an entrance into this life, through the incorporation of one's life and body into the life and body of Christ.

We see this yearning for participation, this being drawn into a life of God that continually reorders Augustine's own desires in his *Confessions*.[27] Here we witness the rather desperate groping for reciprocation of the love that has been extended to him. Yet it is in Augustine's willing toward God, his attempt to receive this love, that we are reminded of Christ's mark of kinship, "the one who does the will of my Father." *Doing* the will of the Father in a way that is complete and full is certainly impossible, as is the admonishment to be holy as he is holy. But what could be meant by such a test of kinship?

Such a test of kinship is not the completion of the requirement, but the desire for those who are loved to enter into an identity of desire and dependence. This desire and dependence is not one of juvenile romantic fantasy, but rather it is a desire grounded in a recognition: there is one without whom we are not. It is entrance into Paul's reminder to the Ephesians that there was a time when we were no people, without God in the world (2:12). Such a desire is not grounded upon a certainty regarding who we are and thus an assertion of what we ought to accumulate or venture into based on that certainty. Rather, such an identity, such a pneumatic existence is predicated upon the assertion that without the will of the Father, the presence of the Spirit which bore me into this new life, my life is illusory and is not. It is a life that hangs upon the recognition that it is in Christ's *willing* our lives that we do not slip into nonbeing.[28]

Thus pneumatic existence is existence born in the Spirit of the Father who sent his Son to recreate human life and lives. Such lives bear the mark of the Spirit and the mark of this new creation insofar as they live into the Father's will. But this willing is the mark not of rationality or intellectual assent, but sheer apprehension (to draw upon Barth's notion of faith) of one's true position in the world. This apprehension does not leave one unchanged with merely a new outlook on life and a new set of precepts by which to guide one's life. Entrance into the will of the Father is the entrance into a new familial structure where kinship is now reconfigured, not through biological, ethnic, or genealogical ties, but is rather stitched together through a common birth and food. Through the baptismal waters the believer enters into a new world through the womb of the will. The will of God is not a distant reality here but a presence which impresses itself upon humanity, taking it up into itself and, as it does so, healing the wounds of resistance and unfaithfulness. Christ's life and work opens up the possibility of this existence as "neither/nor—but." It is recreating human life, welcoming humanity into the reciprocity of his own life with the Father through the Spirit.

In these moments of radical receptivity we see again Augustine's deeply Trinitarian claim particularly expressed in his prayers. It is through these prayers that we not only see humanity seeking to open itself to God, but we also see Augustine's description of God's eternity pressing into time. We find this in particular when we examine Augustine's account of time, eternity, and memory in the later chapters of *Confessions* in light of his Trinitarian conception. Here is the analogy of the singer and lyrics, where God is the one who does not strain to recall what has come nor is God straining to think of what will come. Rather the song rests perfectly within him, unfolding upon the object of those God sings of. Pneumatic existence abides in the perfection of song sung to us and of us. It abides in the new song, the new rhythm of humanity present among us in Christ and his re-creation of humanity.

Thus pneumatic existence is the mark of a deep transgression wherein divinity took upon it flesh, and in doing so reconfigured the possibilities of human participation with God. Such a pneumatic existence is thus a mulattic existence. It is an existence of mixture and the fruit of a blessed transgression which renders the child no longer Jew nor Greek, male nor female (Gal 3:27-28; see also Col 3:11). This mulatto Jesus bears children who can no longer be marked by the biological essentialism of the world, for their life is now bound to the life of the Spirit and thus to new bodies. Jesus' very body, his very presence in the world is the conjugation of what could not be with what is. Jesus' mulatto body is the creation of this new reality, this pneumatic family which thwarts the assertion of religious and biological identity through a desire for the will of the Father, for an abiding in the Spirit of God, for seeking to exist in the midst of the love of the Father for the Son and the Son for the Father.

JESUS' PERFORMANCE OF HUMANITY

Jesus' ministry bears out the embrace or abiding with the poor, the different, or any other group in isolation. In his presence among them, his feeding of them, his healing of them, his love and desire for them, these actions are not moments of exemplification wherein we might take solace or comfort in his being like us. In Christ's presence, his healing, his desire he is continually incorporating those disparate peoples into himself, transforming them and bearing from his womb a new people.[29] In light of Christ's life and work as mulattic, we must now conclude with still deeper reflection of Christ's performative person. It is a performance that leads unto death and brings death to death, rendering the tragedy of our disillusioned identities no longer along lines of racial or national inclusion or exclusion but through the life of incorporation and the many sorrows and departures this life will inevitably mean.[30] The mulattic character of Jesus is thus not one in which peoples of mixed heritage may take solace in or confirmation of their existence, for his mulattic life ushers in the transformation of all biological claims of certainty, requiring them to succumb to the transgression and transformation of the Spirit. His life is ontologically marked by the "neither/nor—but" that incorporates humanity into an "inter" life whose points are fixed by the Spirit's presence and their identity in the birth and sustenance of the life of the church.

In some regards the preceding reflection has tended to move to a more anthropological reflection about Christ's effect upon humanity. Yet this tendency reveals the character of Christ's work and person as the reformation or transformation of human kind. Barth's iteration of the christological formula discussed previously that "Christ is very God and very Man, that the Word of God *is* reconciliation" becomes more radically interpreted here, suggesting that humanity is not a reality apart from God which in its distance must be brought close to God through the mediating work of Christ. Rather, the reconciling work is the transformation of that which is already present in God yet denies and thwarts its own participation in this life.

It is important to note here Barth's conception of participation that circulates around the themes of faith, love, and hope. Within each of these the decisiveness of a complete act is latent within each theme. The possibilities of faith, love, and hope are grounded in the reality of Christ's person and work. Each aspect is in itself full and complete insofar as each arises out of Jesus' faith, hope, and love or more precisely out of the reality that Jesus is faith, hope, and love. But if each of these aspects of humanity is already full we return again to the question of how one can participate within such fullness and of how are such themes operative within humanity's reconciliation with God.

The faith, hope, and love of Christ establish the possibility of faith, hope, and love in humanity's participation with God. In Christ's life and work not only are the conditions of participation broken open, extending the possibility to become what one is not, but Christ's work is a *performance* of our lives. His faith, hope, and love create, performing humanity into its possibilities. The tragedy of our mulattic and racialized life becomes finally overturned, for it frees us from the burden of tragically performing ourselves into a perfection or possibility that is beyond us. It frees us to live into one another and, in doing so, live into Christ. It is through this performative reality of Christ's person and work that we see the finality of the tragic overturned. Our lives, our racially circumscribed lives are no longer left to be performed into or out of on our own part. We are not left to establish our own ends and the means by which we will attain them and consequently recapitulate the deathly discourse that ultimately created the mulatto/a body.

Christ's birth, life, death, and resurrection performs us and performs upon us, inviting us into a life opened up into the possibility of participation with God. Jesus is a performance that welcomes us into the freedom of hybridity, mixture, and becoming dangerously new. This performance is a performance of faith, hope, and love springing out of God's own life, instantiated in Christ's birth and life, welcoming humanity into what has already been accomplished.

Drawing on the language of performance discussed in chapter 2, we see in Christ a life that from its very conception subjected itself to the disciplining of humanity's names and structures. The eternal Word became subject to time and space, but Christ also entered into the rhythm of identity. Jesus learned prayers, entered into relationships, showed himself to be a faithful Jew. These markers of Christ's life are not merely aspects of life one does naturally, but represent the performative character of all lives. Our daily lives and activities are demonstrations of who we are, they are performances of life that serve to indicate who we are and who we are not. The incarnation is a mark of Jesus' presence, as performing humanity in the way that all people do. But at the same time Jesus' performance is also markedly different because in the demonstration, the articulation of his identity, he also articulates all humanity. His humanity does not only represent our humanity, but Jesus *is* our humanity. As such his performance of life lived into and with God is the performance of all of our lives lived into God. Jesus' life is a performance of all human lives, cohering God's own inner life with the life of God's creation. In this performance Jesus not only breaks open a means of participation with him, but also disrupts the structures of unfaithfulness that have demands, performances of identity bound to self-sufficiency and death.

The person of Jesus *is* reconciliation, *is* faith, hope, and love. Jesus impresses himself upon humanity binding his infinitude and freedom to humanity's finitude and creatureliness. This binding or inhering of the Word to flesh engenders a new reality of transformation. The life of Christian hope is the life of transformation, of becoming, of entering into holiness. Yet this becoming and hope always walks before us, incorporating us into the work that has already been achieved in Christ's body. In the midst of this transformation the presence of these new people disrupts the structures built upon the architecture of purity or self-assertion.

The transformation made possible here is one that must be understood to be inherent to the claim regarding Jesus' mulatto existence. The claim concerning his person being born of Spirit and flesh is the mystery of his work that reconfigures notions of high and low, obedience and disobedience, finitude and infinitude, purity and contamination. Barth's own considerations centered upon the dilemma concerning Christ's freedom and human freedom, and in his anthropological work we see the work of Christ making possible human apprehension of its own condition. Yet in this apprehension there remains an implicit transformation. This transformation is made not through our work but through our apprehension in which we come to recognize ourselves as we are. Such a recognition is, in fact, a type of transformation, but one whose implications must be more deeply interrogated, for the apprehension of one's true life and self must be given a deeply pneumatological reading. It is through the work of the Spirit that humanity enters into this apprehension and participates in Christ's enacting of our life and faith.

Such a transformation becomes present in the world through the transgression that is Emmanuel, God with us. The power of this proclamation is the power of the mulatto body that is both divine and human, disrupting the claims to human self-assertion and transforming those assertions into an apprehension. Such an apprehension is an entrance into the life of faith, a willing toward the One who has been willed toward us. Thus this life of faith, this life of apprehension is a pneumatic existence. A life of Spirit and flesh is not merely opened through an act of Christ or the arc of his life, but through his person and his enacting of our lives, our refusals and ultimately our apprehensions. Barth suggests the presence, this reality of Christ,

> is that God Himself in person is actively present in the flesh. God Himself in person is the Subject of a real human being and acting . . . And in being what we are He is God's Word. Thus as one of us, yet the one of us who is Himself God's Word in person. He represents God to us and He represents us to God. In this way He is God's revelation to us and our reconciliation with God.[31]

The power of this representation thus is an enacting of human lives and response. The possibility of participation then is mediating through Christ's life is a performance of human assent impresses itself upon humanity who once denied and resisted.

Bound to the drama of encounter between the one who is created and the one who creates, between the one who exerts power and the one who is exerted upon is the power of particularity of Jesus' human existence. Yet this encounter does not exhibit the tragic betrayal or coercion of the slave master and the bondwoman or the child that is produced in such horror. Rather, the instantiation of this mulatto presence comes through the assent of a girl. Mary's assent is not the victimization of the powerless, but the uplifting of the oppressed to be the temple, the mother of God. In Christ's birth, life, death, and resurrection the nature of his person works upon the world in such a way as to *perform* us. That is, the representation indicated by Barth could be said to still rest too much faith in the possibility of our sight, our apprehension as an intellectual possibility. Rather, Christ the mulatto child reverberates the gift and the disruption of this life through his ministry. His life and ministry are not a work of redemption, but his life is the performance of our redemption, which, in the language of Irenaeus, slowly unties the knot of our disobedience.

This new body offers participation not as an example simply to imitate, but rather Christ's life is itself a performance of human life and faithfulness which humanity performs back into. In modernity our performance has been a response of conformation that offered as white faces, forms of life, and participation in the structures of power and oppression, and children of rape crushed in order to assert and preserve its own power. Instead Christ is given not to crush, but to live into so as to expand human possibilities, distorting and interrupting the rhythms of white hope and assertion and their counterpoints. Thus in Christ's performance of human life the tragedy of self-assertion, the illusion of idolatry becomes shattered beneath the holy mixed one who fragments us only to make us whole and welcome us into his body as new people, whole through the Spirit and engrafted into one another through his body.

This performance culminates in the death of Christ upon the cross and the glory of his resurrection and his ascension. In his resurrection the culmination of Jesus' life is marked by the same pneumatic wonder that conceived his life. The drama of Jesus' life is marked by this movement of redemption and performance that is preparing the way for "another counselor." The resurrection is the culmination of his life and ministry as well as the ushering in of that which will incorporate humanity into his presence. Christ's life as a pneumatic "inter" existence opens up for its followers the possibility of participation with him through a pneumatological presence that marked his life and the life he welcomed his disciples into. This life is the life of the will of the Father, the seeking and conforming and loving which marked his own life, not as an intellectual assent, but as a witness to the eternal unity of the Son to the Father and the love that binds that which is offered to humanity—but only offered through humanity's own rebirth, their own transformation.

But prior to this moment of sending of the Spirit we must face the cross. It is in the cross where the tragedy of mulatto/a existence is marked and visible, for it is here where the refusal of humanity to assent to the presence of Emmanuel is met with a deadly refusal. The tragedy here would be echoed in the sacrificial moments of interracial life examined in chapter 2 where social death (*Autobiography*) or physical death (Rena, Clare, the mulatto of Hughes' poem) marked the reality of mulatto/a life. Their lives are crushed between the competing assertions of purity and wholeness and the continual costs of participation. The tragedy of these lives is marked by the mourning of the mothers who lose their children to this call, who forsake all to enter into the promise of white life and rid themselves of their human stain.[32]

In so many ways Christ, the tragic mulatto, enters into this tragedy as well. Upon the cross he succumbs to the deathly consequence of human self-assertion. Christ enters into an economy of power and powerlessness, of faith and assertion. Christ takes death itself as the fruit of a distorted assertion of purity (washing his hands of guilt) and succumbs to it. In his death he triumphs over the final assertion of possibility and impossibility. Jesus takes death as that which can no longer be overcome and binds it to his own life. Upon his death the end of life becomes bound to the one who gives life. This union of beginning and end is the culmination of his mulattic disruption. It is the final transformation of assertions and their sting into possibility and becoming.

In his resurrection from the tomb, the power of the Spirit again conceives new life, for in his resurrected body he performs our own pneumatic births. His resurrection transforms the stench of death and the tomb of mourning into a womb of promise and the birth of our new selves. Thus his resurrection is the performance of our new birth, our lives and their possibilities in him, for he is both the object of our lives, the end of our hopes, and the womb through which we are named anew. As the Spirit raises him from the dead the reality of mulattic existence is not confined to a miracle or a promise to a young girl, but rather is extended and impressed upon all humanity, ushering those who might believe, who might apprehend their lives, and the calling of the Father into a life transfigured, transformed, and incorporated into Christ's own body. This body has a shape that is not definitive, but rather a form of life characterized by the continual willing for the Father. By this will one is mysteriously transformed into a new person, whose family is now marked no longer by biology but by strange tongues and miracles of relationality.

PART III

IMMERSION

Christian Discipleship or *the New Discipline of the Body*

Chapter 5

YOU MUST BE REBORN
Baptism and Mulatto/a Rebirth

And at that self-same moment, ye died and were born; and that Water
of salvation was at once your grave and your mother.

—St. Cyril of Jerusalem[1]

INTRODUCTION

We are born into a world of race even while we are baptized into Christ.
While Christ encounters humanity as "God with us," born of flesh and
Spirit, the modern world has resisted the transformation Christ's body
calls us to. Modernity's resistance to the mulatto Christ and to modernity's own mulatto/a children demonstrates the wider societal attempts
to discipline difference and stabilize personhood within the confines of
power and self-assertion. In this way the religiosity of race, while still
present in contemporary society has become an ever-widening phenomenon of differentiation even as globalization brings disparate worlds
closer together. In this proximity we are again and again confronted
with difference, with possibilities to become something new, and in these
moments we are again confronted with Christ's question, "Who is my
mother and who is my sister?"

The religious phenomenon of racial logic reverberates in our modern world, forged within the foundries of racial assertion and power. The
question in the face of these powers and principalities becomes present in

the faces of those who are both near and distant. In the faces of the dark, in the faces of the light, in the faces of the foreigners we are confronted with the possibility of becoming something new. But in the midst of these seemingly strange faces we are more profoundly confronted by the face of Christ, one who is both profoundly near us and who is utterly different. We are encountered by a Jesus whose life does not confirm or establish our estimation of ourselves, but requires us to enter into his birth, to enter into his life, and partake in his resurrection. Christ requires our death beneath the baptismal waters. Baptism, as the moment of initiation into the life of the church, but more profoundly into Christ's body, marks humanity's entrance into this rebirth and the death of our racial fidelity.

The baptismal moment is the ushering in of the radical presence of God that transforms its participants into something that they once were not. More profoundly the baptismal moment also transforms their lives into an extension of this moment. Baptism creates lives that utter the possibility that God is with us even now and we must humbly seek to conform to such a presence in our lives, hopes, and prayers—for each of these become declarations of God's transformative work enacted by Christ's immersion into us. Baptism is entrance into the work of Christ's person. It is the initiation into his body *and his people*. As such, this entrance marks the renunciation of the world's claims upon the baptized as well as the renewal, or rebirth, of the person. It is an entrance that requires a departure from the racial economy of the West and its children.

To be baptized is to enter into Christ's mulattic personhood and an economy of negotiation that such a presence is necessarily bound to. I must stress here that the notion of mulattic personhood is more than a clever device for us to imagine a particular people as the ideal of Christian perfection or one among many ways to imagine Christian existence. Mulatto/a existence is a claim that encapsulates the negotiation of identity inherent in our claim to be "in Christ," bound to and iterated within a world where race and ethnic difference is continually and tragically bound to everyone's assertions of identity and belonging. The modern world is a racial world. It is a world whose economies are driven by the processes of identification and differentiation. Even within the societies of "single races," ethnic and cultural differences torment their inhabitants. And within these societies Christians are not only victims but also perpetrators, killers, and killed alike.

This theology of a mulatto/a Christian existence seeks not a spiritualized account of our life in Christ, but seeks to name the embodied challenge to a life in Christ through a description of the kind of people we become. The baptismal moment does not accomplish something for us, but draws us into a drama of God's presence in this world. It is a transgressive presence, a presence that is neither/nor—but, it is a presence that is in-between, disrupting the claims we make about ourselves. This framework of mulatto/a Christian existence does not seek to articulate some bodies into the life of Christ, but to rearticulate *all* Christian bodies as a disruptive presencing of God in the world. It is necessary because it points not only to a spiritual reality, but confesses the nature of our world, which is struggling to account for the remnants of its colonial creation.

This chapter claims that baptism is a moment of "unnatural" transformation wherein the person immersed, dipped, or sprinkled is reborn.[2] They are immersed into the immersion of Christ into us. Thus we are immersed into a performance of Christ's performance of humanity. We are reborn as new people and into a new life made for us, which is a true existence, a true humanity marked uniquely by the intermixture of flesh and Spirit. This intermixture is now the constitution of our persons, of a Christian's "mulattic" character. However, such a transformation does not constitute the reception of a benefit of Christ's work, but rather *is* Christ's work. More precisely it is the remaking of us into Christ's image and person. This remaking creates lives that gather the fragments of particularity, undoing the tragic nature of their confinement within claims of biological or cultural purity to become transfigured within Christ's person and work.

This transformation does not enclose the person within yet another claim of totality or racial/religious purity, but rather into a purity of God's will toward us. This will is one in which the life of faith is the ever-unfolding transformation of our selves and our neighbors into Christ's mixed likeness. That is, the life of the baptized is a life of transformation and conformation. The unfolding of one's discipleship is marked essentially by faithful transformation which does not enclose the boundaries of a people around an illusory, vacuous space of identity. Rather, identity born through the waters of baptism disrupts from within, fragmenting the particular and ecclesial identities and reconstitutes them again through Christ's own body.

This process of transformation continues as more are reborn, requiring the life of faithfulness be punctuated not only by conformity to Christ's life, but the community's reconstitution around those born within it. In this way baptism not only marks the transformation of the individual within a mulattic rhythm of flesh and Spirit, faithfulness and conformity, which requires their own fragmentation, denial, and renewal, but also the fragmentation, denial, and renewal of the body. The birth of the child is the rebirth of the ecclesial community. Its patterns and culture must shift to welcome that new life into its walls. As a man and woman become a mother and a father they become bound to that person whom they welcome and nurture. To give birth is to become something new just as to be born is to walk in newness. The transformative reality of baptism as the incorporation into Christ's immersion into us is both a particular and a communal act. It is the transformation of both aspects within the miracle of Christ's incarnate womb.

Immersion into Christ's Immersion into Us

Christ's immersion into human life is an enacting of human life. In the language of Barth, Christ's incarnation is humanity's response. This response is one that is not external to human bodies and lives but is rather radically uttered from within humanity. This internal utterance is not only humanity's response (its assent to its own sinfulness and an affirmation of what it is not), but more fundamentally this utterance, Christ's presence as response, is the very transformation of humanity itself. Athanasius described this transformation as a renewal of the portrait of humanity's *imago dei*, a reinscribing of the lines of the image of God upon human bodies.[3] This redrawing is now done through Christ's own body and in the incarnation the nature of this body has been filled out. This fullness of the *imago dei*, of the clay animated by the Spirit, is Christ, the one conceived through the Spirit and born of Mary. Christ is the transgression of the temporal and the eternal, created and uncreated. His person is the neither/nor—but that recreates humanity and whose life, imbued and enacted with the Spirit, displays the perfection of createdness and performs its possibilities and its rhythms. Christ's presence sings the song of human life. It is through the waters of baptism that these children of flesh and spirit are born and ushered into the world.

Jesus' life, his immersion into humanity, his performance of humanity, was the beginning of the baptismal moment. His life was the gestation of those in the womb and who were and will be birthed. The transformative possibility of the baptismal moment lies inherently within the claim we make regarding the power of Christ's incarnation. In the Middle Ages the immersive sense of incarnation as told in Athanasius is expressed again in the theologian Bonaventure's christological reflections and his subsequent theological explication of the life of Saint Francis. In *The Tree of*

Life, Bonaventure's description of the incarnation can be read itself as an archetype, the very structure of baptism that is the foundation of baptismal transformation. In the incarnation Christ is immersed within the waters of humanity and in this immersion the human waters become endowed with the possibility of the participation. Bonaventure's reflection on Jesus as the tree of life traces the rather normative explication of his life in the Gospels, yet in this discussion Bonaventure portrays Christ's life as one of deep humility, wherein humanity is thus drawn out of its own desperate condition. Not only is Christ's incarnation significant, but also his life becomes a deepening or impression of the divine upon humanity, which humanity must itself receive.

This reciprocal movement exemplifies how Bonaventure's language draws upon a communication of attributes that expresses not only the significance of the incarnation of the Word. The incarnation establishes the significance of the baptismal moment wherein the attributes or qualities of Jesus' life become pressed into humanity, not only in the moment of the incarnation but through a life of humility which Jesus enters into. As we examined in chapter 5, Christ's life not only witnesses to the coming kingdom, but also performs humanity's response. His life is the enactment of all lives, to follow Christ is to participate in the drama of his life; it is to pray, to heal, to serve, to die, to be risen. Each aspect of Jesus' ministry not only served to display, but to create, to open up a way of existing in the world "in him."

This process of impression and corresponding conformation forms the structure of *The Tree of Life*. Here Jesus—whose origins are fundamentally different than humanity's—is progressively described as taking on the full aspects of human existence. The first fruits emphasize his identity as divine, his origins as eternal, and the narrative ends with a description of humanity's life enveloped in Christ's fullness. The process of Christ's life is a progressive deepening of himself into humanity (and humanity into him). This process culminates upon the cross as the crucial turning point in this transference seen in Bonaventure's description of Jesus' life and suffering. Bonaventure writes,

> See now, my soul
> How he who is God is blessed above all things
> Is totally submerged
> In the waters of suffering
> From the sole of the foot to the top of the head[4]

As Jesus is nailed to the cross his immersion into Christian existence is now complete. His submersion into the water is the making of baptism's power. Submerging into the waters of humanity Jesus sanctifies the water, sanctifies humanity.

Each of the fruits of the tree of life is a description of an aspect of this submersion and is followed with a description of a sufficient human response. These responses indicate how the moments of Christ's life correlate to humanity's participation within Christ's life. It is here that the language of fruit seems to represent this idea of transference. As one partakes there is a subsequent effect. The incarnation is the immersion of the eternal Word into humanity and humanity's incorporation into the eternal Word.[5] Here the baptismal imagery is christocentric where we see the ground of transformation as the Son's incarnation. The response to such an immersion into us is a subsequent conformation into Christ. Baptism is the initiation not only into a community of faith and a life of following, but it is entrance into Christ's entrance into humanity. It is the transformation of one's body and life and marked as something new. Through the Spirit, baptism enfleshes the Word within the participant, allowing them to be named anew upon their ascent. As Cyril of Jerusalem suggests, they rise from the water and "Being there made partakers of Christ, ye are properly called Christs."[6] We see the possibility of the deification of the body. Rising from the waters they are now bound to another. They are the children of this union, of this performance.

THE BIRTH OF EN-SPIRITED PEOPLE

In the baptism established through Christ's incarnation, or immersion into humanity, children of flesh and Spirit are born. These are children who bear the image of God, but now through their renunciation and their confession they seek to press themselves into the life of their creator and open themselves to be impressed upon by the Spirit. Theirs is a life now marked by a fundamental hybridity. They are mulatto/a. To be Christian, to enter into the waters of baptism is to become something new.[7] Eastern Orthodox theologian John Zizioulas describes this moment of initiation or entrance as the establishment of an "ecclesial hypostasis" where

> man can henceforth himself "subsist," can affirm his existence as personal not on the basis of the immutable laws of his nature, but on the basis of a relationship with God which is identified with what the

Christ in freedom and love possesses as Son of God with the Father. This adoption of man by God, the identification of his hypostasis with the hypostasis of the Son of God, is the essence of baptism.[8]

The baptized person becomes a "hypostasis" bound not to biological necessity (kinship or the passions) but in her relation to God.

Baptism ushers in a radical transformation of the relations based upon racial and cultural assertion which now must be radically overturned. No longer can the tragic assertions predicated upon biological difference mediate one's relations with another, for what constitutes the baptized is now a relationship to God that is essential to their person. One's identity then becomes grounded through the historical expression of this relationship, the church.[9] In this overturning "as an ecclesial hypostasis man thus proves that what is valid for God can also be valid for man: that nature does not determine the person; the person enables the nature to exist; freedom is identified with the being of man."[10] The possibility of this freedom becomes grounded in the life of the church, no longer bound to sustaining its own biological or "natural" personhood, but free to love beyond the bounds of exclusivity. Kinship can now be drawn more widely. This possibility of love arises as an attempt to articulate human personhood in terms of a more complicated "inter" existence which is marked by the movement of a certain person from falsity to truthfulness. In this movement, to be truly human is to be in relation to God, allowing one to expand the confines of a biological hypostasis and its limitations to an eternal relationship in its identification with Christ. The mixture of one's life is bound to a fundamental relationship. To be "in Christ" is to be with the Spirit in such a way that we are not whole without the Spirit, without "another."

The relationship of the person to God is certainly constitutive of their "hypostasis" or person, but a pneumatological reading of this transformation must press this point further to make an assertion concerning one's ontological transformation. Persons are different than what they were before not merely because they live in a new "house," but they have been given "garments of skin."[11] That is, the robes of the one lifted out of the waters signify the anointing or the cohering of the Spirit with the believer. The Christian is the one who is "in Christ" not because of his or her confession but because of the person's union with Christ in baptism through the Spirit. This union is not momentary, but now becomes constitutive of the person—they are flesh *and* Spirit. The child newly born through the baptismal waters is one whose person cannot be understood apart from

Christ. But this relationship is not an abstract position of relations, but rather the real instantiation of a presence. The Spirit who came upon the virgin Mary, hovered above Jesus' baptism, and lifted Jesus from the tomb is the self-same Spirit which binds itself to the child of baptism, conceiving their adoption and making them sons and daughters.

This relation is not one of posture but personhood. They are new creatures born of flesh and Spirit whose lives must now press into the form of Christ, in whose image they were made. They must now walk in an existence of neither/nor—but where their biological, racial, and cultural marks are not hidden, but are now marked with new political possibilities. Their lives can no longer press for purity of relations, of kinship, but now the purity of their faith calls them to a life of contamination, transgression, and transformation. Conformation is the pressing into the life of Christ and defiance of cultural idolatry and self-assertion. It is the conformation of the Father's will and love for God's creation opening the newborn unto a life of contamination.

This is a life of transgressing expected boundaries, learning new languages and cultures, and peoples colliding, encountering, and producing new and strange-looking children who confound their society's estimation of what is proper and good. This process of conformation leads to transgression and ultimately a transformation where the lives of the children become punctuated by the inclusions of fragments that seem disparate, yet they are incorporated in such a way as to perpetually transform the follower's estimation of themselves and their own faithfulness—their own purity. Here the hybridity of the Christian child is not an end that encloses and becomes final, but rather the mulattic existence of these children of flesh and Spirit is marked by continual transgression and transformation. They are lives that open themselves up to difference for they are the fruit of difference.

The new creations of baptism are born into a community of faith inhabiting particular habits and patterns of existing in the world. Yet here we must be pressed even further, for the question put to Jesus was, "How can anyone be born after having grown old?" (John 3:4). In Jesus' reply to Nicodemus, "you must be born from above" (John 3:7), we are immediately confronted with the strangeness and improbability of the baptismal claim. We claim that through the baptismal waters the participant's life becomes truly new. While the church's understanding of Jesus' claim regarding rebirth has been a persistent point of contention and reinterpretation throughout the centuries, its nature as transformative of not only our patterns and habits, but our very bodies must be taken seriously. Is this moment a sign of a previous efficacious moment? Is it the impartation of grace? Is it purely a moment of initiation into the church that is the true means of grace given by God? The difficulty of these questions within the traditions of Christian reflection and faith stems not only from the nature of the act, but also from questions of what the act produces.

So far I have highlighted how a christocentric reading of baptism suggests that baptism is a moment of initiation into an *already*. But it is not yet an existence where the salvific work of Christ is complete within the life of the one cleansed. The transformative significance of baptism must also be realized by the participant through a life of discipleship. Thus the moment is both real and a sign.[12] But baptism is a sign in way that differs from all others because of what and who it signifies. In this way we see the transformation made possible through the nature of the one we are baptized into and presence through the Spirit, while the participant's life is itself transformed into a pneumatological witness of this eternal presence in the world. In this baptismal transformation, the eternal is pressed into the temporal, or, the embodied life we live, and our lives become baptized realities, lives of "already, not yet" which are dripping with the eternal. In our prayers, meals, service, and praise the baptismal moment becomes reenacted witnessing to the possibility of God's participation with the world and the creation's response.

What makes baptism's transformative work possible is not something disconnected to it, but it is the fact of Christ present within it. The difference here is that the "sign" of baptism has a profoundly different character than any other notion of the symbolic. The sign which baptism points to is not present through a rational idea or memory, but that which the sign indicates is present through the Spirit. Thus baptism is a sign to the incarnation as the initiation of a baptismal reality, but it is also a sign that such a presence is not distant, but here in the life of the one who is going to enter into the water.

The baptismal moment is one in which the participant is not only ushered into Christ's body, but he or she becomes an instantiation of such a reality within the world. Through the Spirit's binding to them and their binding to the Spirit, their life in the church becomes a presence of God in the world that attests to a different possibility, but also the fulfillment of that possibility in time.

Here Zizioulas seems to echo the claim Cyril of Jerusalem makes in his catechetical lectures that through the baptismal waters "you are christs."[13] Such a dramatic claim is possible only with a pneumatological movement wherein the Spirit is bound to us through the baptismal waters and Christ is present with us. But here again the peculiarity of such a sign or presence must be made. Christ is not present in part, but always wholly. Thus the claim that the Spirit abides with us is the claim that Christ's presence is full, all in all. And thus our rebirth is the presence of God entering into the world afresh through our bodies and lives together within the communion of God.

The question of baptism is consequently also a soteriological question. It is an explication of the movement from being with God in the world to having God. The centrality of baptism to the question of soteriology is a moment of re-creation not in its own validity but the sign to which it points. How baptism is explicated in this regard is thus an expression of the significance of this moment grounded in Christ's salvific work and the subsequent establishment of the baptismal rite. Baptism is the entrance into this new life. Before us in the remainder of this section is a consideration of *what* is created, what is born from the womb of Christ's life, death, and resurrection.

The difficulty of this question rests in the impossibility of the claim concerning the self, who we are, and what is re-created. What is transformed and what is renewed? The questions of our renewal always point to assertions concerning what we were or what we were intended to be. It is not my intention here to trace the development of the self in order to describe the transformation that is wrought through the baptismal waters. The transformation or renewal brought about in the baptismal moment is both a restoration and a fulfillment that is yet to be filled. The person becomes immersed, imbued, inhabited with the Spirit in a way that is both profoundly unique and essential. It is a commingling that does not suggest the body's equality with that which abides in it, yet the body can no longer be understood apart from it.

As I suggested earlier, this ecclesial hypostasis, in Zizioulas' description, is not so much a claim of an essential relationship, but rather, in the language of Eastern Orthodox theologian Panayiotis Nellas, it is an ontological claim where "the biological existence does not exhaust man. Man is understood, ontologically, by the Fathers only as a theological being. His ontology is iconic."[14] Through the baptismal waters the Spirit descends, transforms, and abides with the participants so as to draw them from within to the fullness of that Christ's image now. The indwelling of the Spirit is a life in Christ, but in this claim the centrality of the Spirit to the claim of personhood must not be lost. Baptism reforms personhood as flesh and Spirit, it is an identity that is human in the deepest sense. It is a personhood that is neither/nor, for though we are bound to our fellow creatures we are never identical to another. Though we are bound to Christ, to the divine, we are not identifiable as Christ.

The identity of the baptized is a life between where the fullness of God abides in us and our conformity is measured not only to an external example but to the groans of the Spirit within. We are neither mortal, nor immortal, we are neither fulfilled nor incomplete, we are full, but yet filled. The life in Christ is the opening up of a tense freedom to be in Christ. Our humanity as limited, mortal, and fallible is now bound to that which is unlimited, immortal, and perfect. This presence is not a transcendent presence or connection made through the incarnation alone, thus creating an existential connection between the divine and human, but rather becomes a real presence of Christ imbued within us in the baptismal moment.

Baptized life is one where personhood can no longer be represented either individually or relationally. The identity of the one baptized is now an internal reality. It is an identity grounded within the assertion that the Spirit, God of heaven and earth, dwells among you and *in* you. Selfhood is now possible not through the assertion of who one is, or through an articulation of a network of relationships, but a relationship that must be received and articulated from within. Being grafted onto the tree of life the baptized is now a part of the tree and their person is identified with bearing the fruits of that tree. Baptism is this moment of transformation where identity is no longer tragically performed into with the impossibility of reception of perfection, but rather the performance of this identity is entering into Christ's performance of us. This identity is one that is received and imbued so as to internalize the reality of God's upholding of all.

The structure of the baptized life is not an addition or new creation, but rather a restoration of what Nellas calls the theological structure of humanity.

> Man was the first portion of creation—"dust of the earth" (Gen 2:7)— which was really and truly bound to God, thanks to the "in the image"; he was the first form of biological life and manifestly the highest that existed on earth on the sixth day of creation which thanks to the breath of the Spirit was raised to spiritual life, that is, to a life really and truly

theocentric. Created matter, the "dust of the earth," was thus organized theologically; the material creation acquired a form and structure in the image of God; life on earth becomes conscious, free, and personal.[15]

Nellas describes the centrality to the incarnate Word as the archetype of this creation. Humanity is continually imbued with a presence that is beyond itself. Its creation "in the image" is not an inherent biological quality, but the uniqueness of its creation and its identity as bearing the image of that which creates it. Its identity points beyond itself and yet is inherent to the person. The baptismal moment is a profound intensification of this creative moment, but more than that it is creation's filling out, its fulfillment such that the Spirit now not only organizes the life and gives it its structure, but now abides within and becomes constitutive of that identity. Identity now becomes an articulation of a relationship that is internal. It is a conforming to the one who is within and without. This process of conforming is a process that is both transformative, but at the same time complete.

This transformative reality is complete insofar as Christ is its beginning and its end. We must still be reminded that such a transformation is also not fully realized within time, or that time does not yet recognize that which has happened to it. In the baptismal moment there is full work within us that we must still yet live into. To reflect upon the wonder of the baptismal moment is to be confronted with the question of who we are. It is to be called into a confession of our own impossibility. It is to utter the question of Abraham and Mary anew, "How can this be?" Such a yearning that is both internal and external is profoundly displayed in Teresa of Avila's *Interior Castle*. While her work does not explicitly speak to the mystery of baptism, its underlying force is the question of how one lives into the reality the baptismal moment breaks open for the participant. Her work exemplifies a certain Thomistic baptismal logic wherein baptism is at once a moment and a journey, or unfolding reality within the life of the believer. The question, "How can this be?" is, for Teresa, the question of our own personhood and possibilities. She warns,

> It is no small pity, and should cause us no little shame, that, through our own fault, we do not understand ourselves, or know who we are. Would it not be a sign of great ignorance, my daughters, if a person were asked who he was and could not say, and had no idea who his father or his mother was, or from what country he came?[16]

This question of identity is aroused through the baptismal moment which Teresa wants to press her sisters into more profoundly, leading them away from the exterior of the castle to the interior so that they may

> attempt to discover what we are, and only know that we are living in these bodies . . . because we have heard it and because our Faith tells us so, that we possess souls. As to what good qualities there may be in our souls, or Who dwells within them, or how precious they are—those are things which we seldom consider.[17]

The imagery of body and soul is particularly striking given the profound limitations of women in the sixteenth century. The movement of identity from bodies to soul does not constitute a departure from the material world, but a reconfiguration of the "whatness" of personhood that now transfigures the lives of these women into more than their bodies might indicate in the society they participate in. Here she provides a picture of the yearning that a baptismal life must enter into that does not mark a stasis of the body, but rather breaks open the possibility of a profound transformation.

For Teresa the interior life is one of yearning and humility where the baptismal moment could be understood as the moment of initiation into this life of yearning and seeking. Yet at each turn this work is not only ours but is a submission to the calling of God, perpetually laying down those marks of pride that might prevent us from proceeding further into the life of God. Here I find Teresa helpful in regard to the imagery of baptism, because Teresa's work exemplifies the necessity of the Spirit as both pulling and prodding. The life of the one initiated is not a life ordering, but rather a life of submission to the one calling. In the midst of this response and submission there is also a transformation that occurs to us and through us. The rationality of Thomas Aquinas that seems to be a mark of human seeking after God explodes within the life of the contemplative, as the transformation of the baptismal moment is unfolded and becomes evident throughout one's life.

The culmination of this yearning which serves to transform the shape of one's life unites the faithful with God, "like rain falling from the heavens into a river or spring; there is nothing but water there and it is impossible to divide or separate the water belonging to the river from that which fell from the heavens."[18] This union, this marriage in Teresa's language is the intermingling of flesh and Spirit conceived in the baptismal waters

commingling the rain from heaven and the rivers of the earth. It is calling creation back to itself, transforming the very rivers and streams that
constitute our humanity. Such a transformation also necessitates a different way of being in the world and here we can return again to Cyril of
Jerusalem.

The transformation becomes a moment of interior regeneration arising in the hypostatic hybridity of the participant. It should be said here that
this moment of hybridity is not a hybrid moment identical to that of Christ
discussed in chapter 3. Rather this hybridity is one that is not marked by
the fullness of humanity and divinity within one hypostasis. The hybridity rendered in the baptismal moment is one in which the person is lifted
out of the confines of humanity; it is not simply biologically classifiable.
The identity with Christ is not complete because the perfection of the participant is not generated internally, but rather is constituted through the
identification of Christ with them, which the baptized approximates in
their immersion into Christ's death and resurrection. However, through
this sign, the body is also immersed into Christ's immersion into us. Thus
not only does the water signify the participation of one in the dying and
rising, but the signification points to the very real presence that marks this
moment as more than a bath. The signification points to the transformation of the participant into something more than what they were prior to
their immersion. This difference may be one that is imperceptible, but the
faithfulness of God requires the moment to be understood as marking
the entrance of a person into an embodiment of this new life in Christ.

The resistance to this transformation is what rendered the baptismal practices of slave Christianity so deeply problematic and ultimately
idolatrous. In the moment of the most profound transformation, baptism
was used to concretize or harden one's relationship to the world and was
seen as having no impact upon the embodied life of the participant. The
soul was something distinct from the body and the Spirit's participation
was resisted. Yet, even in the attempts of slave Christianity to police the
transformative power of these practices we see the baptismal moment
being a moment of radical transformation in the lives of Christian slaves
themselves.

Cyril of Jerusalem's central image for the baptismal moment is one
of grafting. In the baptismal moment the participant is being shorn from
their former life and grafted onto the tree of life. The rite of Jerusalem
highlights not only the moment of grafting, but also the cutting necessary in order to be grafted. Prior to approaching the font the catechumen

is asked to face the West and reject Satan, his work, his pomp, and his service. But here these rejections are not spiritual moments, but in fact are embodied realities which now must be rejected as exterior to the life of Christ. In this way the baptismal moment is not merely the transformation of an interior reality, but rather is grounded in an embodied existence that resists the power of the evil one in the world.

The transformation of the believer through their participation in the baptismal waters is one that marks them as new creatures and ones who no longer are marked by the economics, the joys, the passions, or the politics of the Roman world, but rather their first activity as infants in Christ is to partake in the banquet of Christ's body. But even here transformation is not only in the location of eating, but in the politics of eating. The participants take part in the kiss of peace and speak together the Lord's prayer, providing for one another's needs. In these moments the transformed reality of the baptismal moment becomes present in the forgiveness, eating, and prayers of the believers.

The significance of the baptismal moment is not that it makes these realities possible, but that baptism marks the perpetual presence of the Spirit and Christ within these moments of the believer. In these ways, acts of prayer, service, hospitality, and eating are profound extensions of the baptismal moment, not merely practices that are made possible by an act of initiation. Here we see the necessary connection between a rigorously christocentric conception of baptism. If baptism is not a real presence which transforms and ushers into time God's eternal presence and Spirit, then the subsequent practices of the church are merely folks playing, seeking to signify something that has past.

NEITHER/NOR: MULATTIC (PNEUMATIC) CHRISTIAN PERSONHOOD

In baptism the believer is immersed into an interstitial existence wherein their life is an in-between or spatial moment that is articulated between old (without God in the world) and new (you are Christs). Yet, this space is not a vacuous space that resists or erases identity but binds that which is to that which is not. The hybridity of the moment is a union with the Creator through an inhabiting or indwelling. This indwelling transforms the notions of the self so that the one who dwells is, in fact, closer than the one dwelled within. Nicholas Cabasilas suggests this union is one of profound mystery where "His union with those whom he loves surpasses every union of which one might conceive, and cannot be compared with any model."[19] Cabasilas goes on to name how various unions do not truly represent the union with Christ. The reason for this lack of proper analogy lies in the mystery that "it appears that the members of Christ are more closely joined to Him than to their own head, and that it is even more by Him that they live than by their concord with it."[20] This presence, or personhood is not the intellectual, reasoned apprehension of a distant truth which allows one true sight, but rather is a recognition of this reality as embodied and transforming one's very self. Christ is in you.

This presence or transgression of the person and Christ in the baptismal moment is not marked by the tragic entrapment or assertion of purity that cannot be attained. Rather the possibility of purity, of the indwelling of the Spirit, is the fullness of God that has entered that space or that person. Purity then is construed through a greater conformity to the transgression that made the indwelling a possibility. That is, the purity of obedience and desire is not the refusal of difference grounded in racial or ethnic differentiations that require a continual performance and refusal to make them intelligible. Instead, the purity wrought through the union with Christ is the conflation of impossibility and possibility within one's own body. The body becomes iconic of the possibility of transformation and the movement of being one to becoming another. This transformation becomes the mark of the baptized for the very name, which one then claims, *Christian*. This is the confession of a transformation and the transgression which Mary bore and Word incarnate brings to fruition.

Union with Christ in this moment therefore establishes or, what we might say, deepens the claim concerning the hybridity of the Christian body and the ecclesial community as both an ontological and a relational moment. Ontologically, baptism is the filling out of this union, animating body and soul with the Spirit of God which led the baptized into that moment and leads them from it. Baptism is the establishment or sealing of this moment where the creature is "more than," or neither/nor. The union of body and soul to the spirit of God in this moment cannot be named through a rationalistic or biological paradigm. These bodies now rendered christologically defy these very structures or typologies for they are wrought in the image of the Son, who as we examined in chapter 3 is the fullness of neither/nor—but where the interaction or the structure of the person is both neither/nor, with and without. Christ's structure refuses the duality of divinity and creation and thus expands the possibility of humanity. Or as we have noted in Nellas and Zizioulas, displays true and full humanity. This fullness of the baptismal moment is a participatory one wherein the body enters and is entered into. It is possessed.

In charismatic or pentecostal tradition such a moment is marked not by an intellectual assent concerning who one is or is not, but rather there is a baptism of the Spirit which is either present with baptism or subsequent to it. The power of this moment is the filling out of the baptismal moment in an encounter with the Holy One. It is a filling up where the external becomes constitutive of the internal. That is to say, the person upon whom the Spirit comes cannot know themselves apart from that moment or the one who filled or the one who dwells within.[21]

Through this filling the baptized enters into a personhood of communion grounded in the Trinitarian love and movement of the Father, Son, and Holy Spirit, the lover, the loved, and the love.[22] This characterization does not seek to summarize the complex disagreements among charismatic and pentecostal theologians regarding the necessity of such a moment, its content, or its timing. My point here is to indicate (a) the movement of external to internal is not external to Christian tradition, and (b) such a moment indicates not an exception of Christian spirituality or a faulty reading of Scripture, but points to a deep and significant display of the transformation God calls those to in the church. This transformation is not one of simply posture, political maneuvering, or intellectual imagination, but something that comes upon one and becomes a bodily reality within that moment. The notion of a moment following baptism wherein the person comes to share in or experience the indwelling of the Spirit is by no means a modern invention. The baptismal rites of the East in particular point to the progression or deepening of one's bodily entrance into the church and the life of Christ through the rites that preceded and followed baptism. In this case, the chrismation that followed the immersion into the water marked the "partaking or moment of deification."[23] This secondary moment marks the filling out of the baptismal moment. Here the impressing of the Spirit upon the person is the person being drawn into Christ. The imposition of the hands and the anointing with oil signifies a deeper coalescing of Spirit with the body as it absorbs the divine into the very pores.

Reception of the Spirit grounds identity now not within a statement one can offer about oneself, but with a statement regarding what has happened to them, what has come upon them. Identity and personhood must now be expressed not through relationship alone, but through a transformation of what constitutes one's person. It is not about a set of beliefs guiding one's actions or moral life, but rather the baptismal moment is the

initiation into God's own life and the impressing of God into the participant's life. The baptized is no longer their own.

I have previously noted how Teresa of Avila articulates such a transformation as not entirely external to us or internal to us. Rather the transformation is the recognition or apprehension of the external calling us
from within. The transformation is that God now abides with us and has
become the perfect end to that which calls and shapes us. The implication of this transformation now sees the political, familial, and, as we have
noted, the racial structures of one's life and community. The possibility of
lives lived together, of patterns of kinship now also bear the mark of one
grafted onto a foreign tree.

Jesus enjoined his disciples so that they must leave their brothers and
sisters, that they must be understood here not merely in terms of familial bonds but within the confines of deeper structures of relationship and
identity that serve to circumscribe self-understanding in one's society. The
establishment of one's personhood often requires a network of relationships—in the midst of these relationships are certain governing or mediating norms which establish the boundaries of participation. As we noted
in chapter 1 these boundaries and modes of participation were grounded
upon and within a deeply racialized consciousness wherein whiteness was
conceived as an indicator of a profound inner capacity and ultimately a
certain purity. Such a conception served as a religious performance that
worked to coalesce disparate peoples around a common self-estimation
while perpetuating the boundary of blackness, allowing the interior identity to remain intelligible. Through the life of the interracial or mulatto/a
body we saw how these performances became incoherent and ultimately
false, yet continued to perform upon peoples as they performed within
these claims.

In baptism the body becomes re-created in such a way as to confound
such assertions and bonds to kinship predicated upon race by transfig-
uring the complex particularities of personhood within Christ's performance of us. That is, baptism at once requires our renunciation of those
idolatrous modes of participation that are predicated upon external mediating realities that require radical difference to make them coherent. In
baptism the individual participates in the radical conflation of time and
eternity, divine and human, male and female, death and life by entering
into Christ's immersion into us. The baptismal moment is a moment of
transgression transforming the fragments of our tragic lives of denial and
resistance, possibility and promise. Through the water these pieces or

particularities become broken and reconfigured within Christ's own body. The difference inherent to one is not negated or erased as in the racial performance predicated upon an external purity or a mythic transcendental perfection encapsulated in a certain cultural mode or reality. But still these fragments are changed. Lives of disciples are vocations reoriented from the accumulation of wealth toward the eradication of poverty. They are songs of grandmothers and great-grandfathers sung with new rhythms and cadences once thought alien to them.

Baptism is the transgression of flesh and Spirit that requires assertions of cultural or racial purity to be resisted and renounced. But in this baptismal moment there also lies the profound transformation of the community, for with every new member comes the possibility of transformation, change, and adaptation in its inclusion not only for the one welcomed, but for those who welcome. The body of Christ shifts and moves and learns new languages as it adds new members. Its body becomes new as the person becomes new. This transformation is not without shape or purpose. It is a body that recognizes it exists within that in which all difference is found. The church is that transgression of God's mercy against humanity's refusal and disobedience. It is God's presence in the midst of humanity's unfaithfulness. The church thus witnesses to the possibility of creation's transformation in its own transformation and its own incorporation of difference within itself.

New People: Baptism and Mulattic Peoplehood

A consideration of the baptized's personhood as being hybrid or mulatto/a—as one who cannot be known apart from God, who is flesh and Spirit, who has Christ as their head despite their own fallibility and limitation—is grafted into a communal witness of this transformed possibility. These newborn Christians seek to live into Christ's performance of humanity in their present. The paradox or wonder of this moment again is grounded in the miracle of Christ's personhood who is at once an individual and "all in all." He is the one who establishes the community, yet also constitutes the community through his personhood. To enter into this ecclesial moment is to enter Christ's both being a person and upholding all persons. It is in this difficulty of identity, in which all personhood conceived within the life of the church becomes configured around this person yet does not become atomized into individual moments or professions of faith. Christ's entrance into the world transforms the communal witness of Israel, expanding its gaze and its possibilities, sometimes despite itself. The incorporation into this ecclesial life is the incorporation into Jesus' response to Israel, to the promise of God given to Israel. Yet this response required Israel's transformation. The incorporation of Israel by the Word required them to become something they thought not possible. As we explored in chapter 4 this transformation was articulated through the understanding of whom God could and could not be, the expectations of participation with God via the law, and the understanding of who is incorporated and transformed with us.

The body of Christ as the church becomes the expression of this possibility. It is the display of Christ's incorporation of us and our subsequent incorporation of those who will come to believe and follow. This incorporation has a deeply christological structure where the standard of faithfulness does not lie in the propriety of the confession, but rather requires a twofold movement of the people toward the person and the person toward the people. That is, Christ's movement toward us was not one of unilateral movement, but one where the movement was twofold from without and from within. We *had* to respond, transform, and conform. This process was not initiated by a decree that remained distant and apart but was engendered through the conformation of the Word to *us*. This is not to say that Christ is radically other from us, for our personhood is contained *within* God's own life and not apart from it. But the point should be clear here. The movement toward us was a transgression of what seemed possible and appropriate to God and to humanity. The incorporation of the newly baptized into the community of faith likewise is contained within this moment. It is a moment of conformation requiring both the loved and the lover to enter into one another so as to produce something new. The identity of the church and the identity of the person become enraptured within one another so that the child conceived through the water is utterly bound to the body (the church) and the body is bound to the child.

In this regard, to examine baptism within a mulattic structure is to not only examine the transformation of the body and the life that participates in baptism, but it is to examine the effect of this incorporation upon the body itself. Here we must draw again upon the image of performance and discipleship. The baptismal moment is the performance into Christ's performance of humanity and of the individual. It is an assent to the life made possible through his incarnation and the desire to open oneself to a transformation of life and desire. As the formation of mulattic personhood, flesh and Spirit, baptism is the entrance into Christ's performance of us. It is a sign and a declaration of discipleship, but in its most profound sense wherein the participant begins to perform into the utter truthfulness of human yearning and striving, that of the humanity of its archetype.

This transformation, this incorporation, however, is not an individual moment that can be expressed through the description of what happens in the formation of an individual. The performance of baptism in Christ by the participant is a performance that must be received, heard, and lived into by the congregation. The possibility of the baptismal moment is one in which incorporation into Christ is incorporation into a community of persons who have similarly been transformed and are seeking to perform into the perfection of Christ's life. This communal performance, this harmonic of Christian discipleship, is integral to the baptismal moment as the baptized *becomes* a song added to the hymn of faith. In the congregation the song is heard and received and echoed back to the participant as they are welcomed into the tree of life, as they are initiated into a people who are neither/nor—but.

However, the nature, the timbre of the song carries with it a particularity that is not incorporated into the harmony without necessitating an improvisation in the communal song. The reception of the individual is the reception of their particularity and requires the reimagining of communal identity. It is here that the christological claims regarding Christ's mulattic character and the necessity of transformation become exhibited through the baptismal moment. For the body of Christ is not a static moment that is lived into through erasure of the self, but is rather a moment wherein personhood is transformed through a transfiguration. That is, the particularity of the individual is made to radiate God's glory and presence in the world so as to point to the possibilities of creation in relationship to and inhabited by God's Spirit. The incorporation of the new does not necessitate utter erasure. Instead, the communal aspects of this transformation and incorporation also demonstrate a transfigurative moment. The reception of the individual into the communal body of Christ is a transformation of both the participant and the community. The community itself must adapt its timbre, its instrumentation, and its arrangement in its incorporation of the newly born.

This transformation is not to suggest that the communities must continually adapt themselves to the whims and fancies of the newly born. But here I am trying to highlight the way in which the mulattic character and spirituality of being incorporated into Christ's person is mediated not through an incorporation into similitude—but rather it is the reception of difference that produces something new. The possibility of transformation

engendered through the incarnation was the overcoming of the concretization of human forms as idols. The transgression of this moment is a
transformative one where to be made into the image of Christ is to be
opened up to the possibility of the Spirit where one might speak "in new
tongues." The language of tongues is certainly controversial and not universally accepted in the Christian tradition. But the power of tongues
speaking in this context is its conveyance of the possibility of one possessing languages and insights that are alien to them. The possibility of being
"born of Spirit" is to enter into a life where those things that were once
foreign are now native, and things that were once native are now foreign.
This possibility is not an isolated moment that occurs within the baptismal
font for the individual participant.

The creation of an embodied tongue, a living language in the world
through the baptismal font, displays the confounding of language and
knowledge that would, in the early church and in some contemporary
communities, be instantiated as glossolalia, or speaking in tongues. To
pray in tongues expresses the hybridity of our nature as flesh and Spirit.
It displays baptism's transformative work, this rebirth where one inhabits,
or *becomes* a language that confounds the very structure of language and
life. The one who utters the words does not know of what they speak and
they are left to press into them, yearning and searching for the meaning
that their bodies seem to be producing. These utterances must be interpreted by another. They must rely on another to discern the meaning of
the words they speak. Here the structures of certainty and the meaning
of words is not a market of exchange or a discourse of power, but an economy of listening, of hearing, of softening oneself to the Word which comes
upon us.

Yet it should be said that this exchange of utterance and interpretation is not merely a moment of translation for two individuals, but rather
the entire conversation is for the sake of the community. These lives, their
speaking and interpretation is for the sake of all. It is God's word to them,
through their bodies, their speaking and hearing.[24]

We are a people who receive words of which we do not know the
meaning. And yet we are a people whose language, whose utterances,
whose bodies are for the sake of the world. There are those of us who
do not yet live into the possibility of this pneumatic existence. Baptism
is entrance into life as mulattic speech, prayer in tongues, to *be* a strange
tongue in the world where our presence disrupts the very structures that
seem to make the world coherent.[25] Yet it is not only our language, but

the grammars that shape and mark our lives. Race, gender, nation, class, ethnicity— these are the languages we speak and these are what could become confounded by Christian lives, burning bushes and tongues of fire, bodies set ablaze with the Spirit.

Baptism is the entrance into a life of transformation. It is entrance into a life pregnant with the possibility of speaking in new tongues and receiving those people and those practices that once seemed alien. It is the possibility of receiving a new people and in that reception becoming a new people in Christ. This life of conformation as the possibility of the new is the baptismal moment as a communal reality. The reception of a person requires the possibility of a reception of their particularity and their hopes, the fullness of their despair and their triumphs. It is these that are added to the people of God and in the midst of these additions the entirety of a people become something new as they receive and incorporate new people into their midst. The performativity of the baptismal moment is mediated through the instantiation of the practice through Christ or Christ's call to us in his incarnation, baptism, death, and resurrection, and then through the communal response or reception of the participant's performance. The participant's reception is the community's response to the call of Christ. The newly baptized is received into the community. But this reception is again not only marked by a moment of gathering around the table of the Lord, but by the persistent practices of the Lord's Supper, of prayer, confession, and forgiveness. The reception of the initiate is the slow grafting of their lives into the life of the community, including the slow transformation of the community itself as the difficulties, challenges, and hopes of that person or those people received by the community.

This process of conjugation is the performance of Christ's work on us as the community lives into Christ's absorption of our pain and grief, our disobedience, and our resistance. The ecclesial community similarly takes on the life of its newly born and turns itself to them as itself becomes something new in the process. We cannot enter into this body and deny the difference among us. To be in Christ is to enter those strange bodies in our midst, we must be baptized into Christ and bound to one another. To do this is not to move beyond the slave ship or the encyclopedia. Rather, to enter into Christ is to recognize ourselves as bound to both, as children of enslavement and conquerors of knowledge. To enter into Christ is to enter into waters of profound confusion, becoming grafted into realities that once seemed foreign. In baptism something must truly die.

But what is this church of change and transformation? Surely there is something that stays the same, something that grounds the identities of the participants? The character of this ecclesial community, this body of mulatto/as and half-breeds is no longer the assertion of identity upon similitude or proper articulation of practices that can be traced throughout time. Rather, the identity of the mulatto/a is seen as the living into the neither/nor that is grounded upon the reality of the transgression that gave birth to it. It is an identity bound by the in-between, yet grounded in the reality of those people and the practices that constituted their lives. For the ecclesial community a mulattic identity is grounded upon the claim of one's body as bearing the image of the incarnate Word, as being people of flesh and Spirit whose very lives are the fruits of an unnatural union. This unnatural union can find no grounding in a history of ideas or a history of a people except for their constant inter-mixture and perpetual reconstitution over time. The practices that bind these people together are those that brought them into being. In baptism a child is born, but with baptism the community is reborn and the ecclesia must bend itself again toward another. It must look to God's work in the newly born and God's work in the community through the newly added. The estimation of gifts and talents, challenges and pains becomes added to a people producing new possibilities and new marks of unfaithfulness. The baptismal moment is a reminder regarding each member of the community's birth as a new creature.

The community is bound together by the Lord's Supper as they are joined in the memory of the one who became us so that we might exceed our nature and our failures. The eucharistic moment is the moment of feeding upon the one who is different from us, but who *is* us. It is the nourishment of our lives as more than flesh and desires, but it is the nourishment of a body animated and enlivened by the Spirit. The eucharistic moment thus becomes a marker of what we are and what we are to become, what Christ became and what he makes us into. The community is upheld by prayer, which will be explored in the next chapter, but here it should be said that prayer is how the community seeks to conform itself into the will of God and into the lives of one another. These practices mark what it means to be a child of God. They constitute personhood not through the assertion of their own purity or the maintenance of their modes, but they maintain the identity of the person and the community through their conformation into Christ and their transfiguration into the people of Christ. They become a burning bush whose presence, whose

fearsome aberrant beauty declares the glory of God and disrupts all assertions of identity and purity in its midst.

Being reborn in baptismal waters, entering the world out of Christ's
womb is being present in the world in a new way. Being people of flesh
and Spirit, mulattic Christian existence disrupts through its presence and
its demands. These bodies of flesh and Spirit do not exhibit the physical demarcations of racial logic, but defy them through their union with
bodies of difference among them. Abiding within the body of Christ and
the bodies of their mutual foreigners, mulatto/a Christians resonate a
new song punctuated by the questioning of exclusion, by resisting oppression and abiding with one another in ways that confound the rhythms of
modern racial logic and its contemporary permutations. Enspirited bodies transgress tribal fidelity, endure cultural abandonment, and coexist
with the sufferings of their adoptive kin. In this way modernity's power
of enslavement and classification disintegrates in the midst of holy fissures,
blessed gaps that allow something new to enter into a promised land.

Chapter 6

THE POLITICS OF PRESENCE
Prayer and Discipleship

"[I]t has to do with one who is simply and solely nothing else but a groaner."

—Karl Barth[1]

INTRODUCTION

Out of the womb of Christ, the Christian is reborn of flesh and Spirit. After emerging from these holy waters, these enspirited children are confronted not with the world of their blessed birth, but with the world of their death. Infants in Christ, we must begin the life of discipleship, the life of discerning what constitutes faithfulness and what is infidelity. In the modern world this discernment is not only a question of what to eat and drink, or what words to say or not to say. This discernment is more than political ideology or ideals of social justice. The life of discipleship is the life of marriage, sex, and children, of work for and work with, of hopes that transgress boundaries of race and ethnicity and hopes that become present among new communities. The life of discipleship welcomes surprising looking children and is surprised by the questions that simply do not let go of us. It is a life that confounds the logic of master and slave, by worshiping the king who was a slave. Discipleship confounds knowledge as a possession, as an ideal, by conforming to the eternal Word who entered the world as a wordless infant.

But the life of discipleship also confesses the temptation of certainty, of loving similitude and seeking to maintain the boundaries of life together. Confessing dependence upon Christ, the disciple becomes present among strange people and becomes a stranger among his own people. The life of the disciple is one who prays and bends her life into her prayers and into the prayers of the Spirit within. Disciples are those who, like Martin Luther King Jr. who after answering a bomb threat in his home at three o'clock in the morning prayed, "Lord, . . . and felt a presence of God's peace." King's presence, his disruptive call to peace, his nonsensical nonviolent presence disrupted the patterns of racial logic and structural violence. But in many ways these disruptions were bound to that prayer, to King's act of conforming to the call of his birth in Christ. The life of discipleship is the *life* of prayer.

In this way prayer is a politic, a political mode of existence that marks the believer's life as continually open to transformation as they seek to conform themselves. That is, they conform their bodies to Christ's prayer for them in the groans of the Spirit, within, and to the lives of those they pray for, without. In this way true prayer displays the radicality of hybrid existence where the claim to oneself is always bound to the particular life of Christ and to the lives of those who have been created and re-created in him. Through the life of prayer the believer becomes conformed into the life of the one who prays for them. In this way the christological claim that Christ's performance of our lives is mulattic and transformative becomes a mode of discipleship, wherein our prayers for one another are always signs of the ways in which the Christian life is being performed into the lives of one's brothers and sisters. Such prayers are both private and public and thus reveal true Christian discipleship as a public interruption of modern racial-political lives.

This chapter will develop this claim through an examination of Christ's own prayer life, highlighting the way Christ's prayers and his life *as* prayer both establish the act of prayer and the presence of prayer in the life of the believer. I will examine Christ's prayer life as a witness of identity, a performance of humanity, and an opening up of the life of discipleship as one of receptivity and transformation. Through the prayer life of Jesus we see the person and work of Christ to be the basis of our own prayers and our own lives. Lives as prayer thus witness to one's identity in another and seek to perform their own lives into the life of the one who prayed for them—whose lives become marked by the reception of others into their lives as they are transformed in their mutual encounter with the

Son of God. This life of discipleship can be rendered only through the mulattic shape of its birth and life. It is a life of interruption confessing its participation within the claims of racial and cultural particularity and subjects those particularities to the fire of the Spirit. Christian bodies are thus lives of prayer, lives transfigured through the Spirit, lives that cannot be known apart from the one who abides in them, who groans within them. Into God they seek to live and move and have their being.

Upon emerging from the baptismal waters the believer is reborn and remade. They are ushered into a life where their bodies are bound to one within them and outside of them. They are inextricably bound to a people who are likewise bound to them. They exist in the world in ways that disrupt the patterns of racial discipleship, cultural maintenance, or national loyalty. As the "Letter to Diognetus" suggests, they become a strange people who "live in their own countries, but only as aliens. Every foreign land is their fatherland, and yet for them every fatherland is a foreign land."[2] Baptism gives rise to a personhood marked by a peculiar peoplehood imbued with a miraculous and extraordinary presence in and among them. Their lives are now bound together and into the one from whom they were born and into whom they live. This departure and return is the life of discipleship.

This life of discipleship birthed in the baptismal moment bound us to the very bread of life, the Lord's Supper or Eucharist. Discipleship is the daily existence arising out of and stretching toward. This yearning, this conforming between these moments is filled out and marked by the life of prayer, of Christian lives *as* prayer that daily, constantly displays a mulattic re-creation and disruption conceived in the desire of the Father for us. It is birthed through the womb of Christ and enfolded within the enduring presence of the Spirit in our very bodies. This daily display of mulattic creation and disruption is bound to the life of prayer.

The life of discipleship is bound to the life of Christ through the Spirit, given birth through the waters of baptism and given definition through the community of believers who have understood themselves as bound to Christ and to one another. Such a life of discipleship is given definition through the continual confession of their unfaithfulness and their continual praise of God's faithfulness despite their own lives. In these moments of confession and praise they become bound to one another. Such a life of binding and opening is marked by a perpetual interpenetration that welcomes and transfigures the lives of its inhabitants into people who display the calling of God in the wilderness of contemporary society.

In the midst of such an ecclesial life that prayer should be understood as one of the constitutive practices of Christian discipleship. Prayer is an act that is individual and communal, divine and temporal. In moments of prayer we see both the dogmatic and the ethical bound up together in the life of discipleship in a way that is not only located within the life of the church, but explicitly locates the life of the church within the life of the individual, the family, the communal house, the hospital, and so on.[3] This claim is most perceptible through an examination of Jesus' own prayer life. In his prayers and his desire to pray we begin to see both a dogmatic claim concerning Christ's person and work, as well as the implications of prayer in the life of the disciple.

To be a follower of Christ is to pray. Prayer is an aspect of discipleship wherein the believer's life is pointed beyond itself yet through itself. It is through the cares, the joys, the yearnings of one's prayer life that we begin to see the kingdom breaking into the world through those who follow Jesus. It could be said that prayer is one of the most fundamental acts of Christian discipleship, for it is in the prayer of the believer and the believer's struggle to conform and apprehend the Spirit's groans within them that their lives become shaped within the life of the ecclesial community. The life of prayer is a life of conformation into Christ's image and bound to the lives of those who love him and whom he loves.

But what does it mean that Jesus prayed? The brief glimpses of Jesus' prayer life indicate to us three important moments. They offer a glimpse into Jesus' nature, the nature of prayer, and prayer's transformative possibilities in and through the life of the disciples. The christological nature of Jesus' prayer life exhibits not only important aspects of who Jesus was, but also displays the pattern of his work upon humanity and the ways in which humanity participates or enters into this work through their own lives, baptized into the immersion of Christ into us. Prayer is a constitutive mark of participation, but more profoundly, it is the display of a hybrid life, a mulatto/a discipleship wherein the one who prays seeks to conform to the Spirit of God who constitutes their life and person. This process of transformation not only draws one into the life of God, itself a display of mulatto/a life, but also prayer bleeds the boundaries of one into the life of another.

In particular, we see in Jesus' most explicit prayers in Gethsemane profound revelations of Jesus' sonship, and this sonship grounds the lives of those who are created in him through the waters of baptism. Here the prayer life of Jesus indicates (a) the fundamental relationship of the Word to the Father, (b) the performance of human loving which is both uttered toward us and for us, and (c) the ground of desire and reception which marks the Triune God and human participation within the life of God. Each of these marks of Jesus' prayer life also mark the lives of those who would follow him and become his disciples.

THE PRAYER LIFE AS A WITNESS OF SONSHIP

In the prayer life of Jesus we begin to see a witness to the sonship of the Word to the Father. Through the submission of will of one to the other and the return throughout Jesus' ministry to solitary moments of prayer we begin to see that the Son is the one who desires to do the will of the Father. He is the one who knows the will, but even more profoundly he is the fulfillment of the Father's will. To be the Son is not only to be in relation to God—for even creation is in relation—but more profoundly to be the Son is to be bound to the will of God in such a way as to continually bend oneself to it. To be the will of God or to follow the will of God is a claim that constitutes the entirety of one's personhood. The possibility of an identity fixed upon a reality external to this singular claim begins a process of deformation. The shape of Christ's life is constituted by the will of the Father toward those who are loved. Jesus' very birth is the fulfillment of a promise to and in Israel regarding the possibility of a people made from nothing. The will of God was for their restoration filled and given in that child in the manger.

Jesus' life is bound to the will of the Father. The perfection of this obedience and the perfection of his living are undoubtedly tied to the consubstantiality of the Father and the Son. The Son is God. It is not his coherence with the will that marks his divinity as though it were apart from him. Rather, at the same time the will of the Father is understood by Jesus to be that which he must obey, he must live into it. He must follow it. His plea in the garden, "My Father, if it be possible, let this cup pass from me; yet, not what I want, but what you want," (Matt 26:39) demonstrates both the centrality of the Father's will to who he is, as well as the way in which his desire, his love is oriented toward the Father. The will is central to Jesus' personhood. The display of his sonship is given in his obedience. His obedience is offered to us through his prayers as he asks the Father to forgive them, to let this cup pass, as he prays for those who follow him and who will follow him.

Jesus' prayer life indicates what it means to be the only begotten Son, to be a child of God. He is the one who knows the will of the Father. His knowledge and desire to conform is not only witnessed to in his prayer life, but in fact *is* the nature of Jesus' prayer life. In his prayers Jesus confesses himself, makes himself known. His life is prayer.

For those who would follow him, for those who begin to apprehend the world around them as God's creation and their lives as upheld and bound to the Father, Son, and Holy Spirit is to enter into the identity or personhood wrought through the baptismal waters. To be a child of God is to pray. It is to enter into a life of yearning and conforming. Yet the act of prayer is the confession of what is and what will be. The mark of discipleship as prayer thus begins to indicate a crucial aspect of mulattic existence. The hybridity of flesh and Spirit formed through the baptismal waters and fed through the sharing of the Lord's Supper becomes displayed through the life of prayer. Here prayer becomes a mark of this new personhood. It is a sign or indication of one's new kinship.

Prayer as a sign of personhood begins with the following suggestion the fact *that* we pray signifies who we are, *that* we pray confesses something, that we understand who we ought to be. Here the very act of praying begins to demonstrate the inherent claim regarding the birth of an inter-people. Prayer is the assertion of an identity that must be received. This reception is not of a reality external to one, but is an identity bound to and inherent to the fact of one's baptism. It is the confession of who we are. Our prayers seek to utter and conform to the groans of the Spirit within us. We must receive ourselves, our hopes, our ends, from one who is not external to us, but is us. The act is both individual and communal. They are words uttered or reflected individually, but always have an origin and an end both within and without us. Prayer is communion with those who utter words with us and those who utter words for us. It is communion with Christ, who is our prayer, who is the one who hears us and lifts us up and utters his own life for us. Our prayer is the assent to that reality and the attempt to live into that prayer that has already been uttered, lived, and received in Christ's life.

That we pray indicates the possibility of being bound to something beyond us, confesses our own limitations and creatureliness, but more profoundly begins to articulate the mystery that *is* us. That is, prayer is grounded not in the certainty of the world or who we are in the world in relation to one another, but it is a moment of vulnerability requiring us to ask God who we are, to confess the marks of infidelity that riddle our lives and begin to live into those realizations. Prayer is the constellation of moments that mark our utter dependence upon God, but also begins to reckon with the reality that God, who is so distant and so other, in fact constitutes who I am and who I am not. But even more radically, this God of perfection does not see my body as that which is apart from God's own life. But through the baptismal waters, in the life of the ecclesial body, through the indwelling of God's very Spirit, my body is now a temple, a living sacrifice. Prayer is the display of this wonder which confounds notions of personhood constituted either through the articulation of relations or claims of nature. In prayer we see the relation *to be* the natural. The relation *is* the essential.

It is here that theology must be wary of where it enters the discourse concerning essential identities and identities as social constructions. The confession, "Christ is Lord" is to claim something essential about God and thereby to live into an essential claim concerning who we are—we belong to Christ. It is essential, because it is now constitutive of whom we understand ourselves to be. This presence, this relationship constitutes who we are in such a way that to be without would be to render us without an identity, personless. Yet, this essentialism is not something inherent to us, something "natural" that we can point to but is rather made possible by Christ's performance of us through his identification with us. Thus this essential claim is enacted through a dynamic performance of humanity that we must struggle to correspond to. The resulting identity is thus both essential and "made," neither/nor and "more than."

To be a disciple, to be one who dwells in and with God, one who desires to be in his will and to confess those moments when we are out of this will is to pray. Prayer is the mark of this fellowship that constitutes who we are as followers. These are not acts that are done in order to slowly discipline our habits (although this is certainly an aspect of the process), but rather prayer is the display of what is natural and essential to us. *That* we pray becomes a mark of the Spirit that constitutes our lives. The act of prayer is indicative of who we are. The content and forms of these prayers, their ends and our formation is a complicated and difficult process, but *that* we pray indicates something inherent about who we are. It is not the totality, is not representative of a kind of perfection, but nonetheless marks an aspect of our personhood that is essential and tied to the nature of the Christian body as a mulatto/a body, as a neither/nor body, as a conflation of flesh and Spirit established and fulfilled in the incarnation of the Word, Jesus.

Such a claim concerning prayer as an act constitutive of who we are serves to display the shift or transformation that has occurred through the baptismal waters. For to pray is to acknowledge that we are children of

God and that we might call out to God and that God hears us.[4] A mark of personhood, prayer describes us not only in terms of who we were as a historical people, or who we are as a people wrought through the waters of baptism and now an admixture of flesh and Spirit. Prayer is a confession, a display of who we will be. Prayer expresses personhood as not only biologically different, culturally different, but temporally different. We are a people who are bound to time and eternity. We are a people who are stretching into the fullness of God's own eternity yet still moving through a temporal existence. Prayer is the confession of lives constituted and marked by hope, and "therefore in their present life they live as those who belong to the future. That which is promised and He who is promised are seen and heard by them in all their futurity."[5] The neither/nor that marks Christian existence now begins to take shape not only through the body formed through the Holy Spirit, or the community into which the baptized is initiated. Now, in the life of prayer the internal reality of the Holy Spirit and the conformation of the one who prays to the groans of the Spirit within are marked by the confusion of time. Mulatto/a bodies are marked by hope.

The tragedy of interracial existence is that which saw Rena and Clare die at the impossibility of their lives becoming overturned, for the possibility of one's life is no longer bound to the illusion of purity or the negotiation of polarities which require opposition to remain intelligible, rendering the middle a vacuous space of nonbeing. The internal, the space, the transgression is life, it is possibility, it is the promise. Prayer is the confession that the one who is other has heard us. It is the confession that the one who is other is present with us. It is the possibility that the otherness of God is not to be uttered against me, but it has been offered to me. Prayer is the reversal of that tragic refusal, "You are my son, like hell" into "you are my son, my daughter."

Prayer is the daily marking of this life where one begins to enter into the possibility of a hybrid existence that resists the claims of purity requiring the sacrifice of transgressors and transforms the obedient ones into blessed transgressions. The transgression that makes prayer possible is thus rendered upon the life of the one who prays, thus turning their life into one of conformation. This conformation to the will becomes the identity grounded in obedience to the will of the Father. It is an obedience grounded in the conformation of one's will, desires, and hopes to the will, hopes, and desires of the Father. It is an apprehension of one's creatureliness and possibilities. It is an opening up wherein a reconfiguring becomes evident. The Gospels speak of this reordering in Jesus' questioning, "Who are my mother, and who are my brothers?" . . . "Here are my mother and my brothers! For whoever does the will of my Father is heaven is my brother and sister and mother" (Matt 12:48-50). As we see, the will of the Father is the life of hope, the life of prayer; it lives as prayer. This life of prayer is a pneumatological yearning and a bodily witness. Here prayer as the conformation to the *will of God* is a pneumatological claim concerning participation. It is performing into Christ's performance of us through a life being impressed into the Spirit's groans within us. It is the extension of the baptismal moment in its immersion into the will of God.

In the act of prayer as confession and hope it is a profession of identity, an articulation of one's relationship to and in Christ made possible through Christ's calling to them, through the indwelling of the Spirit which stirs them to recall the promises of God and the promise of God which they are. The act of prayer is itself a display of the fact of Christ and the possibility of who one is and will be in him. This preliminary reflection is to suggest the act of prayer itself is an act displaying the hybridity of discipleship, the mixture inherent to the claim that one is called after the name of Christ. This articulation of identity through the groaning of prayer and the conformation to the Spirit is to perform into Christ's performance of us. This performance of prayer is the reception of the name and the articulation that one is called, is heard, and is seen. It is in this being heard which marks one's being in the world. The performance of prayer is the process of conformation into Christ's life, into his prayer for us and in us. Thus discipleship is the life of prayer seeking to press into him who has pressed himself into us. The act of prayer is the intermixture of our hopes, the subjection of ourselves (our lives, our bodies) to his will so that we are not only moving after, but that our very bodies become the prayerful groaning of his coming kingdom both present and possible, already, but not yet. The prayer life of Jesus at once declares his identity, his sonship, and establishes our identities, our adoptions. Our prayers declare our identity *in* Christ and God *in* us. It is the confession and display of our new bodies, our mulattic birth.

THE PRAYER LIFE AS A PERFORMANCE

The prayer life of Jesus indicates not only the dogmatic claim that Jesus is God, but also inhabits the accompanying claim that Jesus is fully man. In this moment we see the two claims bound together, whereas Barth reminds us that Jesus' prayers are not only God's desires for us, but also humanity's confession and reception of God's own life in such a way as humanity could not utter itself. As we examined in chapter 4, the work of Christ was located in his personhood wherein his work was the performance of all personhood, all humanity. The performativity of Jesus' prayer life presses his personhood, his work into the lives of those who believed and would believe. It is through prayer that Christians attune themselves to this work and listen for the false notes that their lives declare. Lastly, through prayer they bind themselves to the lives of those whom Christ loves.

As Jesus prays in the Garden of Gethsemane for those who have followed him and those who would come to follow him, his prayer that they be in him as he is in the Father is visible only within the dogmatic claim concerning the incarnation. "Righteous Father, the world does not know you, but I know you; and these know that you have sent me. I made your name known to them, and I will make it known, so that the love with which you have loved me may be in them, and I in them" (John 17:25-26). The prayer concerning the disciples being in him is the hope for their incorporation into his presence in the world at that very moment. That his disciples might be "in Him" suggests not only the desire to obey and follow, but also such a living into him that their lives become subsumed into his very person. Their very identities are bound to this coming out of and going in. Their lives become bound to the person of Christ such that they come to see their identities grounded in mission and calling. Disciples are people who are called, who call upon the Lord.

The transformation of these lives from autonomous individuals into the very prayers of Jesus, into those who are the mission of God in the world requires more than an intellectual assent, or prayers habitually spoken even with the earnest belief that God hears us. The possibility of prayer is the possibility of the very life of the one who utters and groans becoming like a burning bush. The possibility of prayer is the possibility of transformation found throughout Scripture. In particular it is seen in the life of Moses, whose life, spared from the massacre of children to be adopted by the cradle of power, was marked by the familiar tongue of his mother's people and the privilege of Egyptian power. His presence among the enslaved was a testament to the possibility of redemption, to the possibility of God hearing his people's cry; it is a sign of God's presence among them. Yet in Moses' life we see an intensification of this presence when he happens upon that tree so many years later.

Giving up the privilege of his position, betraying his adopted people, yet remaining a stranger to his mother's people Moses happens upon a miraculous sight. The bush was burning but was not consumed. Even before a word is uttered Moses is given an image of what would become of him. He, a bush of a man who does not know nor understand the power that would inhabit him would come to declare God's redemption to the nations. Moses' life would become transfigured in that moment as his life displayed no longer the language of his people or the food of his youth, but rather the entirety of his person became bound to his mission, this trans- figuration. His life would become one devoted to listening and speaking, to hearing and following, to failing to understand, yet following. His life would become one whose coming and going was predicated upon listen- ing and uttering strange and difficult truths to a resistant world. Moses' very presence before Pharaoh thus indicated the transformation that had been wrought in that miraculous moment in the wilderness.

In Jesus' prayer in Gethsemane, his prayer for those who follow him, we see the utterance of a possibility for following that is grounded in the transfiguration of their very lives. In his prayer any possibility that we have for life, for following him lies in the living into a simple but profound real- ity, the Son is in us. God is in us. We are simple creatures whom God has seen fit to set on fire. The life of discipleship is the life of prayer that seeks to live into this profound possibility. This possibility does not rest in the fact of our doing, but in the performance of Christ's performance of us. It is his life that has transfigured all lives. It is his birth that has rendered all lives possible, all lives truthful. The life of the prayer is the living into his response on our behalf. It is a life where

> Christians do not merely see things differently from other. From God's point of view they are different from others, just as they are different from others in relation to the divine verdict and direction when the Holy Spirit awakens them to faith and love. They do not merely live under the promise, which could be said of all men. They live in and with and by the promise. They seize it. They apprehend it, they con- form themselves to it. And therefore they live as those who belong to the future.[6]

The life of being different is marked by a reality which prayer attests to and seeks to live into. Christ's being for us and as us is the performance of our lives and hopes.[7] Present on both sides of the redemptive puzzle, the prayers of Jesus perform upon humanity and within humanity.[8] Christ's prayer in Gethsemane demonstrates at once the act of this reality and its content. It is the formation of our lives and it is the end of our hope. His prayer in Gethsemane forms the outlines of our transfiguration. It is the establishment of that baptismal moment which our subsequent prayers seek to articulate and repeat and utter through our lives.

Here humanity cannot utter anything beyond what Jesus has uttered in his own prayers. Humanity is left only to conform itself into the perfection that was Jesus' prayer for us and within us, which abides in us through the groaning of his Spirit within us. Human prayers can only ask that God's will be done in us, that we abide in Christ as Christ abides in the Father, that we not be a cause for God's work to be obstructed in the world, that his kingdom come in us and through us.[9] It is the act of confession that seeks to know those aspects that do not conform. It is the "forgive me and deliver me from evil." Prayer is discipleship/performance.

In the process of conformation the politics of presence becomes inherent in the life of prayer. Conformation into Christ necessitates a deformation, a confession, a resistance to the structures of racial formation that inhabit our descriptions of one another but, more importantly, mark the daily rhythms of our lives together. Part 1 described the way racial life in the West has been enacted not only through the major structures of the world, but perhaps more pervasively in the daily realities and desires of our lives with one another. The process of conformation ushers the child of God into a reformation of these desires that binds them to those who were not them. As these mulatto/a children are knit into one another, the structures of separation, the logic of race and its implicit inequalities become challenges to all who claim the name of Christ. To conform into the image of Christ, to pray in Jesus' name is to perform into his creation and into his people. It is to resist the processes of formation, the habitations of desire that are slowly built upon logics of race and power. This resistance (and this conformation) requires more than distant recollecting. Rather, it is a presence that risks transformation, encounters that can bear new children, a presence that disrupts the systems of placedness and homogeneity.

The formation of desire becomes reoriented within the life of prayer in such a way as to resist the formation of racial desire within contemporary society. The performance of prayer is entrance into Christ's life, not as a pious example of a life devoted to God. Rather, it is to enter into a world that is God's. Prayer ushers the one who utters these prayers into the world, disrupting the desires of the one who prays and the conventions of beauty and belonging so long predicated by a logic of racial fidelity. The enfleshment of dispositions within modernity is born in the cultivation of white beauty and Western competence. The groundbreaking study by Kenneth Clark used white and black dolls to demonstrate how negative images of African American children had come to inhabit their psyches. In 2008 the study was repeated in the independent film "A Girl Like Me" with shockingly similar results. African American children had come to inhabit the racialization of desire and beauty at a remarkably young age. The patterns of sexual desire even in interracial marriages exhibits a movement away from dark bodies, with the least common interracial marriages being African American women and white men, while the most prominent number of interracial marriages is Asian American women and white men. The patterns away from desire for dark women are not merely patterns of choice, but are the result of subtle processes of formation that do not result in the violent segregation of white and dark bodies, but more subtly, the pattern is a desire away from dark bodies and toward lighter bodies.[10] The life of prayer as discipleship displays patterns of life that are both repented and hoped for. In this way prayer is not an act of spiritual piety, but the cultivation of practices and possibilities that disrupt the racial fidelity of the modern world and gives birth to new desires and thus new forms of life.

Prayer as performance is the centering of one's life upon the will of God in such a way as to render one's hopes and possibilities to another. Prayer is the performance of Christ's life in that prayer draws the believer into the loss of assertion. Prayer is a perpetual confession of one's necessary obedience. Here the prayers of the two in the temple indicate how prayer is not merely speech directed toward God, but rather it is a bending of oneself toward God. In this bending one is approached by their own incapacities, and their lives are laid down before the one who has prayed for them, who has made this knowledge of them possible. The Pharisee prayed, "Thank you Lord that I am not like that man over there . . ." (Luke 18:9-14). The Pharisee's life of prayer was not confession but an assertion. It was an attempt to delineate his selfhood upon the denial of another. His prayer was the prayer of assertion that sought not to love into the performance of another, but sought to perform himself into God's presence. It was a prayer to idols imaged and molded in his image of righteousness, precipitated upon a self-knowledge and a presumption of his own possibilities.

Prayer as a performance begins with the sinner. It begins with the confession that God has in fact seen us as we are. The prayer, "Forgive me,

a sinner," begins with the confession of one's incapacity to assert themselves as anything other than one who is in need of God, as one who is in
need of another. Not as the negative boundary which makes possible an
illusory center or purity, but rather this prayer recognizes its acting in the
world as that boundary, as that which has sought to resist God's calling
and purpose. The prayer of the sinner here is more than his words and his
utterances, but his groaning, his desperation, his confession of the need to
be something new.

In this way we see prayer as the moment in which mulattic existence
exhibits an identity bound to others, as a personhood grounded in a relationality that is not predicated upon a purity of will or obedience, but
rather is predicated upon the transgression of God that makes that prayer
possible. It is the prayer of Jesus, Jesus' life that makes our confession possible, that makes our apprehension possible. His life instantiates and renews
the infusion of flesh and Spirit that makes true personhood more than
flesh and mind. Prayer is the confession that God is not only calling us to
God's self, but rather it is the recognition that this calling is bound to the
body. Bending oneself to the will of God is a moment of straining to hear
the words rightly, to attune oneself to that which calls from within. It is
the tuning of one's life and the melodic ringing of the Spirit which groans
within to the revelation of Scripture, the word preached and the prayers
of our neighbors.

Augustine writes of this bending, this listening as a process of hearing
a song which God sings with perfection, but we must strain within the
confines of time to hear and utter.[11] Prayer as performance is the struggling to grasp the eternal in the temporal. It is the seeking after the incarnation and living into it. It is the possibility of the eternal seeping into
one's life. As it does so the eternal presses itself into the life of the one who
prays, and as it does so it does not lift up the one who prays, but serves
to remind them of their own creatureliness and the impossibility of their
own act and their own life. This impossibility is the song of God's eternal
perfection beginning to be uttered through our prayers. Contemplative
prayer, or attentive listening, pressing and receiving is the mark of a mulattic Christian existence which is underscored by its marked difference yet
utter connection to those with whom they are in relation. It is similarity
and distance bound up within singular moments that are not reconciled,
but whose interplay reveals the truthfulness of one's life.

The life of prayer is the display of this unity and disjuncture where the
one who prays is bound to God, but utterly different. Yet this difference is

not one to be overcome or constructed in order to maintain one's person-hood. The truthfulness of one's body and life evidenced in prayer is the confession of one being bound to the One who is different, who is utterly Other. Performance here is not the mastery of knowledge that is external, but rather the living into a song that is strange, but has nonetheless been given. This song is both internal and external, within and without. The struggle of the flesh spoken so often of by Paul is the disjointedness of this duality. The Spirit within calls us to the image of our Creator, yet our desires are disordered and wayward. The life of the discipleship is the pressing into that song, despite ourselves, without the certainty of our overcoming, but with the promise of Christ's perfection which resides and calls us from within and from without.

This attuning is not a moment of simple piety, but rather the fear and trembling of faith where we must live into that which is impossible. It is Abraham climbing the mountain seeking to reconcile these two contra-dictory words given to him; "you will be a father" and "take your son." The recognition of God calling us from within ourselves, of God's Spirit becoming an inherent part of us is not a moment of certainty or establish-ment, but enters the disciple into a life of continual instability. It is a per-petually disrupting moment that offsets the claims we make concerning ourselves, for at any moment our certainty is called into question when God calls us to take our sons and daughters up the mountain.

Prayer is the possibility of this transformation, of this change. Reflec-tions on the Lord's Prayer point to this mode of subjection, of the subjuga-tion and transformation of wills being bent into the will of the Father. It is the resistance to evil and confession of sin. It is the pressing into hope for God's kingdom that has come and is coming. But these prayers are not only individual moments of pining and hope bound within the confines of an individual and their God. Here prayer is the performance of hybrid-ity and the extension of the baptismal moment into the life of discipleship because in prayer one is entwined with the hope and pain of others as they seek to conform to the groans of the Spirit within them. As such these communal lives seek to be the witness to the Spirit in the world calling it to conform.

Conformity in this sense is not only the conformity of God's will for the individual, but God's will for re-creation. The possibility of prayer lies in the intertwining of those who pray and those who are prayed for. We are those who receive prayer as well as those who offer prayers. This dialectic of offering and receiving resists the postures of certainty that presuppose and establish the idolatry of racial hierarchy. The one who prays is not the one who knows what ought to be prayed for and mediates on behalf of those who lack knowledge or understanding. Rather, prayer is offered with the understanding that we are also in need of prayer. It is both a sign of our understanding of who we are and our confession of who we are not. But here again, offering prayers and receiving prayers are more than moments of words strung together, but rather prayers are the bending of ourselves into the lives of those who we pray for just as we bend ourselves into the will of the One who prays for us.

This posture of entrance into the lives of those whom we love or hate, those whom we mourn for, or whose lives fill us with worry are not the objects of our words, but become the objects of our hopes. Our hopes are grounded in our hope in the world, in the one who has become hope to the world. Through the moments of prayer, through lives filled with prayerful thought and contemplation, our lives become entwined with the One who hopes for us and became a prayer for us. Christ's life, his performance of us was his bending himself toward humanity. It was Christ's entrance into humanity as that prayer, in this instance, that we seek to follow and participate in. This participation is not only in God's Trinitarian life, but additionally we participate in creation in a new way as we become bound to God's creation as recipients of God's grace and those who bear the mark of the Spirit upon our lives. This bending and transformation marks the final aspect of prayer as a life of receptivity and the possibility of transformation.

The Prayer Life as Receptivity and Transformation

In the prayers of Jesus and the witness of his identity as the one who does the will of the Father we see this not only as a moment which bears witness to a relationship, but we also, in this moment, see within these prayers profound moments of transformation grounded in the reality of receptivity and desire. In the prayers of Jesus we are encountered with the fact that the will of the Father could not be fulfilled from a distance, but through a radical binding. The one who does the will of the Father must also become bound to the object of the Father's love and desire. Here creation is undoubtedly the object of the Word's desire as will, but in the life of prayer the ones who subject themselves to the will of God does not remain unchanged, but rather become bound within God's own life so that the unfolding of the object of prayer becomes bound up with the believer's own life.[12]

Their lives become bound to those they pray for as they become bound to the one they pray to. Disciples' very lives become transformed, commingled with the Spirit, these peculiar people, and even strangers to become something new. This binding requires not only an attentiveness to law or deeds, but also an embodiment of Christ's desire *for* us. This embodiment opens the one who prays to the possibility of transformation, of becoming something new.

The shape of this new life is seen in the very first of those whom Christ called to follow him, and in particular in the life of Simon who would become Peter. Jesus saw Peter and called out to him. In this regard Simon "had heard" and left his nets in obedience. Yet what Simon does not know is that in this new life in which Jesus has asked him into obedience is not enough. His life struggles to discern Jesus' law and conform to it, and is continually rebuffed. His desire is for the fulfillment of the law, not an embrace of the life of the one whom he follows. Simply following the law is not enough.

In this new reality the obedient one will be crushed and re-membered. That is to say, that for Simon the "one that has heard" must find himself crushed and failed until there is only Jesus to hold onto. For Simon to live into his new name his hearing must be transformed. The fragmented pieces of his life must bear heat and pressure until they are transformed into something new. Peter, this rock will not simply appear. It begins as sand and sediment and loose pieces of dirt which are swept away easily by the rain and waters or gusts. To become rock they begin to get ground into the earth and piled upon. Rock is a material that is formed under tremendous pressure, causing the individual particles to begin to give up their particular natures and being solidified into granite or sandstone or marble. The life of discipleship is succumbing to this pressure, this fragmentation so as to be remade within the womb of Christ's body, within the furnace of the Spirit that dwells within us calling us out of and into ourselves.

And this was so in Peter's life. When Jesus called him "Peter" it was not a momentary shift but the beginning of an arduous process of being ground down and made into something new. But Jesus called Simon "Peter" not with an instantaneous transformation in mind, but with a calling to become, to transfix his eyes on the possibilities that God has for him, "I will make you a fisher of men." But we cannot jump to that conclusion too quickly. Jesus' calling to Peter was itself the performativity of prayer, a calling out to those whom would hear. Peter's own life of following is a life that seeks to correspond to this calling, to succumb to the pressure, but in doing so he will ultimately find himself pressed into the lives of those he once thought strangers.

The life of prayer begins with Simon. It begins with "one who has heard." It begins with a people to whom God has said, "I will be your God and you will be my people." And so to pray is to enter into the discipleship of Simon Peter. We must begin to hear the calling of God gently or not so gently seeking our gaze so that we may begin to envision a true existence, a real future, and a presence with him. And upon hearing we must obey, we must follow and seek to conform and bind our lives to the others who have heard. The life of prayer is being pressed into something new, being collected and impressed upon.

Just as the Word's desire or will for us brought about the impression of the divine upon us, our desires bent toward the will of the Father, and the Father's will in our neighbors' lives opens us up to the transformation of our own lives as our lives become marked by a missional identity. It is a life that is marked by a constellation of peoples and commitments that resist classification and confound the world. We are a new people not simply because of a biological identity or the transformation of a relational identity. To be a new people, to be marked by the mulattic is to enter into a life that is resisting the claims of purity and cultural forms that become idolatrous through their traditioning.

The power of the gospel and the new people wrought through the baptismal waters, and those who come continually to pray and bend themselves into the will of the Father and into the lives of one another, become a people who cannot imagine themselves apart from these new strange people. In this transfiguration their lives become bound to one another in such a way as to sing new songs and sing old songs in new ways. It is to incorporate the wealth of dances, foods, tastes, and ways of embracing in new ways. The accumulation of these moments is to create a people who are neither/nor—but. They can no longer return to their former people for they speak with a new accent, their lives are marked by new rhythms, enemies have become friends, and friends have become enemies.

This mulattic Christian existence is one that is continually unfolding and enfolding those who are called into its doors. Mulatto/a Christians are a people who are not entrapped by the totalizing claims of a false purity for they know themselves to exist on both sides. These new children are in and not of, they are part and they are distinct, for there is one in them who is their beginning and their end. As children of God, they do not order their steps but rather their lives are marked by the miracle of their birth and their new life, perpetually impressed with the memory of what they once were and the hope of what they are to become. Bound within the tension of Spirit and flesh, mulattic discipleship is the life of becoming what Christ has made them already. It is the struggle to discern what is to be left behind and what is to be transformed.

The mulattic life is a transfigured life that is continually pressing into receptivity. It is seeking that which has been prepared, and as it does so it receives those who are new and called. The mulattic life does not resist these people or their ways, for they were once strangers in a strange land. The possibility of these new people only serves to remind them of who they once were and the strangeness of who they are to become. For Christ is not captured in the perfection of one people, but in the transfiguration of these peoples' lives together. They are Christ's body incorporated, transformed, and sent. They are a people whose personhood is received from the one whose life they live into and those with whom they live into it.

Transformation is not something to resist for it is transformation, transgression, and "impurity" that make our lives possible. Baptism is the birth of the bastard child, the one born through the waters of many and who struggles into a world that does not receive him and insists his cultural and racial desire be disciplined within the confines of racial propriety. The mixture is an anomaly, a fetish that is entered into by those who do not appreciate the depth of their culture or who hate themselves. In our modern world such claims are sadly true. But they are true because the possibility of any life is pressed into the boundaries of a racialized existence. To be dark is to struggle against the specter of white beauty. To be white is to be continually deluded into your own normativity. The baptismal moment gives birth to those who can no longer live into such tragic realities. Their lives are conceived in the womb of a holy transgression. Their lives are marked by a hybridity requiring the betrayal of a people.[13] It is the entrance into a life that requires not the upholding of a new, stable personhood, but to enter into a prayerful existence where God continually calls us into the lives of our neighbors and our enemies, where we are called from Simon to Peter, where we are confronted with the loss of our children in order to receive them.

Prayer is the inhabitation of this transformation and this danger. It is the promise of change, of becoming something new. Prayer is the political presence of a transformed and transforming people. It is the instantiation and the mark of a transformative reality that resists the temptations of

racial coherence and witnesses to the hybrid nature of being a "new creature." Prayer continually opens one up to becoming something different,
thus ecclesial spaces bear witness to the vulnerability of such transformed
and transforming lives, never the assertion of their finality or purity.
Ecclesial life is prayer life, thus ecclesial life is mulatto/a existence.

As we examined in our discussion of baptism, the moment for the
individual is always a moment of ecclesial and communal witness. The
politics of presence is to confront the world with the questions "What are
you? Where are you from?" It is the life marked by rhythms and rituals
of incorporation that constantly defies and redefines the possibilities of
societal life. Shared existence in this mulattic space is not the competing
assertions of a multicultural people who must be "represented" in order
to be seen, but rather it is marked by the continual offering and reception
of a people whose gifts and lives are being bent into the glorification, the
transfiguration of a people.

The lives of these new creatures are political through their presence,
for they refuse to be named within the confines of racial or ethnic singularity, for these ideas cannot attune themselves to the songs of their
ecclesial being. The names of cultural and racial personhood must resist
innovation and change to preserve them. Yet the Christian life is one perpetuated by its adaptation, its continual impressing and openness to being
impressed upon. It is a community marked by prayer, by baptism, by a
feast of flesh and blood. It is a people marked by songs and new songs. It
is a people whose lives are not marked by the certainty of their melody but
by the possibility of improvisation.

As Paul teaches us, "There is . . . no longer slave nor free, there is no
longer male nor female; for all of you are one in Christ Jesus" (Gal 3:28).
Paul's construction of identity here is neither the erasure of particularity
nor the establishment of a new kind of racial certainty.[14] To be in Christ
in this moment is to occupy a space of utter disruption. It is to enter into a
body that is neither/nor—but. It is the transfiguration of particularity so
as to burn off its idolatry and its certainty, but still declare God's mercy
and justice to the world. The mediatory possibility of our body is one that
cannot be spoken through without change, without transformation. The
necessity of transformation, the necessity of death, and the promise of new
life is the political presence of the inter body; it is the filling out of Israel's
struggle with the alien. It is the incorporation of the peoples into the body
of Christ. It is the creation of a new people who are all people and no
people. They are neither/nor—but.

CONCLUSION

The life of prayer in Jesus here indicates the possibility that is held for anyone who prays. Prayer is a life of receptivity, desire, and transformation wherein the one who prays becomes subject to becoming something different in their desire for God and for the will of God in the lives of those they pray for. The life of prayer is not one of distance, but it is to acknowledge the reality of a God who is near both to the one who prays as well as to the one who is being prayed for. In this unity the distance is overcome and both become open to the possibility of being transformed into something new.[15]

Thus prayer is a kind of intercourse or union where new birth is always possible. The intent here is desire for God and God's will. Its intent is to enter into communion with God, but this communion is not without the risk of procreation, the possibility of becoming mother and father to strange-looking children and connections to people who were once not your brothers and mothers and sisters and daughters.

Jesus' own prayer life is the instantiation of this profound possibility in that it is in his prayers that we are born. It is through his prayers, his being the one who does the will of the Father that we might be in him as he as in the Father. In this way we see the prayer life of Jesus as a foundational aspect of a theological anthropology. Here prayer becomes a witness to the christological claim that Jesus was both human and divine and that in our prayers our humanity indicates something beyond itself. In our prayers we attest to the presence of the Spirit within us and to the transformation wrought through the baptismal waters within us. Here prayer is not a constitutive practice in the sense that it is one among many practices that constitute a "cultural reality." Rather, in moments of prayer we bear witness to the one who prayed for us and from us. Prayer is in itself an iconic reality that is pointing beyond itself and through the one who utters words familiar and strange.[16]

In prayer the believer confesses the reality that their torments and cares, joys and hopes have been taken up within God's own life. This is a moment that not only indicates that we are heard, but that we are *in* Christ and that Christ is in our prayers. Prayer here is a testament to the reality that in the incarnation one's very life has been taken up completely within the life of God. Here again the moment of prayer is a seeking to conform to that in which the believer already exists. They seek to conform to the will and purposes of God unfolding in the midst of them while confessing to the possibility that their will is not that of the Father, and that they may in fact be uttering words incoherent with the one who prays on their behalf.[17]

Here it is not only entering into God's taking up of the concerns of the believer, but as the believer seeks to enter into the will of God they are themselves taken into God's concern for the world, for their neighbor, and for their enemies. As we inhabit Christ's desires and prayers for us we begin to reimagine our relationship and desires for those for whom Christ prays. Here the desires for God's will and to become conformed into the image of the one who does God's will, binds us to those whom God loves, transforming our desires for ourselves into desire for our neighbors. In these prayers my hopes and joys become bound to the hopes, joys, and fears of my neighbors. In this encounter the one who prays becomes transformed. Recall here the literary illustrations provided by Charles Chesnutt, James Weldon Johnson, and Nella Larsen where Chesnutt, in contrast to Johnson and Larsen, highlights climactic moments where it is not the one who "passes" who is transformed, but rather it is often a white individual choosing to forsake the advantages of their race in order to pursue a "colored" love interest.

This transformation is not instantaneous, but nonetheless in these moments of prayer the object of such prayers becomes bound to an ecclesial identity.[18] They become brothers and sisters, mothers and fathers. In these moments of prayer the baptismal moment becomes rearticulated and inflected anew as one arises out of prayer able to see new possibilities and new tragedies in their midst. Through these moments of prayer we begin to imagine ourselves in the world.

Yet these prayers do not allow solely for an intellectual assent or a perpetual distance, but rather are profound moments of presence through Christ. They are moments of entering into strange realities and becoming burdened with new weights that begin to alter the relationships of the church and those within the church.[19] The reality of Christ's presence among them through their prayers, and their prayers as repetitions of Jesus' prayer, are not moments of reflective mourning, but that of bodily desire and yearning that participate in the formation of those who see themselves as strangers in the world and begin to read its text with the eyes of foreigners.[20]

Through the prayers of the faithful and the transformation possible in these moments the participants themselves enter into the risk of the One who prayed for them. The prayers of the faithful lead us to enter into a transgressive love that requires our relationships and desires to confront and disrupt. This disruption is intentional, but also embodies a profound presence in the world that continually defies. Prayerful presence in the world is the divine child born of a virgin whose very being in the world confronts the world with the reality of redemption, and God's presence among the faithful whose lives are defined only by a reception of the call, a "Yes" to God's promise.

Such a transformation within the believer becomes the fulfillment of Jesus' prayer for those who would believe that they might be in him as he is in the Father. Such a transformation could be understood as transfigurative. That is, in the transformation wrought through prayer the believer's life becomes a reality that points to God's call to the world. Those who pray are transfigured into God's presence in the world, God's beckoning that those who are of dirt might become burning bushes, bodies that hold within them and their desires God's hope and possibility within the world.

It is in inhabiting a life of prayer that we begin to see the profound implications for the formation of a political vision of identity. Such a transfiguration is political. These praying bodies become presences. Such bodies seek to inhabit the lives of those who seek, hurt, and yearn in such a way as they become welcomed into God's very body, and in these moments both those who embody and those who receive such a presence become further transformed. The prayers of the people articulate their strangeness to the world, or the way in which the world is sometimes utterly apart from them. Yet they are the world, they are the object of these prayers, of God's mercies. Prayer is always disrupting and articulating. It disrupts the sensibilities and hopes we have concerning ourselves. Prayer is a mode of language that always requires the reception of who we are. It is a practice groping to listen to hear, to be named, and to hear the words of forgiveness. It is the practice of seeking guidance of discerning a way in the world. As such it confesses that though we are of this world it is not our possession. Prayer is not that which we order and establish. We must find our way though it. It is a place that is strange to us. And yet prayer also articulates. It articulates the world as a creation and us as creatures. It declares the possibilities of the world as not within its own possibilities but bound to the possibilities of God who has bound God's own word to it eternally.

Prayers are the yearnings of exiles that have come to call this new place home. They are the utterances and desires for the comfort of the One who knows them and speaks to them softly in their own tongue. Prayers are those lives bent to their author, that sing lowly the melodies of their mothers, but now with new timbres and new accents. Prayers are the lives of those who are redeemed and declare to the world in their refusals the possibilities of redemption.

Through the life of prayer the reality of bodies is revealed to be dirt enlivened by the breath of God. In the life of prayer, such lives become softened to the reality of the life of God in the Other, and in that reality the particularities of differing human lives become interwoven and sutured together.[21] We become Peters. Lives become softened to the fire of the Spirit and once malleable blend into one another creating new particularities that will come to display the glory of God's presence in the world. The politics of presence refuses the dichotomies of identity that render lives within illusions of difference. Prayer refuses these illusions through the perpetual transgression of desires and bodies. In these transgressions, these "mixed" bodies reimagine lives together through their desire for one another. This act refuses conceptions of difference as unsurpassable. The fruit of these children, these en-spirited bodies, these mulatto/a children exist in the world as a witness not only to the illusion of enclosed identities, but more profoundly to God's refusal to abide within these enclosures. Mulatto/a bodies witness to the transfiguration of all bodies, to the transgression not only of cultures and races, but of divine and created, eternal and temporal, calling all people into the certainty of their own transformation into God's children.

To call upon the name of Jesus, to be reborn, to pray, to serve is to conform to the Spirit, to acknowledge the truth of our personhood as bound to the one who both abides in us and calls us from without. The politics of presence is to refuse the logics of race and ethnicity by living into this new birth and the form of life that calls us not to maintain these lines, but subject them to the possibility of becoming something new. As such we present the particularities of our lives to one another and to God and in so doing become disruptions in the world, desiring what the world demands we hate, and hating what the world demands we love so that we might all live this prayer into God and into one another:

> O Lord my God, my one hope, listen to me, lest through weariness I be unwilling to seek You, "but that I may always ardently seek Your face." You give strength to seek, You who have made me find You, and have given the hope of finding You more and more. My strength and my weakness are in Your sight: preserve the one, and heal the other. My knowledge and my ignorance are in Your sight; where You have opened to me, receive me as I enter; where You have closed, open to me as I

knock. May I remember You, understand You, love You. Increase these things in me, until You refashion me wholly. Amen.[22]

BENEDICTION

In Gethsemane Jesus prayed for us that we might be in him as he is in the Father. The possibility of our lives in this world is one that is not without struggle or pain or exile. The question before us as we rise out of the living waters, as we take our first breath upon rising from Christ's womb is this, What will our struggle be? Where will we find sorrow and where will we find joy? For whom will we fight and for whom will we die? Will our presence in the world reiterate patterns of death or will they reverberate the shock of our Lord in the world, calling it once again to itself? The church in the modern world has struggled to negotiate through these questions. Between the slave ships and the encyclopedia it has clung to a purity of body or a purity of thought. It has sought to account for itself in the world apart from the kinship the name "Christian" demands of us: "Hell no you ain't my brother!" The pattern of assertion and refusal marks the human condition, resisting God's claims made of us and the implication that claim makes for our lives together. And yet, God has entered into this condition. God has transgressed the line of Creator and created, divine and limited, to create us anew.

Christ's incarnation was not an apolitical piety that rendered only a faithful sacrifice for our admission into a world beyond this, nor did Christ's life only incite rebellion against the structures of his time. Christ's life, through his transgression of time, his transgression of our humanity, his transgression of humanity's structures of certainty, reordered the very foundations of our world, bringing to death the claims of purity or citizenship that have been so deeply engrained in humanity's history. Christ's life was political not only for what he did, but because of who he was. Christ's life, his presence, was political because he was God among us and refused to allow humanity's narrow conception of what it means to be human, to be a citizen, to thwart the transformation such a presence meant for us.

Upon Jesus' death, while his followers mourned and wept, the Spirit swept upon and through those who loved Jesus so dearly. In their presence among diasporic Jews who spoke so differently, God's presence was announced. As with Moses so long ago, Jesus' disciples became burning bushes, bodies that proclaimed a God who has not regarded humanity as lost but became us so that we might become like God. To claim this possibility in the modern world is not a simple reiteration of an ancient and oppressive doctrine. The confession of the Word enfleshed resists the claims of modernity upon our bodies and the patterns of life built upon the hue of our skin.

To follow Christ, to become like Christ, is to become something new, to enter into an eschatological identity that presses God into the crevices of the everyday, even as we are stretched into the lives of one another. Abiding, straining to hear God's Spirit calling us from within into the lives of those without, our lives become bound and present in unexpected places and in unexpected ways. In Christ, we become sutured together into a new people and become surprised by the people we become in the process

In modernity, race disciplined our lives and structured our hopes. It was not God. Race subtly marked the rhythm of our speech and the shape of our lips, granting us access into one space and obstructing our passage into another. It is these patterns of exclusion and entrance that continue to mark the church today and it is these patterns that must die. We must become bound to one another in such a way that we open ourselves to bearing strange-looking children, children whose very presence in any community confronts the community's people with only questions. The presence of these strange-looking children and their "unnatural" parents forces the community to ask the question why some are in and others are out. Mulatto/a Christian bodies ask the church to reflect upon the desires that lead to separate languages, services, and distinctions between styles, resisting the migrant worker among them or refusing the discomfort of entering into the struggle for a life beyond a veil of color.

Becoming a new people is a possibility that lies before the church. As a people of God, a politics of presence is a possibility that lies before us as Christian intellectuals, as those charged with the task of forming and teaching. Will we draw upon the collective descriptions of the saints, but not as grammatical instruction or letters inked with the blood of the oppressors? Rather, will we draw on our doctrine as descriptions of a God who is deeper than any word, whose encounter with humanity was the Word to us, who desires from us more than our words or our programs, but our whole lives, our bodies set ablaze?

And so this mulatto child, Jesus, the holy mixed one before us requires us to ask, "Why not?" Why not these people? Why do you not desire children with this woman or with this man? Why are these people not our brothers or our sisters? Why are we better when certain people are not among us? Why is their pain not our pain? Why is their oppression not our oppression? The mulatto/a child does not bridge these divides but stands in the midst, and through the mulatto/a's desire for both/and, through the mulatto/a's refusal of the neither/nor, the mulatto/a Christian opens up a possibility for all to enter into the transformative and liberating work of Christ's mulattic body.

NOTES

Introduction

1 The complicity of theology in the colonial project can be seen in the scholarship of Luis Rivera's *A Violent Evangelism: The Political and Religious Conquest of the Americas* (Louisville, Ky.: Westminster John Knox, 1992). Most recently Jay Kameron Carter has outlined how the legacy of racial logic was embedded within European theological reflection in the wake of Immanual Kant, but also how European theology's formation within the Enlightenment has come to be reflected in the responses of black Christian intellectuals in the New World. See Jay Kameron Carter, *Race: A Theological Account* (Oxford: Oxford University Press, 2008).

2 While contextual and "orthodox" theologies obviously vary widely, some examples of attempts to reframe the question theology asked can be seen in texts such as the following: James Cone, *Black Theology and Black Power*; Kelly Brown Douglas, *The Black Christ*; Elizabeth Schussler Fiorenza, *Jesus: Miriam's Child, Sophia's Prophet: Critical Issues in Feminist Christology*; Gustavo Gutierrez, *On Job* and *A Theology of Liberation*; Rosemary Radford Ruether, *New Woman, New Earth: Sexist Ideologies and Human Liberation*. This is by no means an exhaustive list nor does it suggest that there were no critical theological protests prior to the emergence of these within academic theological discourse. Womanist theologians have quite forcefully demonstrated that African American women have been the animating force of the Black Church, and in spite of the perpetual refusal of their bodies and lives, the leadership of black women in these churches serves as a vital and powerful refusal of male domination in the church and in the world. I do think it could be said that since 1960 we have seen a more systematized accounting of the challenges that face people of color and women in the modern world, and in connecting this analysis of the problem we also see an emerging vision of what *could* be.

3   Early in the history of slavery in the Americas, African Christians would decry the religion of "white Christianity." David Walker, Henry Highland Garnett, Frederick Douglass and many others sought to both resist the structural realities of the slave ship as well as pose a theological refutation of Christianity's role in the erection of that structure. More recently, Albert Raboteau would become one of the first to narrate the response of slaves to Christianity in his groundbreaking work *Slave Religion*. Albert J. Raboteau, *Slave Religion: The "Invisible Institution" in the Antebellum South* (New York: Oxford University Press, 1978). This would mark a crucial beginning of African American scholars beginning to rethink the relationship between African reception of Christianity and the demands made by white Euro-Christians. These studies would come to show how early African Christians came to receive Christianity in ways that celebrated their creation as in the image of God, and they heralded God's desire for their freedom. The black theology movement of the 1960s is nothing new in this regard, but rather is a more systematic articulation of a deep and rich tradition of nonwhite creative resistance to and incorporation of Christian teaching.

4   For a helpful discussion of the Enlightenment and the encyclopedia, see Richard R. Yeo, *Encyclopaedic Visions: Scientific Dictionaries and Enlightenment Culture* (Cambridge: Cambridge University Press, 2001).

5   James Cone, *Black Theology and Black Power* (Maryknoll, N.Y.: Orbis, 1997), xii.

6   John Milbank, *The Word Made Strange: Theology, Language, Culture* (Oxford: Blackwell, 1997), 49–50; emphasis added.

7   "[W]e today can claim on the same humanity that was liberated through Jesus' cross and resurrection. Because Jesus lived we now know that servitude is inhuman, and that Christ has set us free to live as liberated sons and daughters of God. Unless Jesus was truly like us, then we have no reason to believe that our true humanity is disclosed in his person." (James Cone, *God of the Oppressed* [Maryknoll, N.Y.: Orbis, 1997], 110). Cone brilliantly places the theological language of communication of attributes within the context of oppression, but also raises questions about whether or not these were the only people Jesus was for.

8   Cone, *God of the Oppressed*, 109.

9   Cone, *God of the Oppressed*, 224.

10   See Milbank, *The Word Made Strange*, 123–44.

11   Graham Ward and Sarah Coakley are notable exceptions to this trend in that both have sought to work through the deep connections between practices and bodies. Whether these investigations begin to account for the racial formation of the modern world still remains an open question.

12   The reality of globalization is not only a question of interethnic children, but the ways in which cultures and societies seek to articulate their existence over or against "foreigners and aliens." The colonialism of the contemporary world is no longer a colonialism of occupation, but of cultural power. Questions of interracial existence, classification, and marriage persist in contemporary society. Recent studies such as Renee C. Romano's *Race Mixing: Black-White Marriage in Postwar America* (Cambridge, Mass.: Harvard University Press, 2003) indicate how patterns of interracial marriage have continued to expand, but even this expansion can be seen to be racially coded. Not only are the numbers of interracial marriages and children increasing, but the interracial identity is itself beginning to coalesce as an identity.

See Kimberly McCain DaCosta, *Making Multiracials: State, Family, and Market in the Redrawing of the Color Line* (Stanford: Stanford University Press, 2007). However, the question of interracial existence is also wider than the binary of white and black. The reality of mixed-race relationships and children can be seen in the widening phenomenon of globalization. One example of this can be seen in Asian migration throughout the world (e.g., Koreans in South America and Indians in South Africa), revealing the pressures of identity and assimilation. Even within the United States the questions of racial identity are becoming increasingly complicated as nonwhite and nonblack citizens of the United States begin to articulate their own refusals of participation as "model-minorities."

13   For an excellent description of the development of racial classification regarding the mulatto in Colonial America see Winthrop Jordan, "American Chairoscuro: The Status and Definition of Mulattoes in the British Colonies," *William and Mary Quarterly* 19.2 (1962): 183–200.

14   See David Goodman Crooly and George Wakeman, *Miscegenation: The Theory of the Blending of the Races Applied to the American White Man and Negro* (New York: Dexter, Hamilton, 1864).

Chapter 1

1   Langston Hughes, "Mulatto." In *The Collected Poems of Langston Hughes*, edited by Arnold Rampersad (New York: Vintage Books, 1994), 100–101.

2   Rebecca M. Blank, Marilyn Dabady, and Constance F. Citro, *Measuring Racial Discrimination* (Washington, D.C.: National Academies Press, 2004).

3   Werner Sollors, *Neither Black nor White yet Both* (Cambridge, Mass.: Harvard University Press, 1997), 112.

4   There are many problems in attempting to classify encounters with racial and ethnic groups. Biologically there is little that distinguishes one group from another, but we must account for the many ways such categorical distinctions have served to reify racial lines and the political advantages such lines serve. Despite the distinctions of these bodies and the generic use of this mixture in this case, mulatto/a points to the sexual encounters among differing people groups that produce children who defy clear classification. In this work the terms "interracial" and "mulatto/a" signify the product of these encounters, although "mestizaje," "mestizo/a," etc. all might serve just as well. Interracial serves as a contemporary description of these encounters while mulatto/a seeks to connect the notion of "interraciality" to its historical antecedent and the problematization of belonging that such interracial lives posed to identities both national and local.

5   There have been no studies of mixed-race identity, although recent articulations of mestizo/a theology are beginning to explain the reality of a culture whose identity is the product of two cultures. The most prominent example of this theology is Virgilio P. Elizondo's *The Future Is Mestizo: Life Where Cultures Meet* (Boulder: University Press of Colorado, 2000).

6   One of the earliest attempts to formally classify "mixed race" peoples was undertaken by Johann Friedrich Blumenbach between 1775 and 1795. See *The Anthropological Treatises*, translated by Thomas Bendyshe (London: Longman, 1865).

7   See Robert Young, *Colonial Desire: Hybridity in Theory, Culture, and Race* (London: Routledge, 1995).

8   Matthew Frye Jacobson, *Whiteness of a Different Color: European Immigrants and the Alchemy of Race* (Cambridge, Mass.: Harvard University Press, 1998), 12.

9   Lydia Marie Child was the first to invoke the term "tragic mulatto" as a literary theme in her abolition fiction. See also Eve Allegra Raimon, *The "Tragic Mulatta" Revisited: Race and Nationalism in Nineteenth-Century Antislavery Fiction* (New Brunswick, N.J.: Rutgers University Press, 2004).

10   For an excellent collection of primary sources and research on anti-miscegenation laws see Werner Sollors, *Interracialism: Black-White Intermarriage in American History, Literature, and Law* (Oxford: Oxford University Press, 2000).

11   Pierre Bourdieu, *The Logic of Practice* (Stanford: Stanford University Press, 1990), 57.

12   Bourdieu makes this point powerfully in *The Logic of Practice*. Paul Connerton also describes how the memory is a social phenomenon that articulates or resists identities and how identity's performativity becomes evident in social memory, particularly in commemorative ceremonies and bodily practices. Connerton writes, "If there is such a thing as social memory . . . we are likely to find it in commemorative ceremonies; but commemorative ceremonies prove to be commemorative only in so far as they are performative; performativity cannot be thought without a concept of habit; and habit cannot be thought without a notion of bodily automatisms." (Paul Connerton, *How Societies Remember* [Cambridge: Cambridge University Press, 1989], 5).

13   *Incidents in the Life of a Slave Girl* is Harriet Jacobs' account of her life as a slave and her eventual escape from her master Dr. Flint. Jacobs (1813–1897) was born to mulatto slaves in North Carolina. Her narrative describes her life as coming into awareness of her life as a slave and the harrowing violent reality of her master's sexual pursuit of her. Finally escaping to freedom after many years hiding in a secret room in her grandmother's house, Jacobs' account reveals how sex was deeply intertwined with the system of slavery, even as white purity was espoused by its purveyors.

14   Jacobs, *Incidents in the Life of a Slave Girl*, 27.

15   Jacobs, *Incidents in the Life of a Slave Girl*, 40. This relationship is, of course, fraught with danger and may or may not exhibit a "true" freedom, for Jacobs is still not free. Her description of this gentleman's affection within the framework of white affection colors her imagination as well, but even given these qualifications the notion of an abiding affection and love between white and "colored" is important here.

16   Jacobs, *Incidents in the Life of a Slave Girl*, 30.

17   Frantz Fanon, *Black Skin, White Masks* (New York: Grove Press, 1967), 45.

18   Frantz Fanon might point to this poem as the delusion of the mulatto/a's own beauty as a dark man in the world. Particularly in *Black Skin, White Masks* such assertions of relation to whiteness are construed in terms of self-hate and desire to ascend. What I want to suggest here is the way in which these claims and denials exhibit a fundamental connection between the two. To assert an acknowledgment of paternity or kinship is not necessarily a desire to ascend, but rather a desire for a kind of wholeness that is perpetually denied any slave. More particularly the mulatto/a slave and inversely the myth of wholeness is perpetuated in the slave-owning families' self-deception. See "The Man of Color and the White Woman." In *Black Skin, White Masks*, 63–82.

19   Stuart Hall, "New Ethnicities." In *Stuart Hall: Critical Dialogues in Cultural Studies*, edited by David Morley and Kuan-Hsing Chen (London: Routledge, 1996), 444.

20   Hall, "New Ethnicities," 444.

21   See Elizabeth Fox-Genovese, *Within the Plantation Household: Black and White Women of the Old South* (Chapel Hill: University of North Carolina Press, 1988).

22   While the formal theme of the tragic mulatto/a can be seen emerging in the nineteenth century, the difficulty of the mixed-race figures and the unions that produce them mark literature as early as the seventeenth and eighteenth centuries.

23   See in particular James Weldon Johnson, *Autobiography of an Ex-Coloured Man*. This is a theme prevalent in Harlem Renaissance depictions of the tragic mulatto/a, where such a figure is often marked with a certain level of suspicion. Here the tragedy does not lie in the absence of place, but in the failure to recognize the beauty or belonging of black life. In this regard we see the formalization of Black Nationalist ideals that seek to resist the hegemony of white claims to purity and beauty by asserting a contrary narrative of the beauty of black "purity."

24   David Walker and Peter P. Hinks, *David Walker's Appeal to the Coloured Citizens of the World* (University Park: Pennsylvania State University Press, 2000), 16; emphasis in original.

25   Frederick Douglass, "Slaveholding Christianity." In *Afro-American Religious History*, edited by Milton C. Sernett (Durham, N.C., Duke University Press, 1999), 106.

26   Karl Barth, *Church Dogmatics*, I.2, translated by Geoffrey William Bromiley and Thomas Forsyth Torrance (Edinburgh: T&T Clark, 1975), 307.

27   While some have come to draw upon Barth's discussion of religion to speak to issues of religious pluralism, it is my contention that Barth's framing of religion as unbelief is intended to capture the wider political and social patterns as exemplifying deeply religious moments.

28   Barth, *Church Dogmatics*, IV.1, 421.

29   My thanks to Willie James Jennings at Duke University for articulating this connection between Barth's theological and cultural concerns.

30   For an excellent consideration of Barth's response to Volk theology and German Christians through the *Church Dogmatics*, see Arne Rasmusson, "Deprive them of their Pathos: Karl Barth and the Nazi Revolution Revisited," *Modern Theology* 23.3 (2007): 369–91.

31   Barth, *Church Dogmatics*, 421–22. Here I am aware that Barth would likely vigorously argue that such a performance of unbelief is the challenge of *all* humanity and that it would be problematic to suggest that one group of people represent this unbelief in a stronger way than another. Yet, it is my hope here to highlight the particular way in which race is seen as a peculiarly religious phenomenon in its own right, in that it shares certain commonalities with the ideals and philosophies that Barth so vigorously worked against. In each of these moments Barth is not merely working against an idea, but rather against a certain material existence that becomes evident in these ideas and philosophies.

32   Toni Morrison provides a compelling description of this violent incorporation through her novel *The Bluest Eye*. The narrator suggests at the conclusion of the book that,

All of our waste which we dumped on her and which she absorbed. And all of our beauty, which was hers—felt so wholesome after we cleaned ourselves on her. We were so beautiful when we stood astride her ugliness. Her simplicity decorated us, her guilt sanctified us, her pain made us glow with health, her awkwardness made us think we had a sense of humor. Her inarticulateness made us believe we were eloquent. Her poverty kept us generous. Even her waking dreams we used—to silence our own nightmares. And she let us, and thereby deserved our contempt. We honed our egos on her, padded our characters with her frailty, and yawned in the fantasy of our strength. (*The Bluest Eye* [New York: Plume Books, 1994], 205)

Here such apostasy slowly inhabits even those who are not at the center of divinity, but in whom such desires become inculcated, thereby inflicting its violence and establishing its authority, even among those on the margins of the claim. This performance of race becomes impressed into every aspect of American life, recapitulating the pattern of differentiation and exclusion.

33   Barth, *Church Dogmatics*, IV.1, 483.

34   Cobb highlights seven aspects of religion: ultimate concern, the holy, moral and ontological faith, revelation and ecstasy, religious symbols, myth, and liminality. (Kelton Cobb, *The Blackwell Guide to Theology and Popular Culture* [Malden, Mass.: Blackwell, 2005], 120) It is important to note here why I draw on Cobb's appropriation of Tillich rather than Tillich himself. In Cobb's attempt to express the relationship between theology and popular culture he draws upon Tillich in order to serve as an interpretive matrix for cultural practices. In this regard "religion" is less of a phenomenological category, but more the various interconnections of daily practices and the meanings they are given by their practitioners. It is in this regard that I find Cobb's work most illuminating for providing the beginnings of a structural account of race as religious performance. I am not suggesting a fundamental congruity between Cobb (Tillich) and Barth. Rather, Cobb expresses the ways in which cultural identity is the codification of practices. Cobb and Tillich use these insights to make a claim concerning religion and culture that is bound to a certain universal notion of religion that I would want to resist. However, their insights concerning how these practices and beliefs constitute a cultural identity inhabited through particular practices is an important observation. For another account of the relationship between practices and cultural memory see Connerton, *How Societies Remember.*

35   Cobb, *Blackwell Guide to Theology and Popular Culture*, 103.

36   Cobb, *Blackwell Guide to Theology and Popular Culture*, 103–4.

37   Lillian Smith, *Killers of the Dream* (New York: Norton, 1949), 83.

38   Smith, *Killers of the Dream*, 83.

39   Sollors, ed., "The Virginia 'Act to Preserve Racial Integrity' of 1924," reprinted in *Interracialism*, 24.

40   Higginbotham and Kopytoff, "Racial Purity and Interracial Sex in the Law of Colonial and Antebellum Virginia," reprinted in *Interracialism*, 82.

41   See also Jacobson, *Whiteness of a Different Color*, for an account of how race played a crucial role in the transformation of European immigrants into white Americans. The rhetoric, debates, and laws enacted to protect the United States from being "defiled" reveal the religiosity of race to be not only a reality for American blacks,

but that it enveloped all people when they entered the United States. Immigrants had to quickly adapt to the religion of the land and determine what they were willing to surrender and to whom their loyalty lay. This difficult transformation of immigrants into white people provides a powerful example of how racialized lives in the West continually incorporate all peoples.

42   The 1915 film *The Birth of a Nation* is a stark example of the logic of racial transgression fueling the formation of collective identity.

43   Arthur Franklin Raper and the Southern Commission on the Study of Lynching, *The Tragedy of Lynching* (New York: Negro Universities Press, 1969), 480.

44   See Ida B. Wells-Barnett, *Selected Works*, edited by Trudier Harris (New York, Oxford University Press, 1991). In particular see "Southern Horrors: Lynch Law in All Its Phases" and "A Red Record: Tabulated Statistics and Alleged Causes of Lynchings in the United States, 1892–1893–1894."

45   See Suzanne Bost, *Mulattas and Mestizas: Representing Mixed Identities in the Americas, 1850–2000*. Athens: University of Georgia Press, 2003.

46   This film is also particularly important in considering the mythic nature of white bodies that I will attend to later in this chapter. See Melvyn Stokes, *D. W. Griffith's The Birth of a Nation: A History of "The Most Controversial Motion Picture of All Time*. New York: Oxford University Press, 2007 and Valerie Smith, *Representing Blackness: Issues in Film and Video*. Rutgers depth of field series. New Brunswick, N.J.: Rutgers University Press, 1997.

47   La Jau, "Slave Conversions in South Carolina" in Sernett, *Afro-American Religious History*, 65.

48   Frantz Fanon allows us to call into question the dynamic of reception that is implicit in such a confession. That is to say the assumption on La Jau's part, that because the slaves recite the words he offers their subsequent reception will somehow be the one that La Jau intends. What Fanon points to in this moment is the way in which production and reception are in fact not always identical. In this case we can see Fanon's understanding of dialect beginning to imagine that the slaves themselves understand the entirety of the baptismal moment in a radically different way than La Jau intends.

49   Raboteau, *Slave Religion*.

50   Again, Jacobson helps us to see the way in which whiteness serves as a type of promise with the fruits of citizenship attached to it. The shift toward whiteness away from Irish, Italian, Polish, etc. were attempts lived into on a daily basis in order to achieve the "American Dream," which bore with it material comforts and helped to eliminate the threat of being labeled "dark."

51   Cobb, *Blackwell Guide to Theology and Popular Culture*, 121.

52   Cobb, *Blackwell Guide to Theology and Popular Culture*, 123.

53   For an excellent account of the relationship between race and the family ideal see Amy Laura Hall, *Conceiving Parenthood* (Grand Rapids: Eerdmans, 2008).

54   "Indeed, to understand identity as a *practice*, and as a signifying practice, is to understand culturally intelligible subjects as the resulting effects of a rule-bound discourse that inserts itself in the pervasive and mundane signifying acts of linguistic life" (Judith Butler, *Gender Trouble* [New York, Routledge, 1990], 198; emphasis mine). Butler's notion of signification is important for our consideration of the way in which

racial lives represent moments of articulation or contestation—where the mundane aspects of one's life are interpreted within a wider set of ideals, possibilities, and limitations serving to frame these actions. The awareness (direct or indirect) of such interpretations is what I am including within the assertion of racial life as a type of performance. Here racial lives are indicative of more than a particular person, but are always bound up within the racialized structures of political and social life. This totalizing and gathering character of performance is what makes it a religious performance.

55   Cyril, *St. Cyril of Jerusalem's Lectures on the Christian Sacraments*, translated by F. L. Cross (Crestwood, N.Y.: St. Vladimir's Seminary Press, 1977), 53–58.

Chapter 2

1   Stuart Hall, "Who Needs Identity?" In Paul Du Gay and Stuart Hall, *Questions of Cultural Identity* (London: Sage, 1996), 6.

2   For an excellent account of the developments in racial classification in the United States see Joel Williamson, *New People: Miscegenation and Mulattoes in the United States* (New York: Free Press, 1980) and Winthrop D. Jordan, *The White Man's Burden: Historical Origins of Racism in the United States* (Oxford: Oxford University Press, 1974).

3   The racial lines were perpetually reinscribed through the legal codification of racial difference. *Dred Scott v. Sandford* (1857), *Pace v. Alabama* (1883), and *Plessy v. Ferguson* (1896) served not only to codify the conditions of participation, but also served to highlight the costs of being on the wrong side of the color line. The "passing" literature of the late nineteenth, early twentieth centuries takes place in the midst of the color line being drawn more deeply within all aspects of American life. These hardening of color lines raised the stakes of being "white" or" colored" in American society, giving rise to people of color "passing" as white, either permanently or on occasion. This idea will be discussed more as the chapter unfolds.

4   Williamson, *New People*, 112.

5   C. Eric Lincoln, *Coming through the Fire: Surviving Race and Place in America* (Durham, N.C.: Duke University Press, 1996).

6   Joel Williamson, *The Crucible of Race: Black/White Relations in the American South since Emancipation* (New York: Oxford University Press, 1984).

7   The recent work of Emilie Maureen Townes, *Womanist Ethics and the Cultural Production of Evil*, highlights the tragic mulatta as a moment of empowerment breaking away from the "tragic mulatto" theme articulated by white authors. Here she suggests the mulatta figure of the Harlem Renaissance and its antecedents as marking a refusal of the inferiority of these bodies and proposing an identification with black bodies that represents a hopefulness inherent to black existence. I quite agree with Townes that the work of African American writers rearticulated these bodies in profound ways. These bodies exhibited levels of independence and power seen rarely in literature of the day. Yet Townes does not account for the recurrence of death that remains in these works. These deaths are sometimes heroic, but more often they are deeply paradoxical. Death surrounds those who hoped to cross over, those who did and refused, as well as those who remained "with their people." The

overwhelming presence of death and exile that pervades these texts mark a distinct pause even within the "people-building" exercise of the Harlem Renaissance and the New Negro Movement. Undoubtedly these texts exhibit the empowerment of darker folk, but they also display the deeply complicated nature of this agency, and in doing so question all notions of agency within our racialized world. See Emilie Maureen Townes, *Womanist Ethics and the Cultural Production of Evil* (New York: Palgrave Macmillan, 2006), 84–89.

8   For excellent accounts of the interpretation of interracial bodies see Sollors, *Neither White nor Black Yet Both* and *Interracialism*, as well as Williamson, *New People*.

9   See Samira Kawash, *Dislocating the Color Line: Identity, Hybridity, and Singularity in African-American Narrative* (Stanford: Stanford University Press, 1997), 22. The concern of Kawash in *Dislocating* is primarily to highlight the disruption of racial epistemology in the mulatto and the passing body. This is a crucial observation considering the deep connection between knowledge and self-assertion or identity. It is my hope throughout this chapter to press this point more deeply to show how such epistemological assertions are born out through the particularities of peoples lives and the ways in which they structure their lives along these precarious lines.

10   See Josh Toth, "Deauthenticating Community: The Passing Intrusion of Clare Kendry in Nella Larsen's *Passing*," *MELUS* 33.1 (2008): 59. Toth suggests that the "passing presence resists complete apprehension. She disrupts our illusion of a coherent and stable reality because she refuses to be fixed or understood via a process of symbolization." Interestingly, Toth notes the necessity of similarity in establishing an individual's place within a community. This suggests the mere presence of one who appears but does not serve to upend the logic of a community and the individuals within it.

11   In both of these terms the variation of meaning conveys a somewhat nuanced understanding of both what the subject is entering as well as the way the activity of passing was understood. That is, to pass into something is to suggest a boundary that is clearly defined where one might be able to measure one's being in or not in. The notion of passing in this regard conveys the way racial identities were not only personal, but rather social or, more precisely, spatial as Buscaglia reminds us. Here to pass into the white world is to occupy a space within a social system. To pass from one life to another again reiterates the religiously grounded language discussed in chapter 1. The second meaning of passing indicates the deeply performative nature of racial existence. Here, to pass does not indicate necessarily that which one is entering into, but rather the perpetual performance of the individual to maintain the ruse. The individual must perpetually display behaviors or actions while suppressing others in order to maintain the illusion of belonging. Yet such notions of passing also indicate the utter impossibility of such a transformation, for one can only pretend to be white. There is nothing in this system that allows one to truly become white, thus foreclosing the possibility of any real transformation, simply a change in fortune or social possibilities. It is rendered from one life to another, from death to life, or life to death.

12   Kawash notes how passing is, in fact, the intensification of the mulatto disruption, "in the figure of the passing body, the signifiers of race are unloosed from the signifieds; the seemingly stable relation between representation and the real collapses,

and representation is suddenly dangerous and untrustworthy" (*Dislocating the Color Line*, 131).

13 M. Giulia Fabi, "Reconstructing the Race: The Novel after Slavery." In *Cambridge Companion to African American Literature*, edited by Maryemma Graham (Cambridge: Cambridge University Press, 2004), 39. Fabi here is highlighting the way in which the mulatto body was often caught within an interpretive vice wherein the lightness of their skin afforded them a certain privileged space within the racial hierarchy, yet was also resisted both by darker and lighter bodies. Literature had tended up to this point to highlight the "tragic mulatto" as a figure caught miserably in between, without the physical prowess or joy of their darker brethren. Also, they could only mimic the lives of their lighter "kin." For more on the literary representation of mulattos see Sollors, *Neither Black nor White yet Both: Thematic Explorations of Interracial Literature*.

14 Fabi, "Reconstructing the Race," In *Cambridge Companion to African Literature*, 39.

15 Such an articulation of interracial figures was new during this time because of the growing influence of the "scientific" study of mixed race children that oftentimes suggested a certain dilution of characteristics in the hybrid man or woman. This dilution resulted in the effeminate or sterile mulatto man or the stunning, but empty mulatta woman. These figures often enjoyed more notoriety among their own people for their lighter skin, but lacked the moral strength to exercise this "gift," well while their attempts to mimic their white counterparts was seen only as a tragic aping or approximation. See Sollors, *Neither Black nor White Yet Both*.

16 George Hutchinson, *The Harlem Renaissance in Black and White* (Cambridge, Mass.: Belknap Press of Harvard University Press, 1995).

17 Kawash, *Dislocating the Color Line*, 123.

18 This reversal of desire of white to live as dark marks many of Chesnutt's novels and in particular can be seen in his explicit discussions of race in his articles "The Future American" and "What is a White Man?" (*The Independent* 41, May 30, 1889, 5–6). These discussions serve to both highlight the absurdity of whiteness as well as suggest the possibility of a "blended" race that does not contaminate, but elevate all people.

19 Recent scholarship has sought to redescribe Chesnutt himself as well as his fiction within a more complicated set of interrelationships regarding Chesnutt's relationships to the African American community, white readers, and his representations of white and black alike. For a helpful survey of recent scholarship see Henry B. Wotham, "What Is a Black Author?: A Review of Recent Charles Chesnutt Studies," *American Literary History* 18 (2006): 7. For a particularly helpful analysis of Chesnutt's major works and his reconception of race see Dean McWilliams, *Charles W. Chesnutt and the Fictions of Race* (Athens: University of Georgia Press, 2002).

20 This is the child of a mulatto and a white person.

21 Charles Waddell Chesnutt, *The House Behind the Cedars* (New York: Modern Library, 2003), 14.

22 Chesnutt, *The House Behind the Cedars*, 16. The theme of the messianic, of a mediating presence, was a theme common to mulatto literature of the nineteenth century. These novels highlighted the gifts bestowed upon those with a lighter hue and emphasized the responsibility (or burden) to lift up those kin marked by ignorance

and oppression. This trope of uplift or what W. E. B. Du Bois would later call the talented tenth is certainly an aspect of the fundamental difference described by mulatto or light skin African Americans.

23   Chesnutt, *The House Behind the Cedars*, 31.

24   Chesnutt, *The House Behind the Cedars*, 135.

25   Edward W. Said, *Reflections on Exile and Other Essays* (Cambridge, Mass.: Harvard University Press, 2000), 186.

26   Chesnutt, *The House Behind the Cedars*, 19–20; emphasis added.

27   Gibel Azoulay's movement toward "becoming" as the deepest significance of the interracial body while disrupting some of its logic could be read as the deepest instantiation of the self in the West.

28   Chesnutt, *The House Behind the Cedars*, 47.

29   Chesnutt, *The House Behind the Cedars*, 52.

30   Jay Kameron Carter observes this dynamic of the relationship between whiteness/masculinity and blackness/femininity in Frederick Douglass' 1845 *Narrative* suggesting that by "positioning himself on the one hand as having overcome the black feminine and the on-the-ground expressions of black folklife, including its so-called feminine-like expressions of Christianity, and on the other hand as having overcome Covey's position of white, racial authority, Douglass can re-present himself as the masculine 'master' of his own fate" (Jay Kameron Carter, *Race: A Theological Account* [Oxford: Oxford University Press, 2008], 304).

31   Chesnutt, *The House Behind the Cedars*, 57.

32   Chesnutt, *The House Behind the Cedars*, 135.

33   Chesnutt, *The House Behind the Cedars*, 101.

34   Chesnutt, *The House Behind the Cedars*, 101.

35   Chesnutt, *The House Behind the Cedars*, 19.

36   In the background of this claim lies Hughes' own fascination with mixed race figures in his poetry and plays. In particular we see the trope of the tragic as a refusal of white paternal recognition. This is particularly clear in Hughes's play *Mulatto* where the protagonist refuses to take the place of a servant and asserts his status as a son in the post-reconstruction South. He ultimately kills the father and kills himself as his mother holds off the white mob gathered to lynch him. See Langston Hughes, *Mulatto* (Alexandria, Va.: Alexander Street Press, 2003).

37   Ariel Balter suggests *Autobiography* reveals a division of the author despite Johnson's repeated assertions that the book was not based on his own life. Butler suggests certain important parallels indicate a "divided self." Yet this assertion regarding a certain division seems to assent to a certain authenticity of African American existence. In my view, Johnson's participation in the African American middle class is no less important, but the way in which the concerns of African Americans became signified *through* this position is crucial. Thus, Johnson's own career exemplifies the attempt to display the decisions the narrator so often refused. These opportunities are those before many, regardless of their capacity to pass. It is the way in which these tools and endeavors are pursued that is important. *Autobiography* begins to unveil how Johnson seeks to live into or identify with the African American cause. The extent of this division as narrated through the life of the narrator is the mark of "double-consciousness" so famously discussed by W. E. B. Du Bois. This is the

mark of dark bodies in the world, and particularly in the United States that cannot be escaped. Thus, this division is not an aspect peculiar to Johnson, but to African American existence more universally. See Ariel Balter, "The Color of Money in *The Autobiography of an Ex-Coloured Man*." In *Complicating Constructions: Race, Ethnicity, and Hybridity in American Texts*, edited by David S. Goldstein and Audrey B. Thacker (Seattle: University of Washington Press, 2007), 50.

38   James Weldon Johnson, *The Autobiography of an Ex-Coloured Man* (New York: Vintage Books, 1989), 153.

39   Johnson, *Autobiography*, 139.

40   Johnson, *Autobiography*, 141.

41   Johnson, *Autobiography*, 154.

42   "Identification is a process of articulation, a suturing, an over-determination, not a subsumption" (Stuart Hall, "Who Needs Identity?" In *Questions of Cultural Identity*, 8). Here Hall points to the way in which identity is always tied to what he terms a process of identification, wherein identity is positional and strategic seeking to place the individual within larger moments of contestation. The central claim here is that such claims are not fixed but being perpetually negotiated, and being pieced together and incorporated into a functional view of oneself and one's position in the world.

43   Samira Kawash identifies this distance or vacillation as a type of negation wherein the action of passing, "the true authentic identity of the narrator can only be told as *not* being: the narrator does not name the truth because the truth (authentic, single, essential racial identity) *is not*" (Kawash, *Dislocating the Color Line*, 144).

44   Johnson, *Autobiography*, 14.

45   His entrance into these lives is marked by a clear lack of tension. The departure is never clear for he is a man without a homeland. This lack of real departure thus gives the title "ex-colored" a deep irony, for it was never clear he was truly colored to begin with. This irony serves to strike both at white audiences, for whom "one drop" is ontological, and African American readers as an ironic dismissal of the claim *ex-*, for he never knew what it meant in the first place.

46   James Weldon Johnson, *Along This Way: The Autobiography of James Weldon Johnson* (New York: Da Capo Press, 2000), 238.

47   Kawash notes, "He has transgressed or perverted the natural order, not because he has moved from one position in that order to another, but because his inauthentic (and therefore guilty) relation to every position upsets the very naturalness of that order" (*Dislocating the Color Line*, 151). Kawash believes the text itself serves to disrupt the epistemological rubric of race, thus opening up a space of racial disruption and the possibility of all lives. I differ with her slightly in this reading. While I concur with her assessment of the narrator's disruptive presence, I differ slightly in the aims of an open-ended becoming. As I will go on to show, the text itself serves as an alternative performance disrupting white notions of race while reifying expectations of black manhood (gendered language intentional here).

48   Johnson, *Along This Way*, 66.

49   Houston A. Baker, *Modernism and the Harlem Renaissance* (Chicago: University of Chicago Press, 1987), 15.

50   Alain Locke, *The New Negro*. In *The Norton Anthology of African American*

Literature, edited by Henry Louis Gates and Nellie Y. McKay (New York: W. W. Norton, 2004), 963.

51 George Hutchinson, *In Search of Nella Larsen: A Biography of the Color Line* (Cambridge, Mass.: Harvard University Press, 2006), 300.

52 Nella Larsen, *Passing* (New York: Modern Library, 2000), 23–24.

53 Larsen, *Passing*, 34.

54 See Zita C. Nunes, "Phantasmic Brazil: Nella Larsen's *Passing*, American Literary Imagination, and Racial Utopianism." In *Mixing Race, Mixing Culture: Inter-American Literary Dialogues*, edited by Monika Kaup and Debra J. Rosenthal (Austin: University of Texas Press, 2002).

55 Larsen, *Passing*, 43.

56 Hutchinson, *In Search of Nella Larsen*, 295.

57 Larsen, *Passing*, 62.

58 For an interesting account of Clare's disruption as one of class and consumption, see Martha J. Cutter, "Sliding Significations: Passing as a Narrative and Textual Strategy in Nella Larsen's Fiction." In *Passing and the Fictions of Identity*, edited by Elaine K. Ginsberg (Durham, N.C.: Duke University Press, 1996).

59 Larsen, *Passing*, 111.

60 Elaine Ginsberg makes a crucial observation regarding the fictive and historical depictions of passing suggesting, "although little is documented about the actual extent of race passing by blacks in the United States, the specter of passing derives its power not from the number of instances of passing but as a signification that embodies the anxieties and contradictions of a racially stratified society" (*Passing and the Fictions of Identity* [Durham, N.C.: Duke University Press, 1996], 8). Ginsberg's observation is a crucial distinction. Here the use of these novels is not to delineate from the historical phenomenon of "passing" certain features. Rather, my aim here is to draw from these literatures both performances of race themselves, as they seek to articulate and rearticulate race, and as such note the way in which passing serves to reinforce or undermine the conscription of racial adherents into the twentieth century. In many ways historical accounts would do little to convey the power of the mulatto figure or the one who passes into white life, for, as these authors note, the true power of these lives is both the performance of racial life internal to their decisions and, more importantly, the reverberations these lives made in the worlds they inhabited. Thus we know historically that these bodies existed, but we draw upon these fictive descriptions to mine for the deeper significance of these lives and their varying receptions.

61 The notion of becoming has developed into a particularly helpful way of resisting the stultifying effects of normative identities in recent cultural theory. Beginning with Judith Butler and more recently discussed by Azoulay and Samira Kawash, the notion of becoming seeks to articulate the centrality of identity within a trajectory of possibility where persons must be free to articulate or declare their own personhood without the fetters of normativity delimiting the claims they make for themselves. Such a narrative is, in my view, peculiarly American, but nonetheless problematic in its lack of attendance to the necessary limitations of any life. We are not free to become, but rather we are bound to those we love and those whom we do not in ways that always complicate our hopes for ourselves. In fact, I am not sure it is possible to

articulate a hope or a desire without one who has hoped or desired for me, or those who have sought to manipulate my hopes or desires. I am very rarely free for I am continuously living into forms of life circumscribed by any number of claims. The question is not a telos of becoming, but what *is* the telos of becoming.

62   More could and should be said about how gender is infused within this economy of passing and transgression, and I regrettably do not have the space to begin to account for it here.

63   Suzanne Bost, *Mulattas and Mestizas: Representing Mixed Identities in the Americas, 1850-2000* (Athens: University of Georgia Press, 2003), 2.

64   Katya Gibel Azoulay, *Black, Jewish, and Interracial: It's Not the Color of Your Skin, but the Race of Your Kin: And Other Myths of Identity* (Durham, N.C.: Duke University Press, 1997), 188.

65   Ginsberg, *Passing and the Fictions of Identity*, 16.

66   The Black Christ is an attempt to claim Christ's body for the inclusion of a people for whom the "white Christ" was a mark of their own inclusion. See Douglas, Kelly Brown. *The Black Christ* (Maryknoll, N.Y.: Orbis, 1994). An important counterpoint within such contextual theologies is the contextual invocation of cultural mixture conceived by Virgilio Elizondo, who describes Christ within the context of the North American borderlands and the peoples who were in one moment citizens of Mexico and, in another, citizens of a United States territory. His research offers some interesting overlaps concerning the Christianity born of colonial Spanish rule, the Latino culture birthed from its presence, and Jesus' location as a Jew in occupied Judea. His work offered an important beginning to the possibility of articulating Jesus as one who broke open a social space where lives and the subsequent church could be reimagined as a mestizo or hybrid people. See Virgilio P. Elizondo, *The Future Is Mestizo: Life Where Cultures Meet* (Boulder: University Press of Colorado, 2000).

Chapter 3

1   Langston Hughes, "Christ in Alabama." In *The Collected Works of Langston Hughes*, 16 vols. (Columbia: University of Missouri Press, 2001).

2   In this way Feuerbach was right to question the relationship between theology and anthropology.

3   Homi K. Bhabha, *The Location of Culture* (London: Routledge, 1994).

4   Bhabha, *The Location of Culture*, 13.

5   Ignatius of Antioch, "Letters of Ignatius: Trallians." In *Early Christian Fathers*, edited by Cyril C. Richardson (New York: Macmillan, 1970), 9.1, 100.

6   In drawing out the personhood of Christ that Chalcedon describes as a negation I am in one sense drawing on a longer tradition of apophatic theology that describes God through negations, or what God is not. I will draw on this discussion in relation to Chalcedon more specifically below. However, in speaking of descriptions of Jesus' personhood through negation I am also suggesting there is a peculiar paradox of presence in the midst of these negations. That is, while we speak of God as not limited, for instance, we struggle to apprehend how God is everywhere, while also present to us. But in confessing who Christ is we are more specifically confessing the presence of one who is not limited to a particular space. In this way, while

Christ's personhood must be expressed through a certain set of negations, he is none-theless actually present, taking up space in the world. This difficulty of negating descriptions and actual presence is a phenomenon not exclusive to descriptions of who Christ is (although there are particular difficulties exclusive to him regarding his humanity and divinity), but this difficulty is constitutive of any anthropological description. The mulatto body raises this dynamic of anthropological description to the fore. It is not exclusive to mixed-race bodies, but constitutes any articulation of personhood. Chalcedon is an example of not only an attempt to describe Christ, but also an attempt to articulate Christ as the ground of any theological anthropology. In other words, can we describe what it means to be human without Chalcedon?

7   It should be said here that Mary's fulfillment of this promise expresses the deepest mark of Israelite identity. The purity of these people lies not only in their "biologi-cal" purity, but rather the way in which they allow their lives to display their pecu-liar character as a people made from nothing. The unfolding narrative of Israel's birth and dependence (or refusal) of God's abiding presence among them is marked at times by biological purity, while at other times their very existence is redeemed through foreigners whose deep faithfulness in the God of Israel sustains Israel's own existence. What these disparate accounts reveal is that the cultural reality of Israel's life, the purity of their obedience is not dependent upon racial purity, but rather a purity of obedience displaying the presence and love of God to the world. See Walter Brueggemann, *Theology of the Old Testament: Testimony, Dispute, Advocacy* (Minne-apolis: Fortress, 1997). This display of obedience creates among these Judaic people a space where aliens can reside, can become grafted into a people. Israel is thus a people whose purity is bound to their faithfulness, opening them up to contamina-tion. The purification of Israel comes not through a biological intermixture, but rather through encounters that serve to tear Israel away from their own faithfulness. This ultimately constitutes who they are.

8   It is not my contention by invoking the term "hybridity" that the discourse concern-ing Christ is hybrid or an amalgamation of theories and doctrines. The varying attempts to explicate the mystery of Christ's person represent, in my view, an unfold-ing and narrowing explication of Christ's person rather than a "picking and choos-ing" of theories that fit an *a priori* philosophical judgment.

9   "The Definition of Chalcedon (451)." In *The Creeds of the Churches: A Reader in Christian Doctrine from the Bible to the Present*, edited by John H. Leith (Louisville: John Knox, 1982), 36.

10   Sarah Coakley, "What Does Chalcedon Solve and What Does It Not? Some Reflec-tions on the Status and Meaning of the Chalcedonian 'Definition.'" In *The Incarna-tion: An Interdisciplinary Symposium on the Incarnation of the Son of God*, edited by Daniel Kendall, Stephen T. Davis, SJ, and Gerald O'Collins, SJ (Oxford: Oxford University Press, 2002), 162.

11   Bhabha, *Location of Culture*, 55.

12   Here I am not suggesting that the participants at Chalcedon had this notion of inter-stitial existence or hybridity in mind. Rather, I am simply seeking to demonstrate how Chalcedon might be interpreted within contemporary theology given the chal-lenges hybridity and interracial identity pose to racial and cultural claims regarding life.

13 Maximus, *On the Cosmic Mystery of Jesus Christ: Selected Writings from St. Maximus the Confessor*, translated by Paul M. Blowers and Robert Louis Wilken (Crestwood, N.Y.: St. Vladimir's Seminary Press, 2003), 125.

14 Maximus' reiteration of Chalcedon came at a time when Chalcedon itself was being invoked in various christological controversies seeking to determine Christ's person-hood. Maximus' reiteration sought to maintain the tension inherent in Chalcedon's claims. It was within this tension, for Maximus, that the redeeming work of Christ was actually found. Within God's own life all difference was found and circum-scribed. To seek to resolve some difference as outside of God was to refuse a funda-mental aspect of who God was and, relatedly, who humanity could become. This reading of Maximus is slightly different than that of some scholars, most notably Hans Urs von Balthasar, who suggested Maximus' reiteration of Chalcedon repre-sented more of a synthesis of opposing views. In my view, the notion of synthesis is to refuse the possibility of holding what appear to be contradictions within a unified vision of humanity or personhood. Balthasar's description of Maximus' thought as synthesis is to fundamentally refuse the mystery of mutually present "high and low" in Christ's own person, thus transforming the low into the high. See Hans Urs von Balthasar, *Cosmic Liturgy: The Universe According to Maximus the Confessor* (San Francisco: Ignatius Press, 2003).

15 Most scholars acknowledge the deep connection between Nicaea and Chalcedon, suggesting that the conclusions reached in Chalcedon were not additions, but merely clarifications. In this regard, even looking at the early formulations in Nicaea regarding the relationship of the Son to the Father we see this paradoxical formula of negation and assertion in seeking to articulate the divinity of the Son. The Son is God, but the Son is not the Father, just as the Father is not the Son. Yet both are God. This difficult admixture of assertion and negation is thus not an innovation in Chalcedon, but Chalcedon simply made explicit this notion regarding the nature of Christ's person *in se*, whereas Nicaea was seeking to assert the identity of Christ through his relationship to the Father.

16 Jay Kameron Carter, "Introduction to Christian Theology" (lecture, Duke Divinity School, Durham, N.C., Fall 2008).

17 I should say here that in suggesting this interpretation of Chalcedon I am not argu-ing that the members of the councils had "inter" existence or notions of mixture in mind. Yet, in their final formulation what we do see is a certain intuition regarding the paradoxical nature of the incarnation and the ways in which it renders Jesus as a sort of "neither nor—but." Here the articulations of Jesus' person seem wary of the claims of purity on either side of the formula, whether they be claims concerning his humanity or his divinity.

18 Cyril, *Cyril of Alexandria*, translated by Norman Russell (London: Routledge, 2000), 135.

19 Cyril, "Commentary on John." In *The Christological Controversy, Sources of Early Christian Thought*, edited by Richard A. Norris (Philadelphia: Fortress, 1980).

20 Cyril, *Cyril of Alexandria*, 136.

21 Nestorius, "Nestorius' Second Letter to Cyril." In *The Christological Controversies*, 138.

22 Cyril, *Cyril of Alexandria*, 141.

23   Cyril, *Cyril of Alexandria*, 141.
24   Apollinaris, "On the Union in Christ of the Body with the Godhead." In *The Christological Controversies*, section 10, 106.
25   Apollinaris, "On the Union in Christ of the Body with the Godhead." In *The Christological Controversies*, para. 9, 108; emphasis added.
26   The transformation of the one who is reflected and lived into this word is exemplified for Athanasius in the life of Saint Antony. His life transfigures, in a sense, the possibility of the mind living into the perfection of the Word where one's life is ordered properly. However, this ordering also becomes impressed into the lives of those who gaze upon the life of one who has been so conformed, so as to be drawn, themselves, into this possibility of transformation.
27   This is not explicitly stated in the text, but the implication of mixture was a common accusation of the Alexandrians. See Frances M. Young, *The Making of the Creeds* (Philadelphia: SCM Press, 1991).
28   Cyril, *Cyril of Alexandria*, 142.
29   Young, *Making of the Creeds*, 79.
30   Apollinaris, "On the Union in Christ of the Body with the Godhead." In *The Christological Controversies*, Para. 10, 108.
31   Cyril, *Cyril of Alexandria*, 101.
32   Cyril, *Cyril of Alexandria*, 174.
33   Cyril, *Cyril of Alexandria*, 143.

Chapter 4

1   José F. Buscaglia-Salgado, *Undoing Empire: Race and Nation in the Mulatto Caribbean* (Minneapolis: University of Minnesota Press, 2003), xvii.
2   Irenaeus of Lyon, "Against Heresies." In *Irenaeus of Lyons*, edited by Robert McQueen Grant (New York: Routledge, 1997), III 22.2, 139.
3   The theological tradition of deification has certainly sought to describe this mysterious "new creature." I am not suggesting mulatto as a theological category serves as a contemporary notion of theosis, although I am drawing strongly upon this body of work. In my view, contemporary expressions of deification have outlined the way modernity has formed bodies in ways that are analogous to, yet a distortion of, this bodily iconicity, and because of this it has not adequately expressed the political realities such a claim makes.
4   While this paraphrase could be considered Barth's overarching theme throughout the dogmatics we see this particular construction of Jesus taking on humanity in *Church Dogmatics* IV.1 §59.1, "The Way of the Son of God into the Far Country" and especially page 158 where Barth writes, "In being gracious to man in Jesus Christ, He also goes into the far country, into the evil society of this being which is not God and against God." Of course there are numerous places in *CD* where this theme is explicated. This is simply one example.
5   Barth, *Church Dogmatics*, III.2, 327.
6   Barth, *Church Dogmatics*, I.2, 156.
7   Barth, *Church Dogmatics*, IV.1, 12.

8   Barth, *Church Dogmatics*, IV.1, 14.

9   Barth, *Church Dogmatics*, IV.1, 15.

10 Barth, *Church Dogmatics*, III.2, 133.

11 Irenaeus of Lyon, "Against Heresies," III, 22.4, 140.

12 See Stuart Hall, "Who Needs Identity?" In *Questions of Cultural Identity*, edited by Paul du Gray and Stuart Hall (London: Sage, 1996).

13 Here I am drawing again on Stuart Hall's important synthesis of critical theory that shows how identities are, in fact, the sum of discourse or processes of naming and differentiation that are both explicit and implicit.

14 This act of identification was described by Balthasar as a connection between Christ's person and Christ's mission. On this point, Balthasar represents an important clarification of Barth regarding the aim of this identity and mission as the instantiation of a "new rhythm" or "pneumatic personhood." Balthasar suggests, "the question of his work implies the question of his person: Who *must* he be, to behave and act in this way? [...this leads from] Christ's overt *function* to his covert *being*." (Hans Urs von Balthasar, *Theo-Drama: Theological Dramatic Theory*, 5 vols.[San Francisco: Ignatius Press, 1988], III, 149; emphasis added).

15 This is not to suggest this transformation is not present in Barth, but in my view is continually suppressed beneath the utter power and totality of God's word. This word and this reconciliation is certainly transformative, but one must work a bit harder to discern the nature of the transformed life in Barth. Balthasar's conception of this unity of person and work I take to be deeply indebted and congruous with Barth and thus the implied transformation. I understand to be crucial Balthasar's clarity of this transformation and the clear connection of this transformed life to a life in the Spirit.

16 Balthasar, *Theo-Drama: Theological Dramatic Theory*, III, 510.

17 Balthasar, *Theo-Drama: Theological Dramatic Theory*, III, 509.

18 Buscaglia-Salgado, *Undoing Empire*, xvii. Buscaglia-Salgado's observation regarding the nature of mulatto existence in the nascent life of Spanish colonial life and what would eventually become Caribbean identity, contains an important point of difference with the development of mulatto identity in the United States. The Caribbean (and some might suggest Latino) cultures which arose from these mixtures would eventually find themselves independent of the physical presence of such colonial markers as Western colonizers eventually returned to their "homeland." The consequence was the negotiation or development of identities that existed in the shadows of their fathers, but without their explicit presence. This is an important difference, for while these cultures are still marked by a profound "calculus of color," they nonetheless developed a certain amalgamation of cultural forms that would soon constitute their own particularities (Jamaican, Bermudian, Trinidadian, etc.). These particularities could still be understood as seeking to perform out of a certain problematic relationship with the West, yet also represent a fruit of this encounter that is *more than* the parts that gave birth to it. That is, there is a real sense in which to not understand the colonial and colonized figures and nations, which is to misapprehend the personhood that constitutes them. They are *more than*. This mulattic structure articulated as birth becomes radicalized, in my view, in the birth of Christ and the performance of his life as he gathers up the articulations of his people and

those whom he encounters and performs them into—himself rearticulating our own lives and hopes, himself becoming something new so that we might become something new.

19   Interestingly, the fact that Ruth is included in the Davidic line that constitutes Joseph's lineage also serves to disrupt notions of identity that are biologically consti- tuted, but nonetheless become present in the constellation of relationships that mark Jesus' life. He is not "of" Joseph, and yet Joseph's listening to Mary binds him to the promise and the fulfillment of the promise as now coming forth through him and his faithfulness.

20   Willie James Jennings. "The Black Church and Christian Identity" (lecture, Duke Divinity School, Durham, N.C., Spring 2003).

21   Dietrich Bonhoeffer, *Christ the Center*, translated by Eberhard Bethge (New York: Harper & Row, 1966).

22   Panayiotis Nellas, *Deification in Christ: The Nature of the Human Person* (Crestwood, N.Y.: St. Vladimir's Seminary Press, 1997), 42.

23   See chapter 3.

24   Jay Kameron Carter, "Introduction to Christian Theology" (lecture, Duke Divinity School, Durham, N.C., Fall 2008).

25   Augustine, *The Trinity* (Washington, D.C.: Catholic University of America Press, 1963), IX.8, 275.

26   Augustine, *The Trinity*, VIII.12, 254.

27   Augustine, *The Confessions*, translated by Maria Boulding (New York: Vintage Books, 1998).

28   Athanasius, *On the Incarnation* (Crestwood, N.Y.: St. Vladimir's Seminary Press, 2003), 30.

29   It is at this point that this theology should be understood as markedly different from the contextual Christologies and their accompanying theologies of the last forty years. Claims regarding the Black Christ or Jesus as liberator of the poor are on one level attempts to articulate Jesus' voice in the midst of a particular human situation, and as this investigation has sought to show this is not extraneous to his person. Yet, his life is marked by a more profound entry into such disparate lives, there- fore such claims do not serve to transform identity, but to reify and harden identity while transforming societies' reception of that identity. The claim regarding Christ's identity is one that transforms the political space, the reception of identity through a reconfiguration of where God can abide. Yet it also transforms those who par- ticipate in this presence by incorporating them into his own life, wherein a personal transformation also takes place. Here the personal becomes bound to the communal life of Christ, the church. Such a transformation is necessarily understood within Christ's person and thus resists any attempts implicit (European theology) or explicit (contextual theologies) to assert an identity as dominant within the person of Christ that does not hold within it the transgression of identity and the patterns of life and loving that are bound to those identities.

30   That Jesus reminds us that those who mourn will be comforted could be understood within this trajectory. It is the inevitability of loss, the death of "family," as one is incorporated into a new family. This among other marks of death and loss are marks of a life in Christ that does not overcome the tragic by bypassing it, but it is entered

into and comforted as those who lose gain a life of wider possibilities, neighbors, mothers, brothers, sisters, and fathers.

31   Barth, *Church Dogmatics*, 1.2, 134.

32   Philip Roth, *The Human Stain* (Boston: Houghton Mifflin, 2000).

Chapter 5

1   Cyril, *St. Cyril of Jerusalem's Lectures*, 61.

2   I should say here briefly that this conception of baptism seeks to make room for traditions of infant and believer's baptism. As I will show in the unfolding of this chapter, the baptismal moment is one grounded in Christ's baptism into us and thus has its efficacy not in its own mode or timing, but rather in its instantiation through the Word's incarnate presence among us. The question is not what is the way we enter into this presence, but rather what kind of people does this practice create.

3   Athanasius, *On the Incarnation : The Treatise De Incarnatione Verbi Dei* (Crestwood, N.Y.: St. Vladimir's Seminary Press, 2003).

4   Bonaventure, *Bonaventure*, translated by Ewert H. Cousins (New York: Paulist Press, 1978), 149.

5   However, in Bonaventure this communication is seen not in universal terms, as we see in Athanasius, in terms of the incarnation of the word. Rather, suffering is the means of this communication. The possibility of this embodiment or communication is seen most clearly for Bonaventure in the life of Saint Francis, who so succumbed to the fruits of Christ's work in him that he himself began to exhibit the qualities of the word of God upon his very body through the stigmata. But here the stigmata is only the intensification of a wider set of markers which were evident in the life of Francis: healing, devotion, sacrifice, wisdom, sight, etc.

6   Cyril, *St. Cyril of Jerusalem's Lectures*, 63.

7   2 Cor 5:17.

8   Jean Zizioulas, *Being as Communion: Studies in Personhood and the Church* (Crestwood, N.Y.: St. Vladimir's Seminary Press, 1985), 56.

9   Zizioulas, *Being as Communion*, 56.

10   Zizioulas, *Being as Communion*, 57.

11   Nellas, *Deification in Christ*. This phrase occurs regularly in this work.

12   Here Calvin's understanding of baptism's initiatory function is helpful. For Calvin, baptism is an initiation not only into the life of the church, but more profoundly an initiation into Christ's life and work. The power of such a moment is its fundamental reality. The baptismal moment is complete insofar as Christ's work is already complete within the life of the one who participates in the rite. Here the nature of the transformation is less a consideration of the believer's state of mind or "faith" as one who is capable of knowing, but rather the nature of Christ's salvific work is what makes the baptismal moment efficacious. It is a complete moment in which the believer must participate. It is a sign not of what preceded in the life of the believer, but rather it is a sign of transformation that entered the world through Christ.

13   Cyril, *St. Cyril of Jerusalem's Lectures*.

14   Nellas, *Deification in Christ*, 33–34.

15   Nellas, *Deification in Christ*, 32.

16 Teresa of Avila, *Interior Castle*, translated by E. Allison Peers (New York: Double-day, 1990), 29.

17 Teresa of Avila, *Interior Castle*, 29; emphasis added.

18 Teresa of Avila, *Interior Castle*, 214.

19 Nicholas Cabasilas, *The Life in Christ* (Crestwood, N.Y.: St. Vladimir's Seminary Press, 1974), 46.

20 Cabasilas, *The Life in Christ*, 46.

21 The importance of baptism's efficacy in this conflation of bodily and spiritual iden-tity is one that does not require the ascension of adult baptism or the infused grace of infant baptism. In this view baptism is an initiation into the life of transforma-tion. This transformation is wrought through the baptismal waters and requires continual participation in the life of the community to convey and infuse the trans-formation of one's identity. This process is a fully participatory one in the case of adult baptism because the new believer participates in the transformation of this self-understanding. In the case of infant baptism, however, the child is conformed into these identities through the participatory confession and witness of the com-munity. In both cases the transformative reality requires the cumulative witness of a community which claims them and to which they see themselves as having been engrafted to. In this regard, the community itself becomes transformed in the addi-tion to the child of God, regardless of its baptism as an infant or adult, for it is the process of discipleship that is both a personal and a communal reality into which the child of God is born.

22 Augustine, *The Trinity*.

23 Cabasilas, *The Life in Christ*, Book III.1, 103.

24 I should say here that we must be wary of making the act of speaking in tongues an achievement, a "necessity" of our humanity which somehow marks us as qualified. E.g., in Mary, her humanity was revealed in her apprehension, her reception of God. Her life was received. Her own humanity was filled out in her own womb. Speaking in tongues is not a mark of our accomplishment, but a witness to our humanity, the possibility of our lives bearing God. In this way it is not a necessity, for our humanity is not established in our acts, but rather in God's bearing us. Our humanity is filled out in the word, the strange tongues uttered to us. Our speaking in tongues is not achieving our humanity, but rather living into it. There are any number of ways in which we resist this just as those who speak in tongues resist, but nonetheless this possibility of speaking, the possibility of interpretation, of healing, etc. must always lie before us as a possibility that may come upon us. What this points us to is that our humanity was established and made full in Christ. It is his person that is our full humanity. It is this intermingling of flesh and Spirit that enlivens us, that marks our humanity and our possibilities. The reception of these possibilities is the reception and formation of lives whose very presence, whose utterances of desire, hope, faith, and love, disrupt the patterns of certainty and injustice in the world.

25 Again, the claim "to be human is to speak in tongues" does not seek to suggest that those who speak in tongues are "more human" than those who do not. The possibil-ity that we might pray in tongues suggests that our humanity must be understood in relationship to the ways in which our bodies are enlivened and imbued with the Spirit. That one speaks in tongues does not give them a claim to a status higher

than others. If it is wielded in ways that serve to determine what another cannot become, then this is to ignore the necessity of their own interpretation. This gap and misuse is certainly present in some pentecostal and charismatic churches, just as it becomes present in many other churches. The claim being made here is not intended to uplift the superiority of certain bodies, but rather suggest that Christian lives must be intelligible in terms of the impression upon them by the Spirit of God. This impression thus leaves no body or life complete or fixed, but opens it to be transformed. Thus communities seeking to conform into Christ's struggle to live into this possibility, mark the struggle of all bodies to be conformed into this image. These bodies of flesh and Spirit continually indicate their fullness through the One who is beyond them and within them.

Chapter 6

1   Karl Barth, *The Holy Spirit and the Christian Life: The Theological Basis of Ethics*, translated by Robin W. Lovin (Louisville, Ky.: Westminster John Knox, 1993), 67.

2   "Letter to Diognetus." In *Early Christian Fathers*, edited by Cyril C. Richardson (New York: Collier), 217.5.

3   This is not to suggest that baptism and Eucharist are not fundamental to the Christian life or identity, but neither can be located within the daily life of the disciple in the way that prayer can. In this regard, prayer does the work of extending the power and the possibility of the baptismal and Eucharistic moment while also adding a certain texture to the claims often made about baptism and Eucharist.

4   Barth, *The Holy Spirit and the Christian Life*, 67.

5   Barth, *Church Dogmatics*, IV.1. 120.

6   Barth, *Church Dogmatics*, IV.1. 120.

7   Bonhoeffer, *Christ the Center*.

8   Barth, *Church Dogmatics*, IV.1. Barth's consideration of reconciliation is helpful here in his description of Christ as "God with us." In this formulation we see the way in which the prayer life of Jesus is both working upon humanity and for humanity. It both confirms Jesus' sonship, yet instantiates something real within humanity that will later become the gift of the Spirit that utters prayers from within.

9   Barth, *Church Dogmatics*, IV.2. Barth is again instructive here as he narrates the ways in which humanity seeks to assert itself even in the midst of God's redemptive work. This theme, ubiquitous in the *Church Dogmatics*, will be drawn upon heavily to outline the way in which racial lives are an aspect of such self-assertion. Also instructive here will be various enlightenment accounts of the self (Kant, Hegel) which outline the way in which the mind's relationship to the body orders identity and the shape of daily life.

10 For example see Cedric Herring, Verna Keith, and Hayward Derrick Horton, *Skin Deep: How Race and Complexion Matter in the "Color-Blind" Era* (Urbana: University of Illinois Press, 2004).

11 For Augustine there can be little distinction between eternity and the Trinitarian relations. These relations constitute eternity inasmuch as eternity describes the relationships. It is this disctinction between time and eternity which thus serves as the basis of our understanding of creaturely existence. Yet, this is not something distinct

from the Triune God, but rather time is that which is made possible through the Triune God whose triune relationship constitutes eternity. The fundamental mark of creation is its createdness. The *imago dei* rests in its abiding in God's eternity, wherein it could love God and move toward God without hesitation.

In this way the fall marks the corruption of eternity in time, the presence of a gap between one's conception of God and one's movement toward God. As one begins to love this gap or distance they become more deluded in the possibility that a fullness of desire or knowledge might actually lie within one's own knowing or loving, one's desires.

In this way, many of Augustine's primary conceptions of the Christian life in *Confessions*, the proper ordering of rationality, memory, love, and will, are as much a matter of time as they are about being properly disciplined. Or to be more precise, their disciplining arises out of their proper conception of time as that which in many ways stands between them and an eternal participation with the Triune God. In this way the restlessness Augustine speaks so eloquently of in the beginning of the *Confessions* is in fact speaking of that gap between time and eternity wherein one can recognize their own creatureliness, and in so doing begin to allow the eternal God to press in upon them. As they do so their memory, their love, their thought, and their hope becomes drawn into a simplicity of loving and thinking and willing that is the *imago dei*, the perfect relations of the Father to the Son in the Spirit that are without time. To be sure, for Augustine this moment of the eternal pressing in upon time is one that is perpetually resisted in the creature's own pride. Thus at every turn there lies the possibility of continuing to wallow in this gap, within time as though it represents the fullness of their desires, their thinking, and their hope.

The relationship between anthropology and the Triune God, for Augustine, is thus a relationship between time and eternity wherein the eternal is the triune and time is the creature. The creature's pride seeks to suggests its time is something more than it is, yet when it accedes to its own reality as that which is created by the eternal, it is lifted up out of its own condition where the gaps that exist between knowing and willing, hoping and loving, etc. begin.

12 See Balthasar, *Theo-Drama*. The notion of the Christian life reborn in God as a new rhythm is crucial here, where the entirety of one's movement, their material reality is caught up within a new time, a new way of counting that renders previous rhythms dissonant or "off" in such a way as can be *felt* within the texture of their life.

13 Willie James Jennings, "Wandering in the Wilderness: Christian Identity and Theology Between Context and Race." In *The Gospel in Black and White: Theological Resources for Racial Reconciliation*, edited by Dennis Okholm (Downers Grove, Ill.: Intervarsity, 1997), 36.

14 This is the fundamental problem with articulations of Christian identity as a "third race." It reproduces an identity bound within terms outside of Christ's own body. Racial identity is one bound intrinsically to a particular aspect of one's body, or at the very least a certain description of a body. Here identity is bound to Christ's body and identity is thus external to one's personhood. Thus the constellation of particularities that forge "a people" are both external and internal, in ways that are continually shifting, but perpetually tied to the abiding and eternal of the presence of God within and without.

15   In Nellas and Zizioulas, the pneumatological aspects of anthropology are crucial.
     Each will help to highlight the ways in which the dogmatic claims concerning
     Christ's life give shape to the claims being made about human lives, and specifically
     the pneumatological claims explicit within a reflection made about prayer.

16   Drawing again upon Barth's emphasis on Jesus' presence on both sides of the equa-
     tion I want to highlight here the way in which the ontological must be political. Spe-
     cifically, Christian claims concerning politics must outline forms of life with who we
     are in light of who Christ *is*. Such claims are inherently political because they require
     not only a response by the world, but the continual attempt to conform to such reali-
     ties within our own bodies. Thus the claim is both witnessing in its confession and
     confessing in its witness.

17   See Augustine, *The Confessions*. Here the way in which the dogmatic claims are
     ever-present within the prayers of *Confession*, as well as its very structure as a prayer,
     highlight the Christian life as seeking to conform to those that are both without and
     within it. It points to the life of discipleship as the continual prayer for faithfulness, a
     life of hope which itself witnesses to the possibility that we can become things radi-
     cally different than we once were.

18   Zizioulas, *Being as Communion*.

19   Barth, *Church Dogmatics*, IV.1. Here I am drawing on Barth's language of apprehen-
     sion to highlight the way in which such a life of discipleship refuses the tendency
     toward self-creation that is often a defining characteristic of interracial life as well
     as contextual theology. What will be important to highlight here is the radical way
     in which receptivity is a politics. It is in prayer that such a politics becomes bound
     necessarily to a spirituality within the life of discipleship.

20   See "Letter to Diognetus" and Ephesians 3. Both of these texts highlight the way in
     which Christian life is characterized through its presence and distance. Such lives
     are marked by neither the absence of "cultural" engagement nor the articulation of
     a contrary culture, but rather a peculiar relation to and within marks these lives.

21   Hans Urs von Balthasar, *Prayer* (San Francisco: Ignatius Press, 1986). Balthasar's
     repeatedly connecting the life of transformation and contemplative prayer are
     important here. See also Gregory of Nyssa, "On Religious Instruction." In *Christol-
     ogy of the Later Fathers*, edited by Edward Rochie Hardy, Library of Christian clas-
     sics, Ichthus edition (Philadelphia: Westminster, 1977). Nyssa provides a profound
     image of wax melting as it encounters the light of the word made flesh. Here I want
     to press this image further in a communal sense, where such softening is a perpetual
     mark of the church. Its members are becoming softened to one another, and each
     member becomes a "hybrid" of those they are near as they all seek to conform to the
     image of Christ who is among them in the Spirit.

22   Augustine, *The Trinity*.

BIBLIOGRAPHY

"Letter to Diognetus." In *Early Christian Fathers*, edited by Cyril C. Richardson. New York: Collier, 2006.

Allen, Pauline, and Bronwen Neil. *Maximus the Confessor and His Companions: Documents from Exile*. New York: Oxford University Press, 2002.

Anderson, Ray Sherman. *On Being Human: Essays in Theological Anthropology*. Grand Rapids: Eerdmans, 1982.

Anselm. *The Prayers and Meditations of St. Anselm*. Translated by Benedicta Ward. Harmondsworth: Penguin, 1973.

Apollinaris. "On the Union in Christ of the Body with the Godhead." In *The Christological Controversies*. Edited by Richard A. Norris Jr. Philadelphia: Fortress, 1980.

Athanasius. *On the Incarnation*. Crestwood, N.Y.: St. Vladimir's Seminary Press, 2003.

Augustine. *The Trinity*. Washington, D.C.: Catholic University of America Press, 1963.

———. *The Confessions*. Translated by Maria Boulding. New York: Vintage Books, 1998.

Avila, Teresa of. *Interior Castle*. Translated by E. Allison Peers. New York: Doubleday, 1990.

Azoulay, Katya Gibel. *Black, Jewish, and Interracial: It's Not the Color of Your Skin, but the Race of Your Kin: And Other Myths of Identity*. Durham, N.C.: Duke University Press, 1997.

Baker, Houston A. *Modernism and the Harlem Renaissance*. Chicago: University of Chicago Press, 1987.

Balter, Ariel. "The Color of Money in *The Autobiography of an Ex-Coloured Man*." In *Complicating Constructions: Race, Ethnicity, and Hybridity in American Texts*, edited by David S. Goldstein and Audrey B. Thacker. Seattle: University of Washington Press, 2007.

Balthasar, Hans Urs von. *Love Alone*. New York: Herder & Herder, 1969.

—. *Prayer*. San Francisco: Ignatius Press, 1986.

—. *Theo-Drama: Theological Dramatic Theory*. 5 vols. San Francisco: Ignatius Press, 1988.

—. *Cosmic Liturgy: The Universe According to Maximus the Confessor*. San Francisco: Ignatius Press, 2003.

Banks, Marcus. *Ethnicity: Anthropological Constructions*. London: Routledge, 1996.

Barth, Karl. *The Epistle to the Romans*. Translated by Edwyn Clement Hoskyns. London: Oxford University Press, 1933.

—. *Church Dogmatics*. Translated by Geoffrey William Bromiley and Thomas Forsyth Torrance. Edinburgh: T&T Clark, 1975.

—. *The Holy Spirit and the Christian Life: The Theological Basis of Ethics*. Translated by Robin W. Lovin. Louisville, Ky.: Westminster John Knox, 1993.

—. *Prayer*. Translated by Don E. Saliers. Louisville, Ky.: Westminster John Knox, 2002.

Berzon, Judith R. *Neither White nor Black: The Mulatto Character in American Fiction*. New York: New York University Press, 1978.

Bhabha, Homi K. *The Location of Culture*. London: Routledge, 1994.

Blank, Rebecca M., Marilyn Dabady, and Constance F. Citro. *Measuring Racial Discrimination*. Washington, D.C.: National Academies Press, 2004.

Blumenbach, Johann Friedrich. *The Anthropological Treatises*. Translated by Thomas Bendyshe. London: Longman, 1865.

Bonaventure. *Bonaventure*. Translated by Ewert H. Cousins. New York: Paulist Press, 1978.

Bonhoeffer, Dietrich. *Life Together*. Translated by John W. Doberstein. New York: Harper & Row, 1954.

—. *Christ the Center*. Translated by Eberhard Bethge. New York: Harper & Row, 1966.

—. *The Cost of Discipleship*. London: SCM Press, 2001.

Bost, Suzanne. *Mulattas and Mestizas: Representing Mixed Identities in the Americas, 1850–2000*. Athens: University of Georgia Press, 2003.

Bourdieu, Pierre. *The Logic of Practice*. Stanford, Calif.: Stanford University Press, 1990.

Brah, A., and Annie E. Coombes. *Hybridity and Its Discontents: Politics, Science, Culture*. London: Routledge, 2000.

Brennan, Jonathan. *Mixed Race Literature*. Stanford, Calif.: Stanford University Press, 2002.

Brown, Delwin, Sheila Greeve Davaney, Kathryn Tanner, and American Academy of Religion. *Converging on Culture: Theologians in Dialogue with Cultural Analysis and Criticism*. Oxford: Oxford University Press, 2001.

Brueggemann, Walter. *Theology of the Old Testament: Testimony, Dispute, Advocacy*. Minneapolis: Fortress, 1997.

Buscaglia-Salgado, José F. *Undoing Empire: Race and Nation in the Mulatto Caribbean*. Minneapolis: University of Minnesota Press, 2003.

Butler, Judith. *Subjects of Desire: Hegelian Reflections in Twentieth-Century France*. New York: Columbia University Press, 1987.

———. *Gender Trouble: Feminism and the Subversion of Identity*. New York: Routledge, 1990.

Cabasilas, Nicholas. *The Life in Christ*. Crestwood, N.Y.: St. Vladimir's Seminary Press, 1974.

Caldwell, Kia Lilly. *Negras in Brazil: Re-Envisioning Black Women, Citizenship, and the Politics of Identity*. New Brunswick, N.J.: Rutgers University Press, 2007.

Carter, J. Kameron. *Race: A Theological Account*. Oxford: Oxford University Press, 2008.

Certeau, Michel de. *The Practice of Everyday Life*. Berkeley: University of California Press, 1984.

Chesnutt, Charles Waddell. *The Journals of Charles W. Chesnutt*. Edited by Richard H. Brodhead. Durham, N.C.: Duke University Press, 1993.

———. "To Be an Author." In *Letters of Charles W. Chesnutt, 1889–1905*, edited by Joseph R. McElrath and Robert C. Leitz. Princeton: Princeton University Press, 1997.

———. *Paul Marchand, F.M.C.* Jackson: University Press of Mississippi, 1998.

———. *The Quarry*. Edited by Dean McWilliams. Princeton: Princeton University Press, 1999.

———. *Charles W. Chesnutt: Essays and Speeches*. Edited by Joseph R. McElrath, Robert C. Leitz and Jesse S. Crisler. Stanford, Calif.: Stanford University Press, 1999.

———. *Conjure Tales and Stories of the Color Line*. New York: Penguin, 2000.

———. *An Exemplary Citizen: Letters of Charles W. Chesnutt, 1906–1932*. Edited by Jesse S. Crisler, Robert C. Leitz and Joseph R. McElrath. Stanford, Calif.: Stanford University Press, 2002.

———. *Stories, Novels, & Essays*. New York: Penguin, 2002.

———. *The House Behind the Cedars*. New York: Modern Library, 2003.

Coakley, Sarah. "What Does Chalcedon Solve and What Does It Not? Some Reflections on the Status and Meaning of the Chalcedonian 'Definition.'" In *The Incarnation: An Interdisciplinary Symposium on the Incarnation of the Son of God*, edited by Daniel Kendall, Stephen T. Davis, SJ, Gerald O'Collins, SJ. Oxford: Oxford University Press, 2002.

Cobb, Kelton. *The Blackwell Guide to Theology and Popular Culture*. Malden, Mass.: Blackwell, 2005.

Cone, James H. *Black Theology and Black Power*. Maryknoll, N.Y.: Orbis, 1997.

————. *For My People: Black Theology and the Black Church*. Maryknoll, N.Y.: Orbis Books, 1984.

————. *God of the Oppressed*. Maryknoll, N.Y.: Orbis Books, 1997.

Connerton, Paul. *How Societies Remember* (Themes in the Social Sciences). Cambridge: Cambridge University Press, 1989.

Cooper, Adam G. *The Body in St. Maximus the Confessor: Holy Flesh, Wholly Deified*. Oxford: Oxford University Press, 2005.

Crooly, David Goodman, and George Wakeman, *Miscegenation: The Theory of the Blending of the Races Applied to the American White Man and Negro*. New York: Dexter, Hamilton, 1864.

Cutter, Martha J. "Sliding Significations: Passing as a Narrative and Textual Strategy in Nella Larsen's Fiction." In *Passing and the Fictions of Identity*, edited by Elaine K. Ginsberg. Durham, N.C.: Duke University Press, 1996.

Cyril of Alexandria. *A Collection of Unpublished Syriac Letters of Cyril of Alexandria*. 2 vols. Edited by R. Y. Ebied and Lionel R. Wickham. Louvain: Peeters Publishing, 1975.

————. *Cyril of Alexandria, Select Letters*. Translated by Lionel R. Wickham. Oxford: Clarendon, 1983.

————. *St. Cyril of Alexandria: Letters*. Translated by John I. McEnerney. 2 vols. Washington, D.C.: Catholic University of America Press, 1987.

————. *On the Unity of Christ*. Translated by John Anthony McGuckin. Crestwood, N.Y.: St. Vladimir's Seminary Press, 1995.

————. *Cyril of Alexandria*. Translated by Norman Russell. London: Routledge, 2000.

Cyril of Jerusalem. *St. Cyril of Jerusalem's Lectures on the Christian Sacraments: The Procatechesis and the Five Mystagogical Catecheses*. Translated by F. L. Cross. Crestwood, N.Y.: St. Vladimir's Seminary Press, 1977.

DaCosta, Kimberly McClain. *Making Multiracials: State, Family, and Market in the Redrawing of the Color Line*. Stanford, Calif: Stanford University Press, 2007.

Douglas, Kelly Brown. *The Black Christ*. Maryknoll, N.Y.: Orbis, 1994.

Du Bois, W. E. B. *Dark Princess: A Romance*. New York: Oxford University Press, 2007.

Du Gay, Paul, and Stuart Hall. *Questions of Cultural Identity*. London: Sage, 1996.

Early, Gerald Lyn, ed. *Lure and Loathing: Essays on Race, Identity, and the Ambivalence of Assimilation*. New York: Penguin, 1994.

Elizondo, Virgilio P. *The Future Is Mestizo: Life Where Cultures Meet*. Boulder: University Press of Colorado, 2000.

Elizondo, Virgilio P., and Timothy M. Matovina. *Mestizo Worship: A Pastoral Approach to Liturgical Ministry*. Collegeville, Minn.: Liturgical Press, 1998.

Fabi, M. Giulia. "Reconstructing the Race: The Novel after Slavery." In *Cambridge Companion to African American Literature*, edited by Maryemma Graham. Cambridge: Cambridge University Press, 2004.

Fanon, Frantz. *Black Skin, White Masks*. New York: Grove Press, 1967.

Schüssler Fiorenza, Elisabeth. *Jesus: Miriam's Child, Sophia's Prophet: Critical Issues in Feminist Christology*. New York: Continuum, 1994.

Fox-Genovese, Elizabeth. *Within the Plantation Household: Black and White Women of the Old South*. Chapel Hill: University of North Carolina Press, 1988.

Gaddis, Michael and Richard Price, eds. *The Acts of the Council of Chalcedon*, Translated Texts for Historians 45. Liverpool: Liverpool University Press, 2005.

Gates, Henry Louis, and Nellie Y. McKay, eds. *The Norton Anthology of African American Literature*. New York: W. W. Norton, 2004.

Gilroy, Paul. *The Black Atlantic: Modernity and Double Consciousness*. Cambridge, Mass.: Harvard University Press, 1993.

————. *Against Race: Imagining Political Culture Beyond the Color Line*. Cambridge, Mass.: Harvard University Press, 2000.

Ginsberg, Elaine K., ed. *Passing and the Fictions of Identity*. Durham, N.C.: Duke University Press, 1996.

Goldstein, David S., and Audrey B. Thacker, eds. *Complicating Constructions: Race, Ethnicity, and Hybridity in American Texts*. Seattle: University of Washington Press, 2007.

Graham, Maryemma, ed. *Cambridge Companion to the African American Novel*. New York: Cambridge University Press, 2004.

Gregory of Nyssa, "On Religious Instruction." In *Christology of the Later Fathers*, edited by Edward Rochie Hardy. Philadelphia: Westminster, 1977.

Gutiérrez, Gustavo. *A Theology of Liberation: History, Politics, and Salvation*. Maryknoll, N.Y.: Orbis, 1988.

————.*On Job: God-Talk and the Suffering of the Innocent*. Maryknoll, N.Y.: Orbis, 1987.

Hall, Amy Laura. *Conceiving Parenthood*. Grand Rapids: Eerdmans, 2008.

Hall, Stuart. "Who Needs Identity?" In *Questions of Cultural Identity*, edited by Paul du Gay and Stuart Hall. London: Sage, 1996.

_____. *Without Guarantees: In Honour of Stuart Hall*. Edited by Paul Gilroy, Lawrence Grossberg and Angela McRobbie. London: Verso, 2000.

Hall, Stuart, David Held, and Anthony G. McGrew. *Modernity and Its Futures*. Cambridge: Polity Press in association with the Open University, 1992.

Hall, Stuart, David Morley, and Kuan-Hsing Chen. *Stuart Hall: Critical Dialogues in Cultural Studies*. London: Routledge, 1996.

Harnack, Adolf von. *What Is Christianity?* New York: Harper, 1957.

Herring, Cedric, Verna Keith, and Hayward Derrick Horton. *Skin Deep: How Race and Complexion Matter in the "Color-Blind" Era*. Urbana: University of Illinois Press, 2004.

Hiraldo, Carlos. *Segregated Miscegenation: On the Treatment of Racial Hybridity in the U.S. and Latin American Literary Traditions*. New York: Routledge, 2003.

Hughes, Langston. *Something in Common, and Other Stories*. New York: Hill & Wang, 1963.

———. *The Ways of White Folks*. New York: Vintage Books, 1990.

———. *The Collected Poems of Langston Hughes*. Edited by Arnold Rampersad and David Roessel. New York: Knopf, 1994.

——— "Christ in Alabama." In *The Collected Works of Langston Hughes*, 16 vols. Columbia: University of Missouri Press, 2001.

———. *Mulatto*. Alexandria, Va.: Alexander Street Press, 2003.

Hutchinson, George. *The Harlem Renaissance in Black and White*. Cambridge, Mass.: Harvard University Press, 1995.

———. *In Search of Nella Larsen: A Biography of the Color Line*. Cambridge, Mass.: Harvard University Press, 2006.

Ignatius of Antioch, "Letters of Ignatius: Trallians." In *Early Christian Fathers*, edited by Cyril C. Richardson. New York: Macmillan, 1970.

Jackson, K. David. *Oxford Anthology of the Brazilian Short Story*. Oxford: Oxford University Press, 2006.

Jacobs, Harriet. *Incidents in the Life of a Slave Girl*. Edited by Paul Negri. Mineola, N.Y.: Dover Publications, 2001.

Jacobson, Matthew Frye. *Whiteness of a Different Color: European Immigrants and the Alchemy of Race*. Cambridge, Mass.: Harvard University Press, 1998.

Jenkins, Candice M. "Decoding Essentialism: Cultural Authenticity and the Black Bourgeoisie in Nella Larsen's *Passing*." *MELUS* 30 (2005): 26.

Jennings, Willie James. *The Christian Imagination: Theology and the Origins of Race*. New Haven: Yale University Press, 2010.

———. "Wandering in the Wilderness: Christian Identity and Theology Between Context and Race." In *The Gospel in Black and White: Theological Resources for Racial Reconciliation*, edited by Dennis Okholm. Downers Grove, Ill.: Intervarsity, 1997.

Johnson, James Weldon. *The Autobiography of an Ex-Coloured Man*. New York: Vintage Books, 1989.

———. *Along This Way: The Autobiography of James Weldon Johnson*. New York: Da Capo Press, 2000.

Jordan, Winthrop D. "American Chairoscuro: The Status and Definition of Mulattoes in the British Colonies," *William and Mary Quarterly* 19.2 (1962): 183–200.

————. *The White Man's Burden: Historical Origins of Racism in the United States.* London: Oxford University Press, 1974.

Jordan, Winthrop D., and Institute of Early American History and Culture. *White over Black: American Attitudes toward the Negro, 1550–1812.* Chapel Hill: University of North Carolina Press, 1968.

Kaup, Monika, and Debra J. Rosenthal. *Mixing Race, Mixing Culture: Inter-American Literary Dialogues.* Austin: University of Texas Press, 2002.

Kawash, Samira. *Dislocating the Color Line: Identity, Hybridity, and Singularity in African-American Narrative.* Stanford, Calif.: Stanford University Press, 1997.

Keizer, Arlene R. *Black Subjects: Identity Formation in the Contemporary Narrative of Slavery.* Ithaca: Cornell University Press, 2004.

Lamb, Robert Paul. "'A Little Yellow Bastard Boy': Paternal Rejection, Filial Insistence, and the Triumph of African American Cultural Aesthetics in Langston Hughes's 'Mulatto.'" *College Literature* 35 (2008): 126–53.

Larsen, Nella. *Quicksand.* New York: Negro Universities Press, 1969.

————. *Passing.* New York: Modern Library, 2000.

Larsen, Timothy, and Daniel J. Treier, eds. *The Cambridge Companion to Evangelical Theology.* Cambridge: Cambridge University Press, 2007.

Leith, John H., ed. *The Creeds of the Churches: A Reader in Christian Doctrine from the Bible to the Present.* Louisville, Ky.: John Knox, 1982.

Lemire, Elise. *"Miscegenation": Making Race in America.* Philadelphia: University of Pennsylvania Press, 2002.

Lincoln, C. Eric. *Coming through the Fire: Surviving Race and Place in America.* Durham N.C.: Duke University Press, 1996.

Lively, Adam. *Masks: Blackness, Race, and the Imagination.* New York: Oxford University Press, 2000.

Louth, Andrew. *Maximus the Confessor.* London: Routledge, 1996.

Lyon, Irenaeus of. "Against Heresies." In *Irenaeus of Lyons.* Edited by Robert McQueen Grant. New York: Routledge, 1997.

Maximus. *Maximus Confessor: Selected Writings.* Translated by George C. Berthold. New York: Paulist Press, 1985.

————. *On the Cosmic Mystery of Jesus Christ: Selected Writings from St. Maximus the Confessor.* Translated by Paul M. Blowers and Robert Louis Wilken. Crestwood, N.Y.: St. Vladimir's Seminary Press, 2003.

McFarland, Ian A. *Difference & Identity: A Theological Anthropology.* Cleveland: Pilgrim Press, 2001.

McGuckin, John Anthony, and Cyril. *St. Cyril of Alexandria: The Christological Controversy: Its History, Theology, and Texts.* Leiden: Brill, 1994.

McLendon, Jacquelyn Y. *The Politics of Color in the Fiction of Jessie Fauset and Nella Larsen.* Charlottesville: University Press of Virginia, 1995.

McWilliams, Dean. *Charles W. Chesnutt and the Fictions of Race*. Athens: University of Georgia Press, 2002.

Milbank, John. *Being Reconciled: Ontology and Pardon*. London: Routledge, 2003.

―――. *Theology and Social Theory: Beyond Secular Reason*. Oxford: Blackwell, 1993.

―――. *The Word Made Strange: Theology, Language, Culture*. Malden, Mass.: Blackwell, 1997.

Miles, Margaret R. *The Word Made Flesh: A History of Christian Thought*. Malden, Mass: Blackwell, 2005.

Moran, Rachel F. *Interracial Intimacy: The Regulation of Race & Romance*. Chicago: University of Chicago Press, 2001.

Morrison, Toni. *Playing in the Dark: Whiteness and the Literary Imagination*. Cambridge, Mass.: Harvard University Press, 1992.

―――. *The Bluest Eye: A Novel*. New York: Plume Books, 1994

Nellas, Panayiotis. *Deification in Christ: The Nature of the Human Person*. Edited by Christos Yannaros. Translated by Norman Russell. Crestwood, N.Y.: St. Vladimir's Seminary Press, 1997.

Norris, Richard A., ed. *The Christological Controversy*. Philadelphia: Fortress, 1980.

Nunes, Zita C. "Phantasmic Brazil: Nella Larsen's *Passing*, American Literary Imagination, and Racial Utopianism." In *Mixing Race, Mixing Culture: Inter-American Literary Dialogues*, edited by Monika Kaup and Debra J. Rosenthal. Austin: University of Texas Press, 2002.

Okholm, Dennis L. *The Gospel in Black and White: Theological Resources for Racial Reconciliation*. Downers Grove, Ill.: InterVarsity, 1997.

Origen, and Tertullian Cyprian. *On the Lord's Prayer*. Translated by Alistair Stewart-Skyes. Edited by John Behr. Crestwood, N.Y.: St. Vladimir's Seminary Press, 2004.

Peterson, Dale E. *Up from Bondage: The Literatures of Russian and African American Soul*. Durham, N.C.: Duke University Press, 2000.

Raboteau, Albert J. *Slave Religion: The "Invisible Institution" in the Antebellum South*. New York: Oxford University Press, 1978.

Raper, Arthur Franklin, and Southern Commission on the Study of Lynching. *The Tragedy of Lynching*. New York: Negro Universities Press, 1969.

Rasmusson, Arne. "Deprive them of their Pathos: Karl Barth and the Nazi Revolution Revisited." *Modern Theology* 23.3 (2007): 369–91.

Regan, Hilary D., Alan J. Torrance, and Antony Wood. *Christ and Context: The Confrontation Between Gospel and Culture*. Edinburgh: T&T Clark, 1993.

Raimon, Eve Allegra. *The "Tragic Mulatta" Revisited: Race and Nationalism in Nineteenth-Century Antislavery Fiction*. New Brunswick, N.J.: Rutgers University Press, 2004.

Reuter, Edward Byron. *The Mulatto in the United States: Including a Study of the Role of Mixed-Blood Races Throughout the World*. New York: Johnson Reprint, 1970.

Ruether, Rosemary Radford. *New Woman, New Earth: Sexist Ideologies and Human Liberation*. New York: Seabury Press, 1975.

Rivera, Luis. *A Violent Evangelism: The Political and Religious Conquest of the Americas*. Louisville, Ky.: Westminster John Knox, 1992.

Romano, Renee C. *Race Mixing: Black-White Marriage in Postwar America*. Cambridge, Mass.: Harvard University Press, 2003

Roth, Philip. *The Human Stain*. Boston: Houghton Mifflin, 2000.

Rottenberg, Catherine. *Performing Americanness: Race, Class, and Gender in Modern African-American and Jewish-American Literature*. Hanover, N.H.: Dartmouth College Press, 2008.

Said, Edward W. *Culture and Imperialism*. New York: Knopf, 1994.

————. *Reflections on Exile and Other Essays*. Cambridge, Mass.: Harvard University Press, 2000.

Schlatter, Adolf von. *Romans: The Righteousness of God*. Peabody, Mass: Hendrickson, 1995.

Schleiermacher, Friedrich, Jack C. Verheyden, and S. MacLean Gilmour. *The Life of Jesus*. Lives of Jesus series. Philadelphia: Fortress, 1975.

Schoenfeld, Jen Lee. "Into the Box and Out of the Picture: The Rhetorical Management of the Mulatto in the Jim Crow Era." Ph.D. diss., Duke University, 2005.

Seigel, Jerrold E. *The Idea of the Self: Thought and Experience in Western Europe since the Seventeenth Century*. Cambridge: Cambridge University Press, 2005.

Sernett, Milton C. *Afro-American Religious History: A Documentary Witness*. Durham, N.C.: Duke University Press, 1999.

Sherrard-Johnson, Cherene. "'A Plea for Color': Nella Larsen's Iconography of the Mulatta." *American Literature* 76 (2004): 833–69.

Shusterman, Richard, ed. *Bourdieu: A Critical Reader*. Oxford: Blackwell, 1999.

Smith, Lillian Eugenia. *Killers of the Dream*. New York: Norton, 1994.

Smith, Valerie. *Representing Blackness: Issues in Film and Video*. New Brunswick, N.J.: Rutgers University Press, 1997.

Sollors, Werner. *The Invention of Ethnicity*. New York: Oxford University Press, 1989.

————. *Theories of Ethnicity: A Classical Reader*. New York: New York University Press, 1996.

————. *Neither Black nor White Yet Both: Thematic Explorations of Interracial Literature*. Cambridge: Harvard University Press, 1997.

————. *Interracialism: Black-White Intermarriage in American History, Literature, and Law*. Oxford: Oxford University Press, 2000.

————. *An Anthology of Interracial Literature: Black-White Contacts in the Old World and the New*. New York: New York University Press, 2004.

Stewart, Charles. *Creolization: History, Ethnography, Theory*. Walnut Creek, Calif.: Left Coast Press, 2007.

Stokes, Melvyn. *D. W. Griffith's* The Birth of a Nation*: A History of The Most Controversial Motion Picture of All Time*. New York: Oxford University Press, 2007.

Stonequist, Everett V. *Race Mixture and the Mulatto*. Durham, N.C.: Duke University Press, n.d.

Strauss, David Friedrich. *The Christ of Faith and the Jesus of History: A Critique of Schleiermacher's Life of Jesus*. Lives of Jesus series. Philadelphia: Fortress, 1977.

Sullivan, Nell. "Nella Larsen's *Passing* and the Fading Subject." *African American Review* 32 (1998): 14.

Sundquist, Eric J. *To Wake the Nations: Race in the Making of American Literature*. Cambridge, Mass.: Harvard University Press, 1993.

Talty, Stephan. *Mulatto America: At the Crossroads of Black and White Culture: A Social History*. New York: HarperCollins, 2003.

Thacker, Audrey B., and David S. Goldstein, eds. *Complicating Constructions: Race, Ethnicity, and Hybridity in American Texts*. Seattle: University of Washington Press, 2007.

Todd, Ruthven. *The Laughing Mulatto; the Story of Alexandre Dumas*. London: Rich & Cowan, 1940.

Torrance, James, Trevor A. Hart, and Daniel P. Thimell. *Christ in Our Place: The Humanity of God in Christ for the Reconciliation of the World: Essays Presented to Professor James Torrance*. Allison Park, Pa.: Paternoster Press, 1989.

Toth, Josh. "Deauthenticating Community: The Passing Intrusion of Clare Kendry in Nella Larsen's *Passing*," *MELUS* 33 (2008): 59.

Townes, Emilie Maureen. *Womanist Ethics and the Cultural Production of Evil*. New York: Palgrave Macmillan, 2006.

Volf, Miroslav. *Exclusion and Embrace: A Theological Exploration of Identity, Otherness, and Reconciliation*. Nashville: Abingdon, 1996.

Volf, Miroslav, and Dorothy C. Bass. *Practicing Theology: Beliefs and Practices in Christian Life*. Grand Rapids: Eerdmans, 2002.

Walker, David, and Peter P. Hinks. *David Walker's Appeal to the Coloured Citizens of the World*. University Park: Pennsylvania State University Press, 2000.

Wells-Barnett, Ida B. *Selected Works of Ida B. Wells-Barnett: Schomburg Library of Nineteenth-Century Black Women Writers*. Edited by Trudier Harris. New York: Oxford University Press, 1991.

Whitaker, E. C., and Maxwell E. Johnson. *Documents of the Baptismal Liturgy*. Collegeville, Minn.: Liturgical Press, 2003.

Williamson, Joel. *New People: Miscegenation and Mulattoes in the United States.* New York: Free Press, 1980.

——. *The Crucible of Race: Black/White Relations in the American South since Emancipation.* New York: Oxford University Press, 1984.

Wotham, Henry B. "What Is a Black Author?: A Review of Recent Charles Chesnutt Studies." *American Literary History* 18 (2006): 7.

Yeo, Richard R, *Encyclopaedic Visions: Scientific Dictionaries and Enlightenment Culture.* Cambridge: Cambridge University Press, 2001.

Yoder, John Howard. *Body Politics: Five Practices of the Christian Community before the Watching World.* Nashville: Discipleship Resources, 1992.

Young, Frances M. *The Making of the Creeds.* Philadelphia: SCM Press, 1991.

Young, Robert. *Colonial Desire: Hybridity in Theory, Culture, and Race.* London: Routledge, 1995.

Zizioulas, Jean. *Being as Communion: Studies in Personhood and the Church.* Crestwood, N.Y.: St. Vladimir's Seminary Press, 1985.

——. *Communion and Otherness: Further Studies in Personhood and the Church.* London: T&T Clark, 2006.

INDEX

CPSIA information can be obtained
at www.ICGtesting.com
Printed in the USA
LVHW021930150621
690291LV00006B/408